T...
As...
Wi...
Wh...
Firs...
Now ...ands are telling lies;
And like a storm arising
His "talent" is increasing.

His crops shoot high,
The country is transformed,
The masses live in shame,
And mock the foul play!
Now it is also proven
What at first was only suspected:
The Good have disappeared,
The Bad band together!

Long after this Despair
Like ice will have been broken,
It will be spoken of
As of the Black Death;
Then children will set up
A straw man on the heath
And thus burn joy out of suffering
And light out of past horror.

Literal translation of Gottfried Keller's poem on pages 252-254.

THE HIDDEN DAMAGE

By the same Author

THE HEARTLESS LAND
SOMETHING WRONG
THE MAN WHO WAS LOVED
THE STORIES OF JAMES STERN

JAMES STERN

THE
HIDDEN
DAMAGE

CHELSEA PRESS
LONDON

© James Stern 1990

Introduction © Stephen Spender 1990

British Library Cataloguing in Publication Data

CIP data for this book is available from the British Library

ISBN 1-871484-01-4

First published in USA by Harcourt Brace, 1947

First published in Great Britain 1990 by
Chelsea Press Ltd
10 Blacklands Terrace
Chelsea
London SW3 2SR

Design: Mick Keates
Production: Hugh Allan

Printed in Great Britain by Bookcraft (Bath) Limited

CONTENTS

INTRODUCTION by Sir Stephen Spender			vii
1.	ENLISTED	NEW YORK TO PARIS	1
2.	FAMILY MATTERS	LONDON	39
3.	GUILTY?	GERMANY	65
4.	BILLETS	DARMSTADT TO STUTTGART	91
5.	A FALLEN LION	STUTTGART TO MUNICH	107
6.	QUESTION AND ANSWER	MUNICH AREA	125
7.	A CIGAR AFTER DACHAU	MUNICH AREA	148
8.	ENCOUNTERS	KEMPTEN AREA	179
9.	THE RECTOR'S TALE	KEMPTEN AREA	214
10.	CHEESE	KEMPTEN AREA	225
11.	THE DEFEATED	NÜRNBERG AREA	257
12.	LIFE IN THE RUBBLE	NÜRNBERG AREA	279
13.	A PEACEFUL PLACE	ERLANGEN AND BAMBERG	309
14.	THE ENEMY	FRANKFURT	321
15.	HOMING	LONDON TO WASHINGTON	353

★

TO THE MEMORY OF
"REGGIE" STERN
KILLED IN ACTION
SWANSEA. FEB. 21. 1941

★

INTRODUCTION
By Sir Stephen Spender

This is a blow by blow account of a sentimental journey. James Stern knew Germany well before the war, and when he returned to Europe as an American Intelligence Officer after V.E. Day, he was greatly interested in the fate of the country and its people after Hitler. The truthfulness of his narrative will immediately impress itself upon those like myself who also participated in the occupation of a Germany already divided into four zones – American, French, British and Russian. Younger readers, many of them perhaps familiar with descriptions of pre-war Germany by Isherwood and Auden, will be struck by the immediacy of James Stern's account of an absolutely changed Germany a few weeks after the war.

The author was a member of the U.S. Strategic Bombing Survey (USBUS) who were sent (via Paris and London) to Germany, where they inverviewed the inhabitants on their reactions to the Allied Powers' "saturation raids". The interviews seem to have extended beyond these raids to the interviewees' whole lives; some of the most interesting were with people living in the countryside, almost undamaged by bombardment.

Obviously the project was of sociological interest. It was one of those ideas – go round and ask the Germans how they felt about being bombed – which, once thought of, has to be put into effect. And yet for the interviewers there was something deeply ironic about it. Stern points out:

> "I had read and reread the two sets of schedules, the *Fragebogen*, the Questionnaires, which had been worded, it seemed to me, in the most peculiar German, and I'd put myself in the place of the interviewee, and wondered how on earth I myself would answer some of these vague, sometimes unintentionally humorous questions."

The first interviewee turned out to be blind, the second stone deaf, but later on some of them, either in their lies or in their truths, were revealing. They provided the material for the account of Germans and Germany immediately after the war which makes up most of this book. Of course none of those interviewed admitted to having been a Nazi, but while some of them betrayed themselves as having views identical with Goebbels, others revealed almost involuntarily how much they had resented the S.S. and the war itself.

I read this book with special interest because while Jimmy Stern, Wystan Auden and their colleagues were on their USBUS mission, I happened to be doing a similar job in the British Zone. This consisted primarily of opening libraries which had been closed for de-Nazification, and also of interviewing German professors in the Humanities about their political attitudes and views concerning "re-education" and so on. My impressions were published in "European Witness".

The librarians were not difficult to deal with. As one lady librarian put it to me, with that air of ambiguous complicity which was characteristic of the more intelligent German officials at that time, "I understand perfectly well what you want: for me to take from the shelves the books by Nazis and put them in the cellar, and take from the cellar the books by Jews and put them on the shelves."

In the towns, most Germans, wandering round and above the heaps of ruins which had been their homes, appeared like zombies. Looking at them through the windscreen of a car of the occupying forces, they seemed inhabitants of a different world. They moved on some plane of time and space, entirely absorbed in their own scavenging and searching preoccupations, scarcely aware of our world. My driver remarked that it was sometimes extremely difficult not to run them down, because they did not seem aware of us in our vehicles. They were in fact in a state of prolonged post-defeat shock. Also many of them were living in a kind of moral vacuum after the defeat of Hitler. Stern describes a group of Germans in Nauheim standing in the street and staring at a billboard on which, under the heading "WHO IS GUILTY?", there were photographs of the inmates of the recently liberated Concentration Camps:

> "These enlarged, rather blurred photographs showed hundreds of naked human skeletons piled high on the open wagons of a goods train: what looked like a mountain of garbage was a mountain of ash and charred human bones; men in striped prison clothes hung from gallows, while children and babies lay on their backs on the ground dead from starvation. Under each photograph a caption informed the observer where the photograph had been taken.
>
> "Standing behind these groups of spectators, I never heard anyone utter a word. A woman would, occasionally, put a hand or a handkerchief to her mouth as though to stifle a moan or cry of horror: an elderly man with his mouth open would stare as though hypnotised for a few minutes: then one by one they would walk slowly, silently away. I tried to put myself in the place of these people, to imagine what they were thinking.... but no mental effort I ever made could have been more vain."

These are the people of Nauheim looking at the victims of concentration camps. But it is almost as if the situation were reversed; as if the people standing in the square felt the skeletal victims in the concentration camp photographs to be staring at them, with accusing eyes.

But perhaps these spectators at Nauheim felt very close to their own immediate past. A spurt of light, like a struck match, is thrown on the situation by a kind of flash-back into the very recent events, when a jeep driven by the Major who was Jimmy Stern's commanding officer runs into a German cyclist, hurting him badly. The Americans are greatly distressed by this accident and when, after finding the address of the cyclist (who does not speak), in one of his pockets, the Major says, "I'd better take him home." the narrative continues:

"Not until he had driven away did we realise that quite a crowd had gathered. The spectators, of both sexes, were a wild looking lot, wearing tattered dirty clothes.... They were Poles, it appeared, who had been transported to Darmstadt, where for several years they had been doing slave labour. In their various ways they were all attempting to express the same thought – their utter bewilderment at the way Americans had treated a German, whom they referred to as *"dieser Hund"*. With their gesticulations they pantomimed how Nazi soldiers would have behaved in similar circumstances. They'd have crushed into man and bicycle, they explained, cursed him up and down from their car, then raced on at breakneck speed, leaving the victim to his fate on the road. Our conduct seemed not only something they had never witnessed, but beyond their comprehension."

The Poles had for a few seconds lifted the curtain between what went on in the streets before that spring of 1945, and what went on after. Strangely enough, on the Rhineland I had a similar meeting with Poles who enacted for me the story of their treatment as slaves by their whipmasters the Germans. For them, all Germans were Nazis.

On my journeys from library to library, I had been struck by the almost uncanny contrast between the German towns – scenes of terrible guilt and terrible punishment – and the innocent-seeming countryside. Stern was also struck by this when his team went to Kempten in the Bavarian Tyrol, visiting some churches on the way. He describes Kempten as "an ideal place for contemplation and vacation", and has lyrical passages describing the landscape of this region. In the house where the team lodged they were waited on by an ideal couple – Hedwig, who did their cleaning and laundry, and Hans, a chef famous in the locality. In the course of their interviewing they discovered the other side of all this: the passionate hatred of the Bavarians for the Prussians who, evacuees from Northern cities, had overflowed into Bavaria, nearly tripling the population.

There were saints, heroes and heroines in this journey as well as bullies and victims. Stern tells a story which I had not heard before about the uprising of a group of students in Munich in March 1943. The team interviewed the parents and brother and sister of one of the student leaders, Schurik Schmorell. This young man seemed even more courageous in his dying than in his rather ill-considered plotting. (One wonders whether the opponents of Hitler did not have some kind of desperate complex of martyrdom which made them give themselves away to the tyranny.) Religious people, unless they be Jesuits, are not skilful in conspiracy, and in his last letter to this family, printed here, Schurik Schmorell, shortly before his death by being beheaded, seems to have entered into a state of religious ecstasy, supremely happy in his belief that after death he and his family would be reunited.

I began this Introduction by describing "The Hidden Damage" as an account of the author's Sentimental Journey. The sentiment cannot be in any doubt in his descriptions of returning to favourite haunts (some of them woefully damaged) in Paris and London. These have the characteristic of the self re-found. In Germany there are a few passages of reunion with old acquaintances in which this also happens. But in this book it is the writer's interior search for a hidden self striving to understand the most terrible events of our century which deepens sentiment with diamond-like determination.

EDITORIAL NOTE

In The Hidden Damage, some names have been changed: "Mervyn", for example, was actually Wystan – W.H. Auden.

NEW YORK TO PARIS

1

In New York the evening of March 5, 1945, turned cold and gray. When I opened the window an icy gust blew in from Third Avenue. Outside Moriarty's, the corner pub, a man stamping his feet and blowing into his hands reminded me of winter nights in Dublin. Turning back into the room, I glanced at the New York *Times* on the table. "The Allies have reached the Rhine," a London dispatch began, "but they have not won the war. . . . This is not the end, nor even the beginning of the end. . . ."

Before I had time to read what the writer thought it was, the bell rang. The ringer was Mervyn, on one of his sudden, periodic visits from Philadelphia. He sat down without saying a word. He seemed distracted, strangely quiet. Finally he muttered: "I think I'm off to Germany!"

I gaped at him. "Germany!" I said. "How? When? You're joking!"

"I promise you I'm not." And slowly, hesitatingly, he proceeded to tell me how he had been put in touch with a "certain man," who was trying to recruit civilians to go overseas. They were to wear uniforms, he said, and to travel under War Department orders with an assimilated rank designated according to their incomes, but just what was to be their function in Germany Mervyn didn't seem to know. I could see now that his calm was forced, that he was highly excited.

"What are the qualifications?" I asked.

"Oh," he said, "I think you are supposed to have spent some time in Germany, and to have some knowledge of the language—that seems to be about all."

I had begun to think hard. "What about me?" I asked finally. "Could I go?"

He looked up in surprise. "You? Do you want to? Aren't you in the middle of translating that long book?"

"Of course I want to go," I said. "As for the book, I've nearly finished it."

"Well," said Mervyn, "I'll give the man your phone number. If a Mr. Nesbit calls, you'll know what he wants."

An hour later Mervyn left and I heard no more for a week. During that time I found it very difficult to concentrate on my work. I had lived and worked in pre-Hitler Germany. But, with the exception of one weekend in 1935, I had not set foot in the country since Hitler came to power. During the intervening years I had spent much time with refugees, mostly writers, trying to teach them English, editing, ghosting, and translating their books. It struck me only now to what extent I identified myself with them. It had not occurred to me that I should ever see Germany again. I now thought of the prospect of returning with a mixture of horror and fascination. I felt that it would be like setting out for a country that didn't really exist, or like going to bed knowing that sleep is bound to reproduce that nightmare in which I, bound hand and foot, am compelled to watch a horizontal slab of Stonehenge dimensions being lowered with terrible slowness over a mass of naked, gagged, and prostrate human beings. The stone slab is operated from each end by a pulley contrivance in the hands of Hitler and Himmler who, as the great weight descends to within a foot of the bodies writhing in their silent agony, burst into mad screams of laughter.

Though that old nightmare did not return, a strange excitement kept me awake at night—until the more I considered the prospect of returning to Germany the more unlikely it seemed. In a few days I had almost succeeded in dismissing the thought from my mind.

Then Mr. Nesbit phoned. He was passing through New York on his way to Washington. He had half an hour between trains. Could I meet him at nine o'clock in a certain waiting-room on 42nd Street? "I'm very short," the voice said. "And my overcoat and hat are brown. What about you?"

"My overcoat is also brown," I told him, "but with rather a loud check. I never wear a hat and I guess I'm above average height."

"The long and the short of it," said Mr. Nesbit's voice.

He was as charming as that remark had led me to believe, and since the waiting-room was almost empty we recognized one another at once. We sat in a corner in leather chairs, and the moment I noticed his alert, shrewd eyes I decided to ask none of the many questions that were on the tip of my tongue. Instead, I answered his. They struck me as only a little less formal that those on the civil service questionnaire I had once filled out for the OWI. Born in Ireland forty-one years ago, I'd arrived in America for the first time in 1929. Yes, I could speak French and German. I had lived in both countries. We then broke from English into German. I had worked in Frankfurt and Berlin, mostly in banks. Was I prepared to sign up for six months, maybe a year? Sure. Mr. Nesbit rose from his chair. I would hear from him within a week. Now he had to catch his train. We shook hands.

"Is there anything secret about this—this mission?" I asked him.

"Er—well, no," he said, with a faint smile. "But it's just as well not to talk about it until you know more."

That night I phoned Mervyn, told him I'd seen Mr. Nesbit.

"Wonderful," he said.

"Is there any chance of us going together?"

"No idea! Hope so."

"What part of Germany do you think we'll go to?"

"Can't imagine!"

"Shall we go by air or sea?"

"Haven't the faintest idea!"

"What's it all about? What happens next?"

"No idea!"

"I'm sure you know something I don't!"

"Not a word, I swear!"

The following week he did. He called me on the phone from Washington.

"I've just come out of the Pentagon," he said. "I'm a Bombing Analyst!"

"A Bombing Analyst! What on earth's that?"

"No idea! But beware of the Pentagon. You won't like it. I think it's wonderful. It was designed by Kafka!"

"How shall I ever get there? You're pulling one of your little strings!"

"I am not! You'll get a telegram from a certain colonel."

"What news about leaving?"

"I'm to be ready in a week. Forty-eight hours' notice."

"Plane or ship? And where to?"

"No idea!"

Two days later the telegram arrived: REPORT AT PENTAGON IMMEDIATELY. I phoned a friend to ask for a bed and caught the next train to Washington.

Mervyn was right. Driving into the Pentagon was like driving into a great concrete cave. Mounting one of its subterranean ramps, escorted by an enormous sergeant, claustrophobia began turning my stomach upside down.

In a bare room a mild man in spectacles introduced himself as Mr. Nesbit's assistant.

"Is Mr. Nesbit around?" I asked.

"Er, no. He went overseas yesterday."

I felt I'd lost a friend.

"You're to be a Bombing Analyst," the man in spectacles' informed me.

"Oh, fine," I said. "What's that?"

His eyes wrinkled up behind the spectacles in a slightly embarrassed smile. "Well," he murmured, "I'm not absolutely sure. I'm new here, you see."

He then sat me down at a table and gave me a sheaf of forms to fill out. I knew all the answers by heart and was through in an hour. Then a girl at a typewriter asked me innumerable questions in a voice gone dead from boredom. Behind her a little man in civilian clothes with a bald head and a brown mustache kept running from telephone to telephone, desperately trying to find a room for the night.

"But leetle bett not enough!" he kept saying. "I tell you, I haf my vife mit!"

A Bombing Analyst in distress, I thought! When the girl at the typewriter saw me smiling, she scowled and asked me grimly if I were married. I watched her type YES. Then she silently escorted me down a corridor to a room where I was finger-printed and another girl asked me where my parents lived. After she had typed ENGLAND, she in turn escorted me back to the first girl, and when I promptly left the room to go to the toilet she came running out after me. "Hi there!" she shouted, "where you going?" Realizing my intentions, she retreated, but before I had reached MEN, out popped the enormous sergeant who stood in the corridor until I reappeared.

"Just a formality," he muttered.

"Oh, sure," I said, and back we went to the grim girl.

"Have you been through the medical?" she asked.

I shook my head. The sergeant then escorted me back down the ramp to a door marked DISPENSARY. Inside, a male nurse conducted me through a maze of corridors to a room where half a dozen men were sitting silently, clothed in nothing but maroon-colored bathrobes. I undressed, put on a robe, and joined them. One by one we were examined by five doctors, the last of whom produced an "Immunization Register" and informed me that I must get my blood typed and be vaccinated for smallpox, tetanus, typhoid, and yellow fever. "You can get that done in New York," he added.

On returning to put on my clothes, I found one massive and one small Negro standing stark naked in the middle of the dressing-room. I looked at them, then pointed to the maroon-colored robes hanging from a line of pegs. For an instant they stared at me wide-eyed, then together they dashed for the robes. As they put them on they began to giggle like children, in high-pitched voices. Then they stood surveying themselves in a full-length mirror and burst into roars of laughter. It seemed a long time since I'd heard anyone laugh.

Before leaving the building I phoned the man in spectacles. "Is there anything more I have to do?" I asked.

"Er, no—I don't think so," he said. "Could you be prepared to go overseas in two weeks?"

"Two weeks?" I repeated. "Sure."

It was just seven weeks later that I left New York for Washington to go overseas. Flags drooped from every building in the perspiring city. Two days before, VE-Day, I had watched the New York sky turn silver as the sun caught the rain of paper that was showered in celebration from the skyscrapers.

Coming out of the Pentagon I ran into an acquaintance, a professor of economics at a Pennsylvania university. Patches of sweat were breaking out through his coat, but from the look on his face I guessed that something more fearsome than the climate of the capital was affecting him.

"Hullo," I said, "what are you doing here?"

"Me?" he growled. "I've been hanging around here for the last month. I'm going steadily nuts. Eight weeks ago I gave up my job. Five weeks ago I gave up my apartment. Now I've spent all my savings. If those . . ."

I took a step nearer. "Look," I interrupted, "have you been told you're a Bombing Analyst?"

His eyes opened wide. His jaw fell. He clutched the lapel of my coat. "Yes!" he said. "Yes! How the hell did you know?"

"Your story sounds familiar," I said.

"Why? Mean to say you're going, too?"

"I'm hoping to," I said. "But you beat me. I've been waiting only seven weeks. I've not given up my apartment, and I've not lost a job. I've only lost some of my savings and my temper over long-distance calls."

"Do you think we'll *ever* get there?" he interrupted with desperation in his eyes. "Now that the war in Europe's over . . ."

"I'm beginning to think we'll make it now," I said. "That

is, if we create enough fuss. All you can do with Bureaucracy is to batter it into action. That's what a friend of mine did. He left two weeks ago—lucky dog!"

That's what I had done, too—but I managed to spare the Professor the news that these tactics had at last succeeded. Instead, I wished both of us luck until we met again on "the other side."

"Now I must catch my train," I lied.

Instead, I caught a bus into town to buy a uniform. I had just an hour before the shops closed. At the end of that time I came out of the store loaded with more clothes than I'd ever had in my life. I felt sure I wouldn't need half of them, but I didn't much care. I was no longer in Washington. Nor was I in America or Europe. I felt suspended in mid-air over no particular place at no particular moment in history. Dizzily I walked into a bar to try and recover my bearings and to sober up. The place was jammed. The only available seat was at a table occupied by two naval officers. One of them was reading a newspaper.

"Gee!" he said as I sat down, "what a guy!"

"Oh, yeah!" said his companion. "Who?"

"This guy Gabbels—says here he committed suicide."

"Gabbels?"

"You know, the German propaganda fellah—Nazi."

"So what?"

"So what? Listen to this. 'The greater the lie and the more often it is repeated the more certain it is to be believed.' You ought to read this, Jack. Just goes to show what kinda bastards they were!"

"Ah, heck!" growled the other officer. "That's all over now!" They both ordered another whisky.

So did I. I was beginning to sober up, to come slowly down to earth—not to the earth of the Western Hemisphere, but to that of a country where for twelve years the voice of a little man called Dr. Paul Joseph Goebbels, a one-time intellectual with parchment skin and a club-foot, had systematically poisoned the minds of tens of millions of people.

Whether his voice would ever be heard again made no difference. What mattered was that it had been heard for twelve years. What mattered was the extent of the infection he'd left behind him. How high was the fever of the diseased? What did the infected look like? What were the surviving inmates doing and saying in the ruins of their prison?

I had not traveled by air since the days when you had to stuff cotton wool in your ears. And I had always paid. Now the tables were turned: no money needed, no tipping. Just Orders—a bundle of paper, the privilege of paper. For once you could cock a snook at a millionaire. It was like being members of a new aristocracy, a strange sensation.

In the airport waiting-room I recognized Colonel Charles Lindbergh in a blue suit. The last time I had seen him was on the morning after his transatlantic flight. An incredibly boyish figure, he had stood on the balcony of the French Aviation Club in Paris, holding in one hand the Stars and Stripes, in the other the Tricolor. The crowds below had screamed themselves hoarse. As I watched him now mount the ladder into the C-47, I wondered if he were thinking the unbelievable thought that drove all other thoughts from my mind: we were heading for the scene of that triumph! The day after tomorrow, maybe sooner, I should see Paris again!

Of the dozen men on the plane, three wore the blue-and-white armband with the large US in the center. Their uniforms, like mine, were new and they didn't fit very well. One of the three I recognized as the little man with the brown mustache whom I'd watched in the Pentagon desperately trying to find a room for himself and his wife. Another sat next to me. His name was Hindler, he told me, and he'd been born and brought up in Berne.

"Chee!" he said. "I never thought I'd get this far!"

He heaved at the safety-belt to fasten it round him, pulling me with it. Then he leaned back and caught the crown of his head on a vicious-looking spike.

"Ouch!" he gasped. "Is this what they call a bucket-seat?"

"I guess so," I said, and we exchanged some not too complimentary remarks about the gentleman who had invented the strip of slippery steel on which we sat.

"How does one sit?" he asked.

"Seems best to lean forward," I suggested.

"Lean forward like this all the way to Scotland?"

"Scotland?" I gasped. "Who told you Scotland?"

"Man in the airport. He said, 'Keep it quiet.'"

"But I have Paris written on my luggage tags!"

"Ha!" smiled Hindler. "You've not read your orders." From his pocket he produced his bundle of papers. "'Most richid discretion,'" he read aloud, "'must be exercised in the divulching of information as to times and places of arrival and departures on overseas moofments.'"

"But that doesn't prove your information is correct," I said. "Where *are* we going?"

"Cod knows!" sighed Hindler, and leaning back he bumped his head again on the spike.

His "Ouch!" was drowned in a sudden roar, followed by another, then another. The forward part of the plane began to shudder. The roar, like tangible air, filled every crevice of the ship. My ears began to ring. Quickly the vibrating shudder came tearing down towards us till I felt my boots shaking on the steel floor. An odd tingling sensation, like a very faint electric shock, crept up my spine. In the overpowering crescendo of noise, I felt the whole cigar-shaped structure might at any moment burst asunder and scatter in a million pieces. Instead, it suddenly bolted forward with such a passion of concentrated power that I found myself smiling. I glanced at Hindler. He was smiling, too. Heaving himself round to look out of the window, he once more pulled me with him. Dusk had fallen, and way behind us, already a thousand feet below, we could just see the dome of the Capitol.

"I've been waiting four weeks for this moment," Hindler sighed, carefully leaning forward.

Fifty minutes later there was a walloping bump beneath us, and we were on the ground again.

"Where the hell have we got to now?"

"Patuxent!" a voice called. "All out!"

"Patuxent? Where's that?"

"Maryland."

Maryland was black. We filed from the plane into a brightly lit waiting-room. At one end of it stood a long counter and at the other a cafeteria with tables and chairs. A stentorian voice from an amplifier suddenly informed "passengers with an overseas destination" to appear at the counter with their orders. Hindler and I stood in line behind the little man with the brown mustache. When his turn came, I heard the official ask him for his dog-tag.

"Tock-tack? Tock-tack?" he muttered, mystified.

Then he wheeled round and scampered away, to return dragging behind him his duffel bag and a ponderous-looking brief-case. The latter he heaved up on to the counter where, with a triumphant grin, he proudly produced its white, cardboard luggage tag!

While my orders were being examined, I asked the official when we were likely to be leaving, and where for.

"In about two hours," he said. "Next stop, Newfoundland."

"And then?"

"Couldn't tell you that," he said.

The first of the two hours I spent drinking coffee and talking to Hindler. He told me he had a friend "in our outfit" who had already left for Germany, but that he hadn't heard from him since.

"Same with me," I said, and I told him about Mervyn. "He sent me his APO number immediately. I've written him two or three times, but I've not heard a word."

"They are probably in London," Hindler said. "I know we must . . ."

The rest of his sentence was shattered by the voice over the amplifier. To my amazement, I heard my name. It was commanding me to "come to the counter."

"I'm sorry," the official was saying, "we have just received orders by phone from Washington that you are not to continue your journey."

I stood there gaping—at a wart, I remember, on the young man's forehead. I started to say something, but I couldn't find any words. I wasn't sure what I wanted to say. I just gaped. I tried to be calm. I finally said, "Can you tell me why?"

"No, I'm afraid not," said the young man. "There's no explanation. If you will collect your baggage, I will call for transportation to take you over to B.O.Q."

"B.O.?"

"Bachelor Officers Quarters."

And I'm neither a bachelor nor an officer, I thought.

"Do you think I shall leave tomorrow?" I asked.

"I'm sorry. We don't know. You will be called by phone when we have some news."

I walked slowly back to Hindler.

"I'm not going with you," I said. "Orders from Washington."

"Cood Cod!" gasped Hindler. I was moved by his look of genuine concern.

"So long," I said, shaking hands. *"Bon voyage."*

"See you in Chermany."

"Hope so," I said.

Outside, a car looking like a Black Maria stood waiting. A Negro pitched my duffel bag into the back of it. I sat behind him on the one wooden bench and we drove away into the night.

In a few minutes I found myself in an intensely overheated room, alone. I sat down on one of four empty double-decker cots, gulped a long swig of John Jameson from my flask and tried to think of nothing. When I felt the whisky beginning to work, I lay back and stared at a Varga pin-up girl on the wall beside the pillow. Standing on her toes, she was lifting a transparent slip half way up her behind. Beneath her I read:

> *February is a month*
> *Of winds and winter snows,*
> *If wolves seek shelter from the cold,*
> *Why, I'll be on my toes!*

The flask was empty and dawn was breaking when finally I fell asleep.

Patuxent seemed to be an endless green desert, like Salisbury Plain. I spent most of that day gazing at it out of the window and waiting to be called to the telephone. The call came at eight in the evening. Transportation would fetch me in an hour. It did. At nine I was driven away in a sumptuous black limousine. The young man with the wart was very sympathetic.

"You'll make it this time," he assured me.

"I hope so," I said. "What held me up?"

"Don't know," he said. I never did know.

At eleven o'clock seven of us boarded a four-engined Naval Air Transport plane. The seating accommodation consisted of four green leather armchairs, one behind the other, and bucket-seats for three. The remainder of the ship's interior was packed to the ceiling with huge cases of freight. By the time I'd climbed the ladder, the chairs were already occupied by a young naval officer bound for the south of England and three men wearing the US armband and ill-fitting uniforms. Two were elderly. The first was a lean-faced, gray-haired Californian called Perkins. He had already informed me that he suffered from stomach ulcers and that his profession had something to do with railroads. "I've been in Europe before," he added, a fact he seemed to consider remarkable. The second civilian, a rotund gentleman with an apoplectic face, had spent most of his life in Germany, where he'd worked for the *Allgemeine Elektrizitäts Gesellschaft* as an electrical engineer. "I quit zat contry in Nineteen-sirty-fife!" he told me proudly. The third was a Ministry of Agriculture employee, called Hale. A tiny man with a huge head, he suffered from hernia and had just undergone an operation for that complaint. It was he who offered to share his chair with me part of the time. When I learned that he was still strapped up after his operation, I gratefully declined and remained on my bucket-seat in the company of two sailors who were traveling to Stockholm.

The bucket-seats were placed opposite the wooden cases, so that our feet and legs became permanently entangled in the maze of ropes and iron bars which we hoped would prevent the freight from collapsing on top of us.

As the engines began to roar I noticed the sailor next to me staring at my armband. "Say, are you guys correspondents or what?" he asked.

"No," I yelled above the noise, "we're going to Germany. I couldn't tell you what for."

He glanced at my colleagues. "Armchair strategists," he grunted.

"Two of them," I smiled, "are suffering from stomach troubles."

He let out a peal of laughter. "Hear that?" he said to his friend. "Stomach troubles! By golly, that's a new one on me!"

Then, like a race-horse let loose at the gate, the plane bolted forward beneath us. The dim lights in the ceiling brightened. I could feel the plane tearing across country; then I knew it must be rising into the air, into the night.

Loosening our belts, we thrust our legs through the tangle of ropes, closed our eyes, let our bodies fall back, our heads fall forwards, fall sideways, fall forwards again. Then we sat up straight, rested our elbows on our knees, chins in our hands. In each position I day-dreamed of Europe, traveling from one country, one city to another in my mind. I was setting out fully conscious of the peculiar guilt that belongs to the unbombed, the uninvaded. The days, the months, the years of howling headlines and radio voices announcing the mounting horror, the ever-increasing destruction of human life and once-familiar cities, had long since anesthetized the imagination—numbing, blurring, and ultimately blotting out all preconceived pictures of the result and aftermath of total war. I thought of my brother who'd been killed four years ago, fighting fires in the blitz; and I thought of the letter I'd recently received from France. "You will never know," the friend wrote, "what life under the Occupation was like. When we meet again you'll find us very changed." I would never know, I knew. Nor would all he could tell me be enough. Even hearing the news of the death of a German friend in Belsen, then seeing the moving pictures of the conditions under which such men had been tortured and left to rot and die, had not been enough. Such sights made the Germany I had known all the more unimaginable. The thought that, years ago, I might have met in the flesh some of the speechless spectators of mass-murder on the screen, only increased my intense curiosity to meet them face to face, hear from their own lips details of how they'd lived, how they now accounted for the crimes committed by their countrymen during the catastrophic decades between.

"Jeez!" I heard a voice saying, and I felt a gentle nudge in my ribs. I looked up. Both sailors had their heads turned and were staring out of the window. I followed their example and promptly held my breath. From somewhere in our region of the sky a colossal Croesus had let fall a jewel-box. Breaking asunder, it had scattered its precious contents over an island which Man has called Manhattan and which Nature has given the shape of a gigantic double-edged saw. The saw's two rows of teeth were studded with stars. Attached to its narrower end shone two concentrated clusters of tiny scintillating diamonds. Each held fast to the ebony blade by a single brilliant, these glittering brooches lay floating side-by-side in a sheen of quicksilver.

"Aircraft carriers," I heard the sailor say.

From tooth to tooth across and along the saw ran string after string of milk-white pearls, meeting and passing through one another to form rectangles of platinum. As we moved seemingly so slow over the great ruby of Times Square and the long jet of Central Park, the creamy spots of pearl merged into dark avenues outlined in gold. Under each minute orange circle of light you could see the tops of toylike trees. Miniature automobiles crawled from gem to gem until the lengths of parallel necklaces began to turn and wind in and out like black, illuminated snakes. The gap of invisible thread between each golden jewel grew longer and longer, till at last only isolated stars flickered from the blacked-out bosom of the country.

"Jeez," said the sailor, closing his eyes and shifting his legs in the ropes, "I guess that's almost worth three thousand miles on a God-damned bucket-seat! Lucky it's a fine night!"

Agreeing silently, I thought what such a night would be like in Paris—Paris in May, just as I had last seen it. . . . The café terraces were crammed. . . . Near the Observatoire the sidewalks were carpeted pink with chestnut blossom. A full moon made ghosts of the drinkers outside La Closerie des Lilas. As I walked home along the river the tall poplars on the Quai de l'Horloge were flickering black and silver. Behind the glass, muslin-curtained door my concierge was sitting at the table, sewing. She looked up, smiled, waved. . . . This is a dream, I kept telling myself, only a dream. . . .

"Wanna have a look at Boston?" the sailor said.

I turned and looked down. I looked again and went on looking.

"That's not Boston!" I exclaimed in dismay. "That's the Hudson! Holy Mother! We're back over New York!"

"By golly! Darned if you ain't right!"

A few minutes later, at one o'clock in the morning, we landed in Brooklyn. The plane's radio equipment had ceased to function.

We clambered down the ladder and into a waiting room full of men snoring on wooden benches. There wasn't a seat in the place, so we sat with our legs dangling from a counter and smoked. Hale, the little man who had been operated on for hernia, showed me pictures of his wife and children.

"This is the first time I've ever left them," he said, "even for a night. D'you think we'll be in Europe long?"

"Didn't you sign up for a year?" I asked.

"Sure," he said. "But we won't be away all that time, will we?"

I said I didn't know, and we went out to look at the plane. Then we came in again and smoked some more. A clock and a calendar told me that the day was the thirteenth of May and the hour two-fifteen A.M. At the counter Perkins was asking the sergeant in charge for something to eat and drink, but the sergeant said there wasn't anything. "Too late," he muttered.

"Well," said Perkins, "if you'd give me some hot water, I could make some coffee. I always carry my own coffee."

"Sorry," said the sergeant, "no hot water. Too late."

Perkins began to curse the War Department. "Who the hell do they think they are, anyway!" he growled.

I thought of telephoning my wife. If she were awake, she'd be thinking of me as somewhere over Europe. I thought it wiser to let her go on thinking that. At three-thirty we climbed back into the plane again.

After ten minutes in the air, one of the crew appeared with life-preservers, which looked like chastity belts. They were flat, yellow, complicated contraptions attached with what seemed to be a whistle. There was also a strap which had to be fixed between the legs, and a list of instructions which concluded with three words of advice in large letters: KEEP YOUR HEAD!

Clothed in this garment, I shut my eyes and tried to recapture memories of Germany, of the places and people I'd once known there; but the pictures my imagination evoked were so dim and distant, and Paris suddenly so frighteningly, so excitingly near and familiar, that no effort I made could keep me off its streets, nor offer me any other suggestion of the city than that I'd always known. To kill time I dawdled, peered into shop windows, dropped in at bistros I knew for a *Calvados* or a *blanc*. Everything was just the same as it had always been—the smell of coffee, French tobacco, the faces of Monsieur and Madame.

I was about to start out on a walk, late at night, from

among the mountains of vegetables in Les Halles towards Montmartre, when dawn suddenly shattered the dream and we looked down to see the early sun shining on the coast of Nova Scotia. Precipitous black cliffs fell sheer into whirlpools of foaming water. Behind them, following bay after bay, a thin ribbon of road wound its way for no apparent reason from nowhere to nowhere. Then, all alone, surrounded by a rolling desert of hills and green virgin forest, a single wooden house appeared, with blue smoke curling from its one chimney. I tried to imagine living there, but the house didn't look real. No part of that lonely landscape looked real. It was all a realistic relief map, an unusually good technicolor movie seen from an uncomfortable seat in a newsreel house.

At ten o'clock we landed at Stephensville, Newfoundland. That was real enough. It was a grim, gray, windswept crater pocked with wooden army shacks and barracks. We ate eggs and bacon in the Transients' Mess, changed our crew, and went on board again at noon, bound for the Azores.

"Seventeen hundred statute miles," the pilot told me.

"How long will that take?" the sailor asked.

"Should be nine hours flying," he said.

"Jeez!" said the sailor.

"No smoking, please!" shouted the pilot as he marched down the plane.

"Oh, my aching back!" moaned the sailor. No occasion, I thought, could have better suited that expression.

We chewed gum and I tried not to think of the hours by gazing out at the sun shining on the limitless expanse of rippling blue damask below. I was trying to imagine what it must be like to lie adrift down there for days and weeks on end, when in the distance I saw a yellow-brown speck. As we drew nearer, it looked like a battleship painted the color of parchment. I nudged the sailor. He turned and looked out. "Iceberg," he said.

I'd imagined icebergs were white, and I thought of the *Lusitania,* the Kaiser's war, and the *Leinster* when it was chased and sunk by a U-boat in the Irish Channel. Then there was another, quite close: shaped like a ship, it looked like a lonely floating island of sand.

In what seemed a strangely short time the sun began to sink over a sea unbelievably serene. On the horizon solid-looking mauve mountains of cloud stood stock still. Below, the water suddenly disappeared from sight as we moved into white powder-puffs of cotton wool. They lay all round us, utterly still and overwhelmingly alone. I watched as the wing, the engine, and the invisible propeller purred into one big ball: it neither scattered nor shied away but continued its static vigil—untouched, impervious to machine and man, waiting for wind to move it or for warmth to melt it into rain.

Then the sun sank and in the darkness the minutes, the half-hours, the hours began to drag. The sailor had climbed onto the top of the chests of freight and lay there with his face almost touching the ceiling, seemingly asleep. The *Saturday Evening Post* had dropped from Perkins' knees; his head was thrown back on his chair; his arms dangled down; his mouth gaped; he showed no sign of being alive.

The door opened suddenly. "Fasten your belts!" a voice called out.

We sat up, stretched, and rubbed our eyes. Bump! We were in the Azores.

In a dark deserted wooden barracks we wolfed cold spaghetti and tomato sauce. Perkins produced a can of coffee from his musette bag and demanded hot water from the one native boy. Raising a yellow, pock-marked face, the boy offered Perkins an uncomprehending stare. I tried to help him out with the few words of Portuguese I had learned years ago in Cintra. And the moment I heard his nasal drawl: *"No agua caliente!"* I felt, with a bound of excitement, that we had "crossed the border" and were back in Europe.

"He says there's no hot water," I told Perkins.

"Little wop!" snarled Perkins. "Why the hell can't he talk English, anyway!"

I glanced at the sailors, who were looking at Perkins. I

thought one of them was going to say something, but instead he shot me a look, shrugged his shoulders and winked.

Half an hour later we boarded the plane again.

"Are we really landing in Paris?" I asked the pilot.

"Sure."

"What time?"

"Nine A.M., Greenwich."

I looked at my watch. It was just after midnight. I now abandoned my walk to Montmartre and began to think of England, of London, of my family and friends, but again the more familiar face of Paris protruded itself and I was back on the crowded Grands Boulevards. I had the intention of walking to my wife's studio off the Champs Elysées, but I lost my way and finally took a Métro as far as the Madeleine. Outside the American Embassy I must, for the first time, have fallen asleep, for when I opened my eyes it was day and the plane was passing over a sea of spotless gray silk. Then the sun rose in a blaze of gold and the water turned into an eiderdown of glittering satin blue. I reached for my binoculars and stared forward. I saw land!

In a couple of minutes we were over a jagged coast. I got up and peered out of a starboard window. The first sight that met the eye was a port town. Through the glasses I could see that none of the houses had any roofs. You could look down into them, to their foundations, which were black. You could see the streets, but they were empty of life. What remained of the town was like a massive burnt skull, gray and charred and dead. I thought at first we must be over Cherbourg. Then I darted back to the port window. A brown-and-green patched quilt spread north as far as the naked eye could see. This couldn't be Cherbourg. And if it wasn't Cherbourg I knew without referring to my pocket atlas that it must be Brest.

In the crystal-clear sunlight the fields of Brittany looked very small, very neat, as though laid out by the all-seeing eye of one man with a tape-measure from a height of ten thousand feet. Not an inch of earth was wasted. There seemed to be place for the small and the large landowner, for the peasant and the man of property. Through the glasses I could see a toy château enclosed by dark green trees—a fairy tale illustration of a king's estate, with its liver-shaped lake and the white speck of a single swan sailing on its inky patch of water. Then it was gone, and through the glasses I began to travel over long ribbons of roads, raven-colored roads and sandy lanes that cut their way through tiny green fields, yellow fields, squares of chocolate earth, then a chessboard of meadows of every shade of green. The lanes led to small farms and the roads to large farms with their manor houses and neat clusters of barns with roofs of terra cotta tiles. Yet nowhere in this garden of civilization did I see any sign of life. It was after seven o'clock, yet everyone in Brittany seemed to be asleep.

"Look," the sailor was saying, "see those round spots . . . ?"

In a field of flowering mustard I saw a rash of sandy circles, like smallpox on an oriental face. The pockmarks were filled with water.

"Bomb craters," the sailor said.

Looking north, we could see the mouth of the channel. I glanced at the atlas. That town must be St. Malo—because out in the water all alone lay the unmistakable island tower of St. Michel. The distant darkness of the receding map must be Normandy, that barely visible mass of stone and brick, Avranches. . . . I tried to imagine the fearful activity there had been, only a few months ago, upon these now lifeless roads.

"See that bridge," the sailor said. "There's another. . . ."

They were the remains of bridges, their spans invisible under water and their steel or stone ends sticking up helplessly, ridiculously, like feet without legs, on the river banks.

"I think that's Pontoise," I muttered, and I thought of the times my wife and I had driven our twenty-year-old Talbot across that now sunken bridge. Staring down at the Seine as it wormed its placid way through the rich, serene, cultivated country, I thought of Pissarro, of Monet in his garden at Giverny, of Seurat in his stipple haze, surrounded by long-skirted women under parasols on the Island of La Grande Jatte, and I marveled that the wars waged, the machines invented since their century had not wrought even more indelible scars on the face of France.

Immediately under us I recognized the dark green gardens, the sun glittering on the lake of Versailles. For the first time I began to feel sick. I couldn't look out of the window any more. I fastened my belt and closed my eyes. *"In a few minutes,"* a voice kept saying, *"you are going to see Paris."*

The plane lurched sideways. My hands were cold and wet.

I opened my eyes. From the window opposite I saw, instead of the sky, the panorama of a sunlit city almost upside down—a river running under many bridges, thousands of houses in a gray jumble, a star of streets all converging on a single arch. . . .

There came the bump. I felt so sick I didn't dare move. I was last out of the plane. I stood still on concrete in the blazing sun and shivered. I felt deaf and dazed. I was breathing the air of France and every man in sight wore an American uniform.

Mechanically I got into a jeep. I found myself in the back with Hale. Perkins was in front beside the driver, a sergeant. No one spoke.

I didn't know where we were. I could see nothing but an endless flat plain of long grass with concrete runways cutting across it. This was not Le Bourget.

"What airfield is this?" I asked the driver.

"Orly," he said. I had never been in Orly.

"How far are we from the city?"

"Forty-five minutes by bus," the driver said.

An appalling thought flashed into my mind. Supposing this was as near as I was going to get to Paris! Supposing we'd have to fly straight on to London, never set foot in the capital!

The jeep drew up outside an ugly brick building surrounded by trucks, bull-dozers, weapons-carriers, jeeps, G.I.s.

Engines roared, men yelled, and everything was covered in a thick layer of yellow dust.

We entered the building and stood in front of a long counter—Perkins, Hale and I. A young man in civilian clothes leaned over and took our orders.

"Gentlemen," he said in a slightly French accent, "where do you wish to go?"

"London!" snapped Perkins in a loud voice.

"Yes, London," murmured Hale.

I said nothing and held my breath.

"Gentlemen," said the civilian, "I regret that we have no room in a plane for London today."

Could you reach out and shake the Frenchman's hand? Then I heard a burst of abuse from Perkins.

"No room!" he was shouting. "I'll be damned if I'll stay here, man! I have very important documents to deliver in London tonight. Very important indeed."

He turned round, and with a flushed face he muttered in fury, "Stay here amongst all these God damned frogs! Who the hell do they think I am, anyway!"

Heaving my duffel bag onto my shoulder, I went out into the sun. I never saw Perkins again.

In the yellow haze of dust I recognized the familiar shape of a snub-nosed Paris bus. It was empty, but a stocky little man with a red face protruding from a leather wind-jacket sat hunched over the wheel.

"What time d'you leave?" I asked him.

"Ah ça!" he said with a hopeless shrug of his shoulders. *"On ne sait jamais, vous savez! Vingt minutes, peut-être*—maybe twenty minutes, maybe forty. *Ça dépend!"*

"Merci, Monsieur," I said, and smiled. I began to feel at home. After we'd dumped our baggage in a large airy dormitory and shaved, Hale and I went to breakfast in the Transients' Mess. In a room jammed with American officers, we found ourselves sitting opposite the only two civilians. They were young Frenchmen, and though they talked almost in

whispers I managed to gather from their conversation that they had worked in the Resistance. While they talked I noticed that every few minutes they glanced furtively over their shoulders. My God, I thought, a quarter-of-an-hour in France and already the *Deutsche Blick!*

Hale complained that he was too exhausted from lack of sleep to finish his dish of hash and canned vegetables, and I replied that I was too excited. As we laid down our knives and forks on the half-eaten food I saw, with a pang of shame, the eyes of both boys staring at our plates.

"We've just this minute arrived from New York," I explained. "We're too thrilled to eat!"

At the sound of their language, they glanced up with a shocked look. "I used to live here," I said, and handed them a pack of Camels across the table. They beamed and in return offered us each a *Gauloise Jaune.*

"For the sake of old times!" one of them said, and he promptly embarked on a description of the city during the last great days culminating in its liberation.

"*Ça c'était quelque chose!* That was something! We fought in the streets for a whole week!"

"And saved Paris!" I said. "That's the one miracle of the war!"

We shook their hands, and as we left I heard them ordering from the French waiter another round of hash.

"*Bon appétit!*" I called back.

"*Merci!*" they laughed. "You needn't worry about that!"

We were just in time to catch the bus, already packed with G.I.s. Despite his state of health and exhaustion, Hale insisted on seeing what he called "the sights."

"They'll be running trips for Americans, won't they?" he asked.

"I guess so," I said, and I told him to inquire at the Place Vendôme, where the bus stopped. "I'll be getting off before," I added. "I want to look up some friends."

As we approached the city I began to recognize names—Kremlin-Bicêtre, the Avenue de Choisy.... It was ten o'clock on Monday morning, yet in the streets all the shops were closed, the shutters up, the sidewalks strangely empty. An air of Sunday penetrated even into the bus, bringing with it a drab, funereal feeling.

I noticed the hammer-and-sickle chalked on many doors. The flags of the allied nations drooped from window after window, but without the sound or sight of people the colors seemed only to intensify the atmosphere of Sabbath gloom.

Clattering through the Porte d'Italie, down the Rue Monge, past the Halle aux Vins and out onto the quays, I recognized and inwardly hailed every corner and crossing. From the bus the streets, the corners, the trees were there, just as they had always been; yet the houses looked grim and lonely, with a shut-up look, as though their owners had gone away and were not expected to return very soon.

"There's Notre Dame," I told Hale. Gray and timeless, it made me think as much as ever of a great elephant. The thick ropes of ivy, like the long hair of women, still hung from the walls, almost into the water. But the ancient houses along the quays, the houses that once had color, seemed to have changed. Their façades had faded; the plaster on their walls was pealing off; they looked lifeless, uncared for, parched, as though thirsting for company and a coat of paint.

"Here's where I get off," I told Hale. "Take it easy. Those trips are damned tiring."

I stood at the corner of the Boul' Miche and wanted to walk in all directions at once. The expanse of sky seemed immense, the buildings strangely low. I tried to absorb the atmosphere of Paris in a minute and succeeded in absorbing almost nothing. Only by closing my eyes and seeing my concierge's face could I make up my mind which way to go. I set off towards the Quai de l'Horloge. In the flower market there were no flowers, on the river no barges. The restaurant of the Vert Galant was shuttered, the chestnut-shaded Place Dauphine deserted. Only the slender poplars on the quay, their leaves flickering green and silver, looked alive.

I glanced up. From the long windows of the studio on the

top floor of Number 31 hung the colors of the Cross of Lorraine. A little weak with anticipation, I walked into the shade of the porch, peered through the familiar curtained window of the concierge's door. A thin, middle-aged woman stood in the middle of the room, her arms in a basin of water. I knocked. A worn, disgruntled face glanced up. I opened the door.

"Excusez-moi, Madame," I said. "Is Madame Grillet in?"

"Madame who?"

"Grillet, *la concierge* . . ."

"Ha! Madame Grillet! She's been dead two years!"

"Madame Grillet dead," I muttered. "What from?"

"Didn't get enough to eat. She wasn't the only one. . . ."

For a minute I couldn't think of anything to say. I thought of all the kindnesses the dead woman had done us. Finally I asked: "And Monsieur?"

"M. Grillet? He's gone. I don't know where he is."

"Does Mlle. Tarbord still own this house?"

"Naturally," said the woman. "She's sick."

"Merci, Madame," I said, closed the door and walked away. I crossed the street and stood leaning over the wall. Below, on the cobbled patch of ground beside the water—where by night the *clochards,* wrapped in sacks, used to sleep, and by day lines of men sat on boxes, hour after hour, fishing—now only a yellowed scrap of newspaper was being shifted, in jerks, by the gentle breeze.

I walked slowly under the poplars towards the Pont Neuf, turned the corner, and—as much from force of habit as from preconceived intent—dropped into the *tabac.* Madame Perier's once fleece-white hair had turned the color of dirty hay and her bust was no longer huge. For several seconds we gazed at one another in silence, until I took off my cap and stretched out my hand. She then let out a shriek and, howling for her husband, came bustling round the counter.

"Enfin!" she cried, grasping both my hands. "At last! At last! Pierre! Pierre! *Viens voir qui est arrivé! Mon Dieu,* what a surprise!"

M. Perier came limping up the stairs. His cheeks had fallen in; the loss of his *embonpoint* made him look strangely frail and small.

"*Pauvre Pierre*," sighed his wife. "*Les sales Boches*—he's had sciatica ever since he first saw them!"

"*Tiens!*" panted M. Perier, taking my hands in his. "*Tiens! Un ami! Comme il est beau* in his uniform! *Alors*, an excellent excuse for one more celebration. What shall it be? *Rouge, blanc?*"

"Ha!" snapped Madame, clapping her hands. "*Blanc*, indeed! I know what Monsieur likes. I remember. Out of the way, Pierre!"

Disappearing beneath the counter, she came up with a labelless bottle. Filling three small glasses, she glanced at me, raised one to her lips, threw back her head and emptied it. "*Vive les Américains!*" she cried.

I sniffed my glass. It was Calvados.

"To you both," I said, drinking. "To Paris. And to France." I put the glass down. "Fancy you remembering!" I said.

"Ha! Me remember? Ask Pierre! Do I ever forget a man who likes our Calvados, Pierre?"

M. Perier lowered his bleary eyes, glanced sheepishly at me. "Catch her!" he said.

Madame burst into roars of laughter. "Ha! You should have seen him the day the Boches cleared out! *Oh là-là!* They were all lined up outside the door here, all the way along the bridge—generals with monocles, colonels, hundreds of men. Six of us went down to our secret cellar. The Boches, they thought they'd drunk us out of house and home four years ago! *Les idiots!* We came up with magnums of champagne and cases of Calvados. We gave every civilian in the street a bottle. Then we all stood in front of the Boches and drank and shouted as they marched away: '*Vive la France! Vive de Gaulle! A bas les cochons.*' *Oh là-là,* what a day! Pierre passed out at three in the afternoon. *N'est-ce pas,* Pierre?"

M. Perier turned his eyes away. "Calvados and champagne don't mix," he muttered.

"No more than we and the Germans!" snapped Madame, clearing her throat in disgust.

Suddenly her face clouded over. *"Dites,"* she said, looking at me out of sad, serious eyes. "do you think the old days will ever come back? Do you think there can ever be peace so long as Germany exists?"

"I'm going there in a few days," I told her. "Maybe I'll find it easier to answer that when I get back."

"You're going to Germany?" she said in almost a whisper. Then she threw up her head, banged her fist on the counter. *"Les salauds!"* she shouted. "They killed our Jean in 1940!"

Then she lowered her head and wiped one eye with the corner of her apron. *"Excusez-moi, Monsieur,"* she murmured. *"Quelquefois la vie est triste."*

I glanced at M. Perier. He slowly nodded his head at me, shot a glance at his wife, then raised a silencing finger to his lips.

I went over to them both and shook their hands. "I wish I'd been here," I confessed for the first time aloud.

"Monsieur," said Madame Perier, leaning over and holding on to my hand, "we thanked *le bon Dieu* for every friend of ours who was not."

In the market in the Rue de Buci, where we used to buy our vegetables, a single woman was sitting behind the one-sheet newspaper, *Libération*. In front of her lay two boxes, one containing some dust-covered strawberries, the other a few yellow asparagus. The strawberries were priced at fifty francs, a dollar a pound, the asparagus at sixty cents. When I looked into the boxes, the woman glanced up at me, then quickly turned back to her paper.

On the terrace of the Deux Magots the chairs were piled one on top of the other and the door was locked. In a wheel chair outside the Café Bonaparte sat a small man with a bald head and his arm in a sling. As I passed him to go into the *bistro,* he looked up.

"Pas possible!" he exclaimed.

It took me several seconds to recognize him as a French journalist I used to know. This was where we used to sit, drinking *apéritifs* in these chairs. "I was unlucky," he said, as he saw me looking at his arm, at the wheel chair. "Only just got out of hospital. The bastards plugged me in the arms and legs the day before the end."

He wheeled himself inside. *"Alors,* patron! A face from the past!" he cried.

Several men stood at the bar, drinking ersatz coffee. They all began to stare. When the patron recognized me, he brought out a bottle of cognac.

"I'll not drink that," I said, "unless everyone else drinks with me—and I pay. One doesn't arrive in Paris every day. . . ."

"Nor is it every day," said the patron, shrugging his shoulders, "that we see an old face again!"

He lined up a number of liqueur glasses on the bar, and I handed round a pack of Camels.

"Dites, Monsieur," he asked, "what are they saying in America? Tell us about New York. When did you leave?"

"The day before yesterday," I said.

Everyone gasped. *"Pas vrai! Mon Dieu! Imaginez-vous—* New York the day before yesterday . . . !"

"Alors, tell us—*on mange bien là-bas?* How's the food? What's the price of a bottle of wine?"

In the silence I felt everyone hanging on my words, like a new prisoner among men long in jail.

"A bottle of wine?" I smiled. "French or American?"

Everyone laughed. "French, of course!"

"I don't know," I said. "I'm not a millionaire!"

"Tiens! So dear!"

"Does America really grow wine?" someone asked. "How much for a bottle of *ordinaire?*"

"It's nearly all *ordinaire,*" I said. "Forty, fifty francs."

"But that's worse than here! How much can you buy at once?"

"As much as you like."

An "Aaaaah!" went up from all along the bar.

For half an hour I answered question after question about the details of living in the United States. I told them that meat was obtainable almost only on the black market, that butter and sugar were scarce, that cigarettes—except in midtown nightclubs at three times their normal price—were virtually non-existent.

"Incredible!" they muttered, wagging their heads. "A black market in New York! We always heard America had more than enough of everything!" As I paid and walked away I didn't think I was believed.

The Café Flore was open. On the leather benches a few men sat in silence—reading, writing. Pascal, the *garçon* with the enormous brown eyes and skull-like face, looked more than ever like a ghost; and when he saw me walking in he threw up his hands as though he had seen one in me. I sat down by the open door and we talked of mutual friends.

"Madame Reynolds is back from America," he said. "And Monsieur Paul. They were in here last night. Soon it will be like old times."

When I asked for pen and paper to tell my wife where I was sitting, I realized I was not sober. I told Pascal as much and asked for a cup of coffee.

"Voilà!" he smiled. "Like old times already!"

The coffee—just seven times its former price—tasted a little like charcoal.

I sat on the terrace in the shade of the awning, gazing out through the plane trees at the Boulevard St. Germain, trying to collect my thoughts. But in the strange, uncanny silence of that perfect May morning I couldn't think, concentrate, or keep still. I walked up to the rue de l'Odéon, bought some French magazines at Adrienne Monnier's bookshop. Opposite the Palace in the Luxembourg Gardens the statues of the Queens gazed down on empty flowerbeds, on the empty vases on their pedestals of stone. No children played on the rim of the Round Pond, no toy boats were sailing on its water. Near the ridiculous reclining figure of George Sand a single G.I. was sitting under a chestnut tree, writing a letter. Under another tree a girl was waiting for her lover, or just waiting. . . . A spray of water from a hose was swinging round and round over a patch of sandy, grassless ground. On a flight of stone steps I stood still and listened: all I heard was the sound of water falling, falling on the parched earth. Then I walked quickly under the trees towards the river.

On a wall at the corner of the rue Bonaparte and the rue Vaugirard, over a plaque commemorating those Parisians who had died for France in the First War was another plaque, white and new, in honor of those Parisians who had died for Paris between the years 1940 and 1945. On the Quai Voltaire, the sunken-cheeked old genius no longer leaned his face on his hand; only his pedestal remained as a reminder of the seat he used to occupy. In the Tuileries the grass was high and there was earth where in May the mass of tulips and pansies used to grow. But Jeanne d'Arc, ablaze in a fresh coat of gold, was still astride her horse on the rue de Rivoli. All round her, on a wooden floor painted red, white, and blue, lay heaps of bouquets and wreaths of flowers, in celebration of her recent birthday. Opposite the Comédie Française, always one of the busiest, most clamorous corners of Europe, I stopped once more in the hot sun. Closing my eyes, I listened to the tinkle of a bicycle bell, the slow shuffle, the sharp wooden clack of feet on the sidewalk, the clip-clop of a tired horse as it trundled by.

On the Avenue de l'Opéra I passed women carrying market bags. They moved slowly, dragging their legs. They wore no stockings and on their feet were slippers or shoes with wooden soles. Their faces were white and worn, and they gave the impression of wandering painfully to no particular place. The men, either very young or aged, looked sullen or bitter; the young were thin, and the old, in clothes that hung from their gaunt shoulders and ballooned round their waists, looked haggard.

All the café chairs under the plane trees on the Grands

Boulevards were occupied by G.I.s. They sat there in rows, drinking watery beer at fifty cents the glass, staring out in silence at the passing bicycles, the buggies, the barouches.

Opposite the Trois Quartiers stood a line of four-wheelers. The horses hung their heads; the sun emphasized in silver the skeleton of their ribs. A *cocher,* the image of Aristide Briand, sat motionless on his footplate, his hand hidden in his long, hay-colored mustaches.

"How much would you charge," I asked him, "to take me as far as the Etoile?"

The old man didn't even raise an eyebrow. Then, over his hand, as though tugged by an invisible thread, his mustaches went up and down. *"Quatre cents francs!* Four hundred francs" came out in a mumble from under them. Eight dollars—for a mile!

"Mais, Monsieur," I began to protest.

"Ecoute, mon vieux," he interrupted. "See that old mare? I make that journey to the Etoile once more today—*eh, bien!"* —he spread his hands—"tomorrow I sell her carcase to the butcher!"

I walked down into the Métro, but when I saw the size of the crowd waiting on the platform I came up again and crossed over to the rue Royale. The Place de la Concorde looked like a bicycle racetrack. I noticed bullet-marks over the entrance to the Crillon. On the curb outside the hotel stood a charabanc jammed with G.I.s. I wondered how Hale was enjoying "the sights."

All the trees and rhododendrons between the Concorde and the Rond-Point were orange with grime, the iron benches and chairs chipped and brown with rust. A huge military sign hung outside the Théatre des Ambassadeurs. The bowls of the fountains at the Rond-Point were dry; their rabbits of Lalique glass had gone.

Crowds milled along the wide *trottoirs* of the upper Champs Elysées. American MPs—looking strangely smart, virile, healthy, tall—stood at the entrances to the Métros, wandered about among the weary-looking, shabbily-dressed Parisians. Here, more than anywhere else—from out of open doors and from the proximity of so many people—I smelled the stench of poverty: the unmistakable odor of unwashed bodies, unwashed clothes; unaired, unheated homes; empty stomachs and decaying teeth.

A crowd formed suddenly in front of me. Men and women were converging upon one unshaven, emaciated figure. He wore steel spectacles and blue- and white-striped pajamas. I had a vision of concentration camps and tried not to look. The crowd grew quickly larger and people began to mutter. The muttering became a babble. The man raised his arms and tried to say something, but the crowd wouldn't let him. Suddenly a woman shouted: "Don't trust him! *Sale Boche!*" Someone repeated the woman's words, then another, until the refrain became a chorus. Then a single voice cried out *"Juif!"* and the man's face dropped into his bony hands.

Turning the corner of the rue Washington, I ran into a French acquaintance who used to deal in antiques. As impeccably dressed as ever, he hadn't changed in any way. We shook hands. "Welcome back, *mon vieux!* What about dinner together tonight!" he suggested. "I know a little place where we can have quite a good meal."

"For how much?" I asked.

"Well, 'round fifteen hundred francs," * he said, and added, "with a decent bottle of Bordeaux, of course."

"Thanks," I replied, "I think that's a little beyond my means."

In the courtyard in front of my wife's studio an old man and a child were lying on the patch of unmown grass, playing with a kitten. I walked up the steps and knocked at the concierge's door. It was opened by an oldish woman with deep holes in her cheeks.

"Is Monsieur or Madame Dérain in?" I asked.

"Monsieur and Madame Dérain? *Mais non,* Monsieur. Monsieur Dérain was taken off to Germany long ago. Madame—

* At that date: $30.00.

we don't know where Madame is. When her husband was taken, she went away with *la petite*. . . . We have not heard from her since."

I introduced myself to the old woman, asked her if Madame Joubert still occupied the studio. "Ah, Monsieur knows Madame Joubert?" she said, and when she opened her mouth and smiled I saw she had no teeth. "Yes, Monsieur, I think she is at home."

I was on the stairs when I heard the old woman call my name. I turned back.

"Monsieur," she said in a low voice. "Monsieur will not inquire after Madame's boys. . . ."

Noticing the question in my eyes, she added: "Young Monsieur Lucien, he is still a prisoner. Marcel was—well, they caught him in Nice last year. Madame has had no news of him. She is very sad."

Dropping her eyes, the old woman patted my arm and turned indoors.

"Thank you, Madame, for telling me," I said.

I stood still at the bottom of the stairs, feeling slightly dizzy, slightly sick. Then I slowly mounted the familiar wooden steps. I hope she's not in, I thought, I hope she is, I hope she's not. . . .

She was; but I didn't at first recognize the stooping figure with white hair. She stood in the doorway, the once dark and handsome woman now frail, bent and old. Only after I'd muttered my name did she throw up her hands with the shock of recognition.

Her arm through mine, we walked over the threshold, saying nothing. In a dream I saw an old bookcase I'd made, years ago, in another part of Paris. A few well-thumbed books, more familiar than any face, seemed to stare at me accusingly as inanimate objects do in dreams. I saw the low, enormous bed, the cheap counterpane I'd bought during the 1920's in a London store. The orange curtains a French aunt had given us years ago were torn; the brown mat-carpet was stained and threadbare. An early original Picasso hung on the wall. A painted screen stood in the place of the writing table. I looked at it and wondered what it hid.

Madame Joubert followed my gaze. "You can stay the night?" she asked, speaking for the first time.

"It's awfully kind of you," I said. "I mustn't." And I told her I had to sleep at Orly and leave for London at dawn.

"London?" She glanced up and smiled, then looked away. "I was there in '43," she murmured.

"You were in London? During the war?"

"Yes, I managed to get across. I did a little—underground work. With the help of—of friends." I noticed her eyeing the screen. "British flyers; nice boys," she muttered.

Then she walked—or rather, limped—across the room, took a bottle from a glass-fronted cupboard. "Cherry brandy," she said, smiling. "There's just enough for two to celebrate!"

"Please keep it," I protested.

"Keep it? What for? *Mon cher,* do you know what it means to us to see an old friend again . . . ? Wait, I'll just call up Louise, and tell her you're here. She'll be so excited. I'm dining with her tonight; you must come along. . . ."

Louise was the young and beautiful daughter of a mutual friend, a Spanish painter.

"I really mustn't," I protested. "I've no way of providing food, and I'm certainly not going to eat . . ."

"*Ça va! Ça va!*" she said, "Louise has just got six eggs from the country. We can make a beautiful omelet."

"How's Louise?" I asked, after we'd both spoken a few words to the girl over the phone.

Madame Joubert lowered her eyes. "Ah, poor thing," she sighed, moving her white head from side to side. "She had a bad time, very bad. I'd rather not tell you, but since you will see her it is as well to be prepared. She will give you details. You will find her changed. The Gestapo got her, though only on suspicion. They could prove nothing, and she never spoke. . . . They stripped her, and for forty-eight hours they immersed her, first in boiling water, then in cold. . . ."

All of a sudden, with a wave of nausea, I saw the floor rising towards me, the ceiling receding, and I missed the end of Madame Joubert's sentence.

I stayed with her half an hour longer, but I cannot recall what more she said. I remember only her last words in the doorway as she saw me looking down at her swollen ankle.

"Oh, that," she said, "that was when they nearly got me, too. The concierge, God bless her, tipped me off—but only at the last minute. I heard them already on the stairs—you could always recognize them by their walk, their boots—and I managed to get out of the window. Only twenty feet. Shouldn't have broken the ankle. But," she laughed, "maybe I was heavier then!"

I didn't get to dinner with Madame Joubert and Louise. I only just managed to walk as far as the Place Vendôme. From there, sad with shame, I lied over the telephone that I'd been ordered, suddenly, to leave for London that night.

In the airport dormitory Hale was lying on his cot.

"Boy, I've had a wonderful time," he said.

LONDON

2

WE hung around in the dust of Orly until three in the afternoon.

The trip from there to Bovington airport was like an hour's pleasure cruise, the Channel a wide river and most of southern England an endless green estate.

In the plane two young British officers, with wiry mustaches and pipes, alternately read the *Daily Mail* and conversed in a language it took me minutes to believe was not meant to caricature their particular breed.

"I say, old boy," one called to the other across the aisle, "whatcher think o' this?"

"What?"

"Says here that bloke Blum landed at Orly from Germany this morning!"

"Ha! That's rum! Let's see, he was the Socialist chap, wasn't he?"

"That's right. Sit-down strikes and all that. Wonder why those Nahzi buggers didn't bump 'im off!"

"Jew, too, what? That's what I always say about the Nahzis—bloody well can't rely on 'em!"

"Bloody right! Wouldn't trust one o' those bahstards the length of a ruddy barge pole!"

With their aid I had re-absorbed one strata of English society before the Bovington bus started off for London—a trip that took almost as long as that across the Channel.

The roads into the suburbs were like roofless green corridors, the windows of the bus all but scraping the high hedges on either side. I kept wondering what would happen if another bus, heading towards us, were suddenly to appear round one of these blind corners. Fortunately we encountered nothing wider than a woman on a bicycle, and she promptly dropped to her feet at sight of us.

"Gee, look at all those flowers!" Hale said, expressing my own thoughts. To the red brick walls of the squat suburban cottages, each "standing in its own private grounds," clung clumps of purple clematis. Higher, under their eaves, hung heavy cushions of crimson roses.

"My wife'd sure like these gardens," Hale said. "What I can't figure out is why they fence them in!"

"Ah," I muttered, " 'the Englishman's castle. . . .' " And I thought of what in England Henry James found that could not be defined as private property: "When I have mentioned the hedgerows and the churches I have almost exhausted the list."

Near Lord's Cricket Ground we passed a London bus. Once, I remembered, New York's Fifth Avenue buses had reminded me of London buses painted green. Now a London bus reminded me of a Fifth Avenue bus painted red.

Very suddenly we emerged from Edgware Road into the circus of Marble Arch. The Arch looked unbelievably small. Hyde Park seemed different, larger, more beautiful. Then I realized the black spiked railings had gone. I glanced back. All the way down Bayswater Road the Park was free and open. The sidewalks of Oxford Street, which made me think of Main Street in a provincial American town, were jammed with men in khaki. Queues of sootily-dressed men and women stood mutely waiting for buses. All the windows flew flags. Over the corner cinema hung huge colored posters of Churchill, Stalin, Roosevelt.

At the terminal in Welbeck Street Hale and I stood in line at a counter. A sergeant handed us little maps of London's West End and with a red pencil marked a street near Paddington Station.

"Your billets," he informed us. "Best we can do at the

moment. Now you'd better scram and report at Grosvenor Square. This is how to get there. Take . . ."

"Okay," I said, "I know."

He looked up. "Golly, that's unusual!" he smiled.

We walked out into the street. "Let's try and get a drink first," I said.

We went to a pub I knew in the next block, but we couldn't get near the bar: there were too many G.I.s.

It was eight years since I'd been in London, and fifteen since I'd lived there: I'd lost contact, knew the addresses of very few friends, and felt like a foreigner—a foreigner, however, in familiar surroundings, among people until now more familiar than the natives. For the West End streets were so filled with uniformed foreigners that a British face came as a surprise and a relief. Oxford Street gave the impression of being owned by G.I.s, who seemed strangely at home. They had formed the British habit of standing perfectly still and speechless, as though in a trance, outside the entrance to pubs. Some, the younger ones, even looked like Englishmen— in American uniforms. The soft climate of the Islands seemed to have already affected their complexions, turning their naturally sallow, even-colored faces a slightly blotchy purple. But in or out of uniform the best guide to their nationality was, now more than ever, the whiteness of their teeth.

From ground level the houses along Oxford Street looked shoddier, smaller, lower, the sky even more immense than that over Paris. It was not chance that prompted Hale to ask for the name of "that big building with the flower-boxes."

"Selfridge's," I said. "Department store."

"Selfridge's? The Washington papers said it had been hit by a V-1."

"I believe the New York papers did too," I said.

Then we saw—by the absence of one, if not two houses across the street—how narrowly it had been missed.

At Headquarters in Grosvenor Square we "signed in" at a table, behind which sat a tired-looking captain.

"I thought you were never coming," he yawned.

"So did we!" we chorused. "Can we get something to eat here?"

"Not here," said the captain, looking at his watch. "And I'm afraid the mess'll be closed now. I really don't know what to suggest."

"We'll have to pick up our baggage at the terminal," I told Hale. "I know a hotel next door."

"Don't need to report here till around noon tomorrow," the captain said. "You're probably in need of sleep."

"How long shall we be in London?" I asked.

"God knows," he yawned. "We're doing our best to ship you over as soon as possible."

"Where to?"

"Either Bad Nauheim or Darmstadt. Better keep that under your belt for the time being."

I asked him if Mervyn were still in London. "Oh, no," said the captain, "he left a couple of weeks ago. Darmstadt, I think."

"Will I have time to see my parents?" I asked. "They live in the country—about three hours out of town."

"Parents?" he smiled. "Sure they're parents?"

"Well," I said, "that's what I've been calling them for more than forty years!"

"Oh!" he laughed. "I guess the colonel'll give you leave for that."

Outside, dusk was falling over the empty square. In the block ending at Upper Brook Street there was a gap between the houses, like a missing incisor in a row of decaying teeth. A large green weed was growing from a cavity in the partly shattered wall next door. Years of black, indelible-looking grime had eaten into the pores of the houses' faces; cracks cut across their soot-coated cheeks, and between the windows of their eyes lay the brown scars of burns. But out on Park Lane, facing the free, unenclosed green of the grass and trees, the great hotels and un-Londonlike apartment houses looked clean and as full of wealth as the sound of their site suggests.

American officers had taken charge of the Cumberland

Hotel. During the hour we sat in the lounge, waiting for a table, I thought of telephoning to my parents, whom I had not seen in eight years. They had no idea I was in England, since we had not been permitted to tell anyone we were coming. Then I looked at my watch and remembered that they seldom broke the habit of retiring to bed at ten.

In the hotel dining room dozens of American officers and a few British were dancing to a loud orchestra. To the accompaniment of whining saxophones we ate an omelet of powdered eggs and a potato, followed by a thimbleful of brandy for which I willingly paid an extravagant sum.

Unable to find a taxi to transport our baggage to our billets, we found our way there on foot. My so-called billet turned out to be a comfortable attic, looking out on to a tree-filled *cul-de-sac*. Over the tops of the trees, strangely white under the moon, I could see a garden of high weeds where once a house had stood. It seemed weeks since I'd been alone.

Next morning I got up early, leaving Hale asleep next door. On the stairs I ran into Mrs. Craig, the landlady. She was a small, good-looking woman with a beautiful skin and brown hair done up in a duster.

"Oh, 'ullo," she said brightly, "are you one of the ones what come in last nigh'? 'Ope you slep' well. Don't know 'ow long you'll be stayin', I s'pose? No good askin' for breakfast. Got no eggs, no sugar, nuthink like that. Shall I warm y'up a nice cup o' tea? Do you good, tea would—whether you like it or not."

At this first contact with real Londonese I felt, with startling suddenness, that I had known Mrs. Craig all my life.

I thanked her for the offer of tea and told her that if I could reach the Officers' Mess in Upper Grosvenor Street by eight o'clock, I'd get breakfast there.

"Oh," she said, "better look sharp then, 'adn't you? Know 'ow to get there? Two ways—tube right at the back 'ere, or bus along the Park."

"Yes, thanks," I said, "I know the way."

"Fancy!" I heard her breathe as she climbed up the stairs. "A reg'lar Mister Knowall!"

After a breakfast of real eggs and bacon, I walked back to the bus terminal to fetch my duffel bag. While waiting there I thought I'd drop into the Cumberland Hotel and telephone my parents. I wanted to make the call from a hotel because I guessed it would be both difficult and long; I had a vision of juggling with florins and shillings, sixpenny bits and coppers in a phone booth, and I hoped that a hotel would relieve me of that part of the operation. I also had to admit to myself that I'd actually forgotten how to make a long-distance call on an English phone.

Just inside the lobby I noticed a small cigar store, and behind its counter a youngish, mild-looking man in spectacles.

"Do you think I could possibly make a long-distance call from here?" I asked him.

"Oh, I think so, sir," he said. "Just ask the 'otel clerk over there—that's right, sir—the one in uniform."

The man in uniform asked me if I were staying in the hotel, and when I said no he said he was sorry, I'd have to go across the street to the postoffice.

I knew that postoffice well. It hadn't changed. I was standing at the counter, figuring out with the girl behind it just how many coins of different denominations I should need for a six minute call, when I felt a hand on my shoulder. Looking round, I recognized the young man from the cigar store.

"Beg pardon," he said in a voice of quiet concern, "didn't they let you phone from the 'otel?"

"No," I said. "You see, I'm not staying there."

"Oh, I *am* sorry," he said, as though he shared the guilt. "They shouldn't ought to 'ave done that. 'Ere, let me give you a 'and. It's sort of complicated with all them coins and things, i'n't it?"

"Oh, please don't bother," I said, falling into English. "I can manage perfectly well. It just happens it's so long since . . ."

But I could see there was no stopping him.

"Just leave it to me," he said, and he started gathering up the pile of coins on the counter. "Won't take a jiffy—promise it won't."

A moment later, with his hand on my arm, he was guiding me towards the line of booths.

"Now then," he said, in the tone of a nurse to a child, "now then, let's see, what's the number?"

"Templecombe 868," I told him, "but I do wish you wouldn't bother. . . ."

"No bother at all, old man," he insisted. "Now then—Templecombe, h'm, let's see, that'll be a toll, won't it?"

Toll? I thought. What distant bell does that word ring?

"Er, no," I said. "I don't think it is a toll. It's the other thing—it's long-distance—I mean it's further than a toll."

"Ah, trunks!"

"*That's* right!" I said. "Trunks! Fancy forgetting!"

He was in the booth, piling the little tower of coins over the slots, lifting the receiver. "Templecombe? Let's see, that's Dorset, i'n't it?"

"Somerset," I said.

"Somerset! Course! What am I thinkin' of! Beautiful bit o' country round there, i'n't it? You're stationed there, I s'pose?"

"No," I said, "my mother lives there."

"Your mother? Well, I never!"

"Haven't talked to her since 1937," I said, for the sake of something to say.

His eyes and mouth opened wide. "Go on!" he breathed.

"Yes," I said. "I've just arrived from New York."

"My, won't 'alf get a surprise, will she! Coo! Nineteen-'undred-and-thirty-seven! That is a time. Sort of 'ard to picture, i'n't it? Does she know you're on this side, your Ma?"

"No, she doesn't," I said. "I couldn't let her know."

He let out a whistle through his teeth. "Lummy," he said. "Fair take the wind out o' 'er sails, won't it? ('Ullo? Yes, Miss. 'Ere we go! One shillin', two, three. One penny, two, three, four! 'Ullo? Thanks ever so. 'Ullo? Templecombe

868? 'Alf a mo', London calling!) 'Ere you are, old man. Talk loud!"

"Thank you very much," I said, quickly taking his place in the booth and closing the door. I did not immediately recognize my mother's voice. It was hard to believe that anyone off the stage could sound quite so quietly English. Nor did she recognize mine, nor even the name she once had given me.

"Jimmy? Jimmy who?" she kept repeating.

"Stern," I said, "Stern!"

"Stern? But that's our name! I don't think I know a Jim—I'm afraid you must have got the wrong . . . *What?* My son? Son? Good-gracious! Where-are-you? London? Why-didn't-you-let-us-know? When-did-you-arrive? How? Where-are-you-staying? What?"

As is invariably the case with the members of one family, we all share certain definite characteristics. In ours the first, the most conspicuous is an almost eccentric undemonstrativeness; and the second, common to country-bred people, a deep-seated suspicion of the electric or mechanical device. To my mother, and particularly to myself, a telephone to this day is an instrument of portentous evil. Its black, shiny, anonymous face can neither speak nor smile, only ring, ring, and ring. When she dropped the receiver and I heard her voice: "Guess who's here! Guess who's here!" echoing excitedly through the faraway country house, I felt, for the first time in many years, the lump the child knows rising into my throat.

Then my father came. "Most surprised to hear you're here! Can't get over it! When are you coming down?"

I answered all their questions and told them as much as was possible in six minutes. At the end of that time I emerged from the booth in a state not unlike that of waking from a vivid but highly unlikely dream. I felt oddly exhausted. I wanted to sit down and think. But at that moment I saw my friend from the cigar store.

"Didger get 'er?" he asked excitedly.

"I did, indeed," I said. "I'm most awfully grateful to you for your assistance. Let me," I added, thrusting my hand into a pocket, "please let me reimburse you in some way for all your trouble. . . ."

But he immediately put up his hand and I could see he was embarrassed. "It was a pleasure, old man," he said.

"Well, all I can say is very many thanks."

"Don't mensh," he said, and with a wave of his hand he was gone.

The colonel had no objections to my leaving town. "Try and get back tomorrow night," he said. "You might have to leave early next day."

Mrs. Craig had warned me to be at the station at least an hour before the train was due to leave. "Standin' in line, starin'," she said, "that's travelin' nowadays, like everythink else. Not worth it, I say—bombs or no bombs. As I was tellin' Mr. Craig last nigh': 'Frank, I says, know what I'm goin' to do when the 'olidays come round?' 'What?' says 'e. 'Sleep,' I says. 'Stay 'ome and sleep,' I says. 'None o' this runnin' off to the seaside. Times 'ave changed, and we with 'em. We ain't so young as we was,' I says. Course," she added, glancing up at me, "if you're goin' to see your Mum and Dad—well, that's diff'rent."

Mrs. Craig's warnings were not exaggerated. It was Whitsun Week (I had forgotten the frequency of Britain's public holidays) and Waterloo station's huge area of concrete was crawling with perspiring vacationists. Pale-faced, colorlessly dressed, the English people stood behind train-boards in wide blocks of lines. Orderly, patient, uncomplaining, polite, murmuring in slow subdued voices to friends and strangers alike, they hugged their hampers, held a child's hand, rested their weight for five minutes first on one foot, then shifted it to the other. I stood in a narrow, slow-moving crocodile to buy a ticket, which seemed enormously dear. Then, before joining the crowd, I dropped into the public saloon. A hedge of human beings, three and four deep, concealed the long bar from sight. A group of men—with peaked caps, purple faces, and only two or three front teeth apiece—were discussing the prospects of a dog-race. The tepid, amber "Mild" tasted watery, insipid. I must have grimaced at the first gulp, for the white-skinned, fuzzy-haired barmaid lowered her eyebrows in a flirtatious frown.

"What?" she squeaked. "Dontcher like it? Don't wonder, after what you bin used to!"

"How d'you know what I've been used to?" I asked.

"Coo, I like tha'! Whatcher take me for—dumb? Not our dumb, neither—your dumb, I mean!" She pointed to her forehead.

"You *are* in a temper!" I said.

"And who wouldn't be, I'd like ter know—muckin' abaht all day in this Gawdfersaken 'ole!"

"What's wrong? The war's over!"

"War z'over, my eye! What's the diff'? Better when war z'on, if y'ask me! S'all righ' f'you—you're a Yank!"

"Why, what's wrong with England?"

"What's wrong? What's righ', more like!" She suddenly dropped her head, kicked at a bottle on the floor. "Ain't no future 'ere!" she muttered. "Not fer the likes o' me."

"So that's it. You want to go to the States?"

"Course I wanna go to the Stytes, silly! Anyone's balmy what don't."

"*I* know," I said. "You've got a G.I. boy friend!"

"No, I 'ave not—thank you very much, Mister Clever. I've 'ad enough of men."

"But not enough . . . dough?"

Her eyes lit up. She flashed a golden tooth and blushed. Then she burst into a peal of laughter. "Now you're talkin'!" she said, and I watched her continue laughing to herself while she served another customer.

She was one of the three or four English people I met who expressed a desire to emigrate to America.

Even when the gates were opened, only a few of the crowd made a rush for the train. An expatriate accustomed to Manhattan subways, I confess I was among those few—with the

LONDON

result that I got a corner seat in a train which, strangely enough, was not so overcrowded. The carriage, the windowed corridor, the seats facing one another in small closed compartments, the faded photographs of Salisbury Cathedral, Bath, and Basingstoke under the baggage rack, but more than any sight the smell of soot and smoke, brought back in wave after wave the years—beginning, inevitably, at the beginning, the last spring of the last year of the Old World, then the four frantic years that followed: the arrivals with my small brother at dawn at Euston, after a night on the *Irish Mail*, seasick among the Tommies, to go to school; the taxi drive across London, to bed in Grandmother's Kensington home; the hushed talk of "subs" and "zepps"; then the hateful last lap: other people's parents waving hands and handkerchiefs here at Waterloo; the unshed tears; the smell of plush seats, and soot; the thunderous shunt-shunt of the engine shash-shashing to the glass roof; the fearful farewell to privacy, the last defiant, sickening cigarette.

Where the treble-voiced sons of English gentry once had squabbled and smoked there now sat a blond, dignified, good-looking American captain, a couple of Wacs, two soft-speaking middle-aged Londoners, and at the last moment the compartment's quota was filled by a tall, dark, powerful-looking G.I. sergeant.

"Christ!" said one WAC, opening a copy of *Collier's*, "I'll sure be glad to get the hell out o' this country!"

"You telling me!" groaned the other. "Those hours at Edinburgh, the night in the waiting-room at Crewe, bedbugs in London—and now Tidworth again! Hell, I'm through with the Army!"

She leaned back in her corner, her powdered cheek against the glass, and closed her eyes.

"See, was you in Battersea, Bill, back in '41?" asked one Englishman, leaning towards the other and lighting his pipe. "Time our place was 'it—remember?"

"That April raid—'Awful Wednesday,' you mean? Na. I was on a job then, travelin', for Marx & Crossman. Up in

'Arrogate, Yorks." He put a hand in his pocket and produced a pack of Player's. "Fag?"

"Thanks, Bill. Got me pipe."

"Oh, beg pardon. H'm, 'Arrogate, that's where I was. Let's see, you 'ad to move three times all told, eh?"

"Four. Last was the worst. Blimey, that was a nigh'! Talk abaht 'eat! Missus still keeps 'arpin' on them fires. Doctor says she won't never be quite the same. Let 'er run on, though, he says—good for the nerves. What's this? Basingstoke?"

"Lummy, that ain't bad. No more 'n 'alf-'our behind time."

"Ha, sayin' that puts me in mind o' that travelin' job. Blimey, in those days if I got to a place on the righ' day, let alone the 'our, I'd 'ave to reckon meself lucky!"

"Ah," breathed his companion, knocking out his pipe on his boot heel, "Jerry fair kep' it up in those days, didn't 'e?"

"Not 'alf!"

Since the train had left Basingstoke the sergeant and the captain had begun to talk: the officer making monosyllabic comments in a soft southern drawl; the sergeant, who continuously eyed the Wacs, in an increasingly loud, penetrating voice which no one but the captain showed a sign of hearing. To him the sergeant had been boasting of his experiences in Germany whence, it seemed, he had recently returned: of the "Fräuleins" with whom he had fraternized, the white wine he had consumed, the "God-damned Krauts" he had infuriated by the seduction of their daughters and girl-friends, but above all of the trophies he had managed to "liberate" and bring with him. Apparently to prove this he suddenly unbuttoned his blouse, and with a glance round the compartment in the hope that his actions were being observed (the WACs by now were both fast asleep, the Englishmen still deep in wartime reminiscence) he displayed, hanging back and front from his trousers-belt, four black and shining *Lugers*. At sight of these the captain, who'd been listening in dignified silence to the sergeant's stories, failed to suppress a smile.

"Get them in combat?" he asked, chuckling.

"No, sir!" said the sergeant, opening up a weapon and,

pointing its muzzle towards the window, squinting down its barrel. "No, sir! Just a simple job of liberation."

I then decided to ask a question I'd always wanted to put to a collector of firearms. "Tell me," I said, "what are you going to do with them?"

The sergeant looked at me as though he were not sure he'd heard right. "What am I gonna do with 'em?" he repeated, his eyes wide. "Why, I . . ." He hesitated as though considering the problem seriously for the first time. Then an inspiration seemed to strike him. "Why, God damn it, man, these things are valuable," he said. "Guy already offered me fifty bucks for one. But I ain't selling! No, siree! Get seventy-five back home."

At Salisbury one of the Englishmen got out.

"Well, ta-ta, Bill!" he called to his friend.

"S'long!" said Bill. "Safe 'ome!"

The fields, the hedges, the woods of Wiltshire looked even greener than I'd remembered, their silence and quality of peace more intense. Like the quiet, amicable unanimity between the two natives, everything on the landscape seemed to have acquired a quality of *finished* harmony—the gray stone houses of the occasional villages to have been there always, the ancient oaks and elms to be immortal and never to have been young, the smallest meadow to be cared for as a garden, even the cattle, stretching their necks against a strand of wire, to be chewing the cud of confidence and content. No wonder, I thought, as the train trundled into Templecombe, no wonder the nearest this land came to a revolution was a bloodless general strike!

Instead of the family Austin to meet me, there was a brown tub-trap; between its shafts a fat bay pony, and in one corner seat, holding the thick reins in kid-gloved hands, an oldish man in black coat and bowler hat.

"Evenin', sir!" he said, touching the bowler's brim. "Nice evenin'."

I had thought, three hours earlier, that the train's smell of soot had transported me back to the "beginning." Those days had been, perhaps, a beginning—the first experiences for the boys alone, thinking, acting, traveling by themselves. But the moment I'd stepped on the trap's footplate and, with much the same sense of timid excitement as gripped the child in the palmy days, had asked to "hold the reins," back I was swept to memories of longer ago and years ago forgotten. The family "trapper" in that careless, carefree era when Edward still was Ireland's as well as England's king, went by the name of Nightingale. A shiny-coated, long-tailed bay with a brass bell everlastingly ringing on his chest, Nightingale had the fascinating habit of dodging—of his own accord despite his black blinkers—the areas of sharp stones shoveled into the rain-holes on the lonely Irish lanes. Then one day, notwithstanding his caution, he stumbled, fell, and broke his knees; and for the first time I saw a horse, an immensely wide leather girth round its belly, all four legs dangling a foot above the ground, as the animal hung suspended from its stall's ceiling in what the stablemen called a sling.

"Whoa, me beauty!" the old man said, as the pony pulled at the reins and slithered. "Better catch 'old of 'is 'ead a bit, sir, down this 'ill. Tarmac's likely to be slippy. Besides, never know what's comin' round corners these days."

No sooner were the words out of his mouth than an American army truck came crashing round the bend, missing the trap's wheel by no more than a foot.

"Phew!" breathed the old man. "Didn't oughter drive like that, they didn't! Downright dangerous, I calls it!"

Union Jacks fluttered from the gateposts of my parents' home; my father stood in the shadow of the creeper-covered porch.

"Very pleased to see you," he said, passing a practiced military eye over my uniform. As we shook hands I saw, with amazement, how little the eight awful years had changed him. "Sorry that infernal train was so late," he said. "When've you got to leave?"

"Tomorrow, I'm afraid," I said.

"H'm, that's very short. Well, look here, there're two afternoon trains. You do what you like, of course, but if you want my advice . . ."

Then my mother appeared, dressed in what used to be known as a tea-gown, of green and gold brocade. Her back was straight, her figure as young as ever. Only her hair had grown grayer.

"You haven't altered a scrap!" we both exclaimed at once.

"Dinner won't be a minute," she said, moving into the house. "You must be starving."

"A very good evening, sir," said the butler from behind the door. As Spencer took my bag and I saw again his flushed theatrical face, the gap in his teeth which had always gripped his pipe, I felt just what his friendly, understated greeting seemed to imply—that I was down again for the weekend from the City, where, after twenty years, I was still clipping coupons in the basement of a bank.

"We've put you in the double room!" my mother called.

"Okay," I said, and in silence to myself: Funny, this old house has probably never heard that word before!

On the threshold of the drawing-room, I watched her arranging with her expert hands a bowl of flowers on a rosewood cabinet. Then, over her shoulder, I caught sight on the wall of a remarkable likeness, in oils, of my brother in the uniform of an officer. I was thinking what the loss of this gentle, sensitive person who had shared their instinctive understanding and love of horses, must have meant to his parents, when my mother looked up and said, "Of course, you've never seen it, have you? I'm not sure I really like it. There's something a little wrong about the mouth."

"I think it's excellent," I said, marveling, as I had so often in the past, at her calm self-control in the face of tragedy and danger.

Over the rug-chest at the foot of the stairs I saw Cuyp's painting of cows standing munching in a marsh. Odd, I thought, to think that that belongs to me! As a child, in Grandmother's London morning-room, I'd stared at it for hours in wonder. When, four years ago, she'd died at the age of ninety-one, she'd left it to me in her will. And on the wall above the stairs, there she was, a serene and lovely girl in a pale-gold satin gown, by Millais. Even as a boy, in her ornate Victorian drawing-room so seldom used, I'd never liked the painting. Now I thought it awful: in the gown there breathed no body, behind the innocent limpid eyes no life. . . . Snobbish, money-minded Mr. Millais hadn't cared.

The double room smelled of lavender and *pot-pourri* of roses. Every object in the room I traced back to Bective, to their original nooks and corners in that long, low, ivy-covered Georgian house, with the panorama from its windows over the River Boyne, the Hill of Tara, and the lush, emerald meadows of Meath. I looked at the wide bed and saw a younger self sinking, sinking into its bosom of feathers and Limerick linen as into a pool of cool cream.

In the dining room the same family "silver," the exquisite Waterford glass collected by my mother over the years, shone from the same shining sideboard; but the precious tapestry fire screen, before which I'd watched my father and his brothers so often bend and unbend their knees, had since traveled from under the London morning-room's marble mantel to my parents' simpler hearth of brick.

"We've only just got this room back to normal," my mother said. "I held my Red Cross meetings here all through the war."

"Decent room," remarked my father, casting his eye over the oak-paneled walls. "Queer to be sitting eating here again. Just like old times."

"You know Aunt Flora and half the family were nearly killed in Sherborne?" my mother said. "Out shopping in the middle of the day. Bomb only missed them by a few feet."

"Yards," corrected my father. "Bally lucky," he added, "it didn't get you!"

"Wasn't it just!" agreed my mother. "I used to drive in

there three times a week, to my canteen. Just happened to be a Wednesday, and Wednesdays I didn't go!"

"Was there much damage in the immediate neighborhood?" I asked.

"Got the station," my father replied. "Direct hit. Winter of '41 I think it was—made the divil of a mess. Eighteen casualties. Infernal noise."

"We're still down to two-course meals," my mother said, as my mouth began to water over the plate of lamb, new English potatoes, and fresh English peas. "I hope you'll have enough."

"You'd have to pay a good deal," I told her, "for a meal like this in America."

When I informed them what was short and what prohibitively expensive in New York, they registered the customary astonishment.

"Got to go easy on sugar," my father said, and he pointed out to me the only change I'd noticed on the glistening mahogany table—in front of each of us, on theirs their name inscribed, a small glass bottle.

"Can't see anything wrong with saccharin meself," he added. "Ate it all through the last war in France."

"We were staying with Uncle Frank last summer," my mother said. "There were some Americans there—a colonel and his wife—really awfully nice."

"Yes," agreed my father, "very decent people—very decent indeed."

"What's it *like* out there?" asked my mother. "At all like here? The country, I mean, of course."

"Well," I said, wondering how many times of how many countries in precisely these words she had asked me this before. "Well, America's pretty big. There's almost every kind of country. Yes, parts of New England are not unlike here."

"You never run into Lily, I suppose?"

Lily was our one relative who, having married an American naval officer, had settled in the States with her husband and in-laws.

"No," I said, "Lily lives in Arizona—about two thousand miles from New York."

"Poor girl!" exclaimed my mother. "What a long way away!"

In the library—a forest of family photographs, of men on horses, women on horses, children on ponies, of military prints, medals and mementos—my father lit his pipe. Then he leaned over and stared closely through his spectacles at the pinkish trousers of my uniform. "Funny color, that," he muttered. "Must show the dirt." Then between his fingers he examined the lapel of the blouse. "Good solid stuff, though. Heavy. Thick. Should wear. Know when I bought this suit?" he asked, patting the gray Donegal tweed covering his knees. "Nineteen-fourteen—just before the war. Sandon's. Just as good as new."

It struck me only now that this was one of the few occasions on which I'd seen my father sit down to dinner in anything but black tie and evening clothes.

"I suppose you'll be very busy in Germany," my mother remarked.

"I suppose so," I replied.

"Oh, clean forgot," said my father, turning in his chair. "What you going to do there?"

"Strangely enough," I laughed, "I don't yet know!"

I saw my mother shoot my father a look. "Probably not allowed to tell," she said in an undertone, and added, "Be awfully interesting, I'm sure."

"Course, you've bin there before," my father observed. "Extr'ord'nary people, the Germans—damned if I know what to make of 'em!"

My mother yawned. "Heavens!" she exclaimed, pretending to eye the Chippendale clock on the mantel. "Can you believe it! It's half-past nine! How time flies!"

"Missed the news," my father said.

"Well, don't know about anybody else," said my mother, "but I'm for bed." And to me: "You must be dead!"

"Thought you went to bed at ten?" I said, surprised by this revolution in the family's evening routine.

"Well," murmured my mother, "during the war, you know . . ."

Placing the palms of his hands on his knees, my father rose slowly to his feet. "Saves 'lectricity," he said, and I caught my mother's indulgent, smiling eye.

I woke, in bliss, to the sound of birds and to the sight, through the small latticed windows, of honeysuckle on the walls of the gardener's cottage across the lane. Then I saw, and never with greater wonder, that the all-but-forgotten morning miracle had already been performed: there, over the chintz-covered chair, lay the blouse and trousers brushed and pressed, and under them, side-by-side on the soft maroon carpet, the shoes unrecognizably shined—all by Spencer's super-professional hand.

"Just striking eight, sir," he said, as he stood arranging my shaving things on the glass-topped dresser. "A warm bath and a sunny morning await you. Not to mention breakfast, sir, at the customary hour." Then, with his hand on the door-knob, he hesitated. "Shall you be likely, sir," he asked, "to return to the still sunnier land of dreams?"

I laughed, not only at his phrasing of the question, but at the flood of morning memories it brought back.

"Doubt it, thanks," I said. Then, "Know what?" I added, falling unconsciously into the family vernacular, "I think I've changed!"

"If I may make so bold, sir," he said, his eyes alone expressing mirth, "it is not remarkable!"

At the ultra-typical innuendo from this man of matchless humor, I burst into laughter.

"I have!" I insisted. "Listen, d'you realize that since we last met I've been living on my wits?"

"Oh, sir!" he groaned, his mouth agape with simulated horror. "I am deeply grieved. I was not aware that things had come to such a pass!"

"Oh," I laughed, "the pass has its compensations!" And

I wanted to add: "It compares favorably with the days when you and I used to catch one another's embarrassed eye over the barrier between the Saloon and Private bars in the class-conscious village pub!—It's a pity we could not have been together," I wanted to tell the perfectly-adjusted, never-servile servant, "in the one dark room in the cheap New York rooming-house, in the wooden shack without electricity or heating, in the crammed cafeterias or the Third Avenue taverns, where your employer's son is known by his first name to bums and barmen who do not recognize a butler from a banker, a butcher from a baron, dub no man a gentleman nor address anyone as sir!"

I would have liked to whisper that and more into Spencer's proud ear. But I would like to have been believed. "I note, sir, with pleasure," I could already hear him say, "that for your chosen craft you are properly endowed. Imagination is to the scribe what a master is to me!"

At nine-fifteen my parents were already in the dining-room.

"Sleep well?" my mother asked, over our eggs and bacon, tea and toast.

"Like a dog," I told her.

"Oh, that reminds me," said my father, "did I tell you? Old Buster died!"

"Ah, yes," breathed my mother, "poor old man! But he was getting so stiff, and beginning to smell. Poof!" she snorted, wrinkling her nose.

The bedroom conversation interested me more.

"Spencer hasn't changed," I said, drawing what that man used to call "a blow at a denture."

"No," said my father, "but some of his duties have!"

And suddenly they both began to laugh. Laying down her knife and fork, my mother leaned back in her chair and resigned herself to a paroxysm of mirth. Then, with a tiny white handkerchief, she began dabbing the tears from her eyes.

"Duties?" I repeated, mystified by this most unusual display of hilarity. "What's so funny about them?"

"He—he . . ." But again my mother burst into a fit of helpless, now silent giggles. "He—he turns-down-our-beds-at-night!" she finally managed to say. "And-puts-in-the-hotwater-bottles!"

"Makes the beds in the morning too," my father added.

"Good gracious!" my mother said, recovered at last from her bout and rising from the table. "You've not seen the garden yet!"

"And my chickens," my father said. "And what about my rock-garden? Don't know why you always pooh-pooh my rock-garden!"

"Pooh-pooh, indeed!" scoffed my mother. "You know it's a jolly good rock-garden. As for your chickens, I don't know what we'd do without them."

"By Jove!" my father suddenly exclaimed, as he took his hoe-stick from the rack.

"What?"

"Where the blazes is my hat? I wonder who the divil—? Spenc-ERR!"

I listened to the familiar roar echoing through the house. When the pantry door opened I could see, rising from the fist behind the butler's back, a barely visible wisp of smoke.

"Where's my hat?" demanded my father.

"Hat, sir?" said Spencer, grimly. "A little above your head, sir—on the peg."

"Good Lor'!" muttered my father; and my mother: "Well, *really* . . ."

We spent the remainder of the day in the garden, my mother picking an odd weed from the herbaceous border aflame with flowers, my father giving the plantains and dandelions a vicious prodding on the lawn.

"Bally difficult to keep grass decent," he observed, "with only one man."

The rock-garden—long ago described to me by an Irish stableman as "the Major's wee hape o' stones"—was now indeed a place to boast about. A tiny stream of gurgling water—winding its way in and out among moss- and gentian-coated boulders, past little patches of jonquils, dwarf-iris, toy-like Oriental pines—flowed out finally as a miniature torrent down a mown slope of lawn, between beds of peonies, and into a plantation of blossoming cherry trees which, my father informed me, had been imported from China and planted here with his own hands, before the war.

"They have some bigger ones at Kew," he said with modest pride, and he picked a sprig of the pink petals and pulled it through his buttonhole.

Under the pale mauve wistaria, clinging in clumps to the garden wall, I saw the scarlet lamps of salvia, slender sky-blue rods of delphinium, chalk-white bunches of phlox, whose perfume filled the air.

"Don't know what I'd do without the garden," my mother remarked. And as she spoke I saw her glance up at the row of shuttered stable stalls. I knew what she was thinking and I decided not to speak.

"Oh, dear," she said, "what ages it seems since we used to feed the horses—at just this time of day."

Then she sighed, and bending down over the blazing border, she slowly plucked a weed.

Since it was the Sabbath, a day of rest for the old coachman and the pony, the one village taxi—of ample proportions and uncertain age—had been hired in my honor.

"Well, good luck!" my father said, as I climbed in. And my mother: "Let us know when you get back!"

"Maybe I'll be here for Christmas," I said.

"Santa Claus," murmured Spencer, placing the suitcase at my feet, "visits us once a year—and you, sir, once in ten!"

From the train near Gillingham, between the green hedgerows of a quiet country lane, I saw a strange and most incongruous sight—a dark-chocolate-colored Negro, in American uniform, walking all alone. His slow wandering gait did not suggest that he himself felt foreign or out-of-place; he looked as much at home, in fact, as the boys outside the pubs in Oxford Street.

After the paper-strewn dinginess of a Manhattan subway, a London tube seemed a paragon of elegance and comfort. Between each upholstered seat, covered in gaily patterned plush, an arm-rest could be pulled out or pushed in, according to the passengers' wishes. The lights, instead of flickering on and off, retained a strange and steady brilliance. On the platform of each station a guard shouted out its name. At the top of Piccadilly's moving staircase I noticed the most revolutionary spectacle wartime London had so far offered: a gigantic poster, a vast VD, warning the world against the infection of venereal disease. Out on the Circus, crowds surged in solid blocks from corner to corner. Eros, the pivot of the "Center of the World," either had been removed or had survived under wood and concrete.

In the Café Royal I ran into an American friend who'd been working for the OWI in London. "What's that large drink you've got?" I asked him, sitting down.

"Gin & It," he said. "Double. No one ever drinks anything but doubles nowadays. Even George won't serve me more than a couple of drinks an evening."

"George!" I said. "Is he still here?"

"Sure. There he is."

Like most waiters in London's West End, George was an Italian. We'd known one another for more than twenty years.

"You're too thin, George," I couldn't help remarking, as I stared at his shrunken frame.

"Lost d'irty po'nds!" he said, glancing down at the pants hanging loose round his waist. "I see my feet now, widout bending over!"

"Well," I laughed, "you've not lost your humor!"

"Hoch!" he chuckled. "No laugh, no live!"

The Gin & It cost only a little less than the tasteless *paté maison*, the excellent fried sole, and the dull dessert of prunes.

After dinner I walked westwards along Piccadilly. Every vestige of the elegance I associated with this region had vanished; in its place the people, the traffic, the houses were haunted by the ghost of wartime squalor. The windows of St. James' Church were gaping, glassless oblong holes; through the roofless rafters the last rays of the evening sun turned the white marble rubble on its nave into blocks of molten gold. Tommies and G.I.s, their arms round their girls, walked slowly, aimlessly past the shuttered windows of Hatchard's, where I'd once bought my books. In the wide street of buses, trucks and taxis a private car was rare, a shining limousine a sight to stand and stare at.

Outside the Ritz I boarded a bus. "Fares, please! All fares!"

For an instant I could not believe my ears. Here in paper-famished Britain the same little tickets, their price and color varying according to the length of your journey, were still being sold by a patient, perspiring Londoner whose profession—because someone had presented me with a toy ticket-puncher at the age of six—was the first I'd ever coveted.

ARRIVAL IN GERMANY

3

THE rotund, fidgety little sergeant stood in the center of the room looking very important.

"Gentlemen!" he said in a tone that suggested he was about to reveal a long-kept secret to a large congregation. "Gentlemen, I trust you all have ten copies of your orders. You will assemble here tomorrow morning at eight o'clock. Please see that you have had breakfast." After a glance at a sheaf of papers in his hand he added, somewhat lamely: "You may not get anything to eat again for some time." Then he darted out of the door.

I looked round the bare room. There were about eight of us present, officers and civilians. I didn't know anyone.

The sergeant reappeared. "Gentlemen," he said, "you will assemble here tomorrow morning at seven-thirty. Please see that you have had breakfast."

Then, referring once more to the papers in his hand, he read out a long list of articles—sleeping-bag, helmet, belt, blanket, water bottle, canteen, etc.—that we were already supposed to have acquired. "Please see that these are downstairs before midnight," he said.

When it was all over, I was approached by a tall lieutenant with a genial, red face.

"Ma name's Frank Knox," he said in an enviable southern drawl. "Aren't you a friend of Ethel Deane?"

"Sure," I said, shaking hands.

"Ah saw her last week. She told me to look out for you. See you tomorrow."

Early next morning I took leave of Mrs. Craig. I gave her one of several lipsticks I had brought from New York.

"Coo!" she said. "Thanks ever so. One thing abaht you Americans: can't call you mean, that we can't. Always 'andin' things out, you are—lipsticks 'ere, powder and soap there."

As she stumped up the stairs I waited for the inevitable final crack. There it came, a little breathless and not quite to herself: "Reg'lar Mister Plutocrats!"

A weapons-carrier, with a trailer attached, was waiting in Grosvenor Square, and round it stood the group I had met the day before, including Frank Knox with a *New Republic* tucked under his arm. We climbed on board and sat wedged in, facing one another, over a well full of baggage, on opposite benches. A weapons-carrier allows you to see out only from the back. Since I was last on board, I managed to get a rear-end seat, from which I could watch the streets disappearing behind us—streets that were shining wet from one of those London drizzles that looks as though it will never end. We drove south, over Vauxhall Bridge, through some of the sprawling capital's grimmer districts where the prevailing color had always been a grimy black. Now, in the rain, the few men plodding to work in their dark clothes and peaked caps, the rows of mournful weeping houses all the same, the cleared gaps which even weeds seemed to disdain, all looked grimier, older, blacker than ever.

At the airport there was the usual wait, the inevitable rumors. The weather was too bad to fly. We were going to be sent back. The plane was leaving in ten minutes, in half an hour. I joined a queue and changed some pounds into Occupation Marks—a currency with an appearance even more spurious than that of the million- and billion-mark bills of the inflation period after the First War. An hour later we took off.

I sat next to Frank Knox on a bucket seat. We had been gossiping about New York and London, contemporary literature and mutual acquaintances, when the plane banked and someone remarked that we were about to descend on the Brussels airport.

"To hell with airports!" I muttered, gazing down at the

ugly waste of anonymous land. Airports bear towards the cities they serve, I thought, a relation far more remote even than docks or distant suburbs. After a drink in a harbor tavern, a traveler by sea can usually wander into some part of the town in a few minutes. But an air-passenger, even if he can find a drink on the field, is strongly advised not to drink it; and unless he is very hard up for exercise and willing to stay the night, he'd be very foolish to attempt footing it into town.

Leaning over the counter with a cup of tea and a ham "sonvitch," trying to recapture the atmosphere of the nearby capital with the aid of a Brussels newspaper, I thought of a Belgian uncle—a man with a beard climbing to his eyes, an unpredictable temper, and a brilliant mind—in whose house in the Avenue Coghen I'd spent part of a summer vacation. My parents had once invited Uncle Pierre to Bective where he'd been promptly bitten by a flea. That night he had managed to have himself sent a telegram, and next morning, growling unprintable epithets at *la saleté de l'Irlande,* he had fumed back to Brussels. In that city he considered I should "improve my mind" (his desire, of course, was simply to get me out of the house), so he sent me off alone to see the sights. The first evening I spent in La Monnaie, where I slept through my first opera, *Boris Godounov.* Afterwards, to my consternation, I found that Brussels suffered even more than London from a form of prohibition. This was a rude shock to my love of life wherever French was spoken. I had to bribe a barman to get me a drink, which he served, as later I was served so many in American speakeasies, in a coffee cup. One morning, during these lonely peregrinations through the city, I found myself in the vast Palais de Justice. A little man was standing at my elbow, drawing my attention to a slight hollow in the stone floor. He then raised his head and pointed to the roof of the unbelievably high dome.

"Up there, during the Occupation, only five years ago," he said, *"les sales Boches* took out all the copper fittings. But one day one of them fell—*zip, vous comprenez—plomp!*" We then lowered our eyes to the hollow in the floor. "Aha!" grinned the little man, "must have been a fat one, *n'est-ce-pas,* Monsieur . . . ?"

A few days later Uncle Pierre—who'd risked his life a hundred times during that Occupation by delivering mail, clandestinely, to out-of-the-way places in the Ardennes Forest (where he owned a château)—took me to a village in that part of the country. Pointing to a wall beside the road, he growled between his teeth: "Against that, in 1917, the Boches swine shot six hundred men and women of this village. Only one survived." Seeing my incredulous stare, he then led me across the street to a small *tabac*.

"*Voilà!* There he is!" said Uncle Pierre, pointing to a one-legged man on a chair. The man, with the help of a crutch, staggered to his foot and handed me a pamphlet he had written (and which had been translated into broken English), describing in detail the day of atrocity and how, by feigning death under the hill of corpses, he had managed to survive.

Standing munching my "sonvitch" in the airport and thinking of these incidents, I remembered mentioning them, years later, in Portugal, to Christopher Isherwood. He had remained silent for some time and then, when I imagined his thoughts to have passed far from the Belgian scene, he had exclaimed in his enthusiastic and very English voice: "My word! The food in Brussels . . . !"

"Fishcakes!" someone (knowing his passion for that British concoction) had said; and with a burst of boyish laughter Christopher had begun telling us stories of Brussels in the company of "Mr. Norris." In the midst of them the radio had been turned on, and in the small Cintra house which we'd shared during that faraway, fearful summer of 1936, we listened to the first news of the civil war across the border, to reports of murder and rape in Seville.

"This is the beginning, only the beginning," Christopher said, expressing my thoughts, and we glanced at one another, then away, as though to conceal our certain knowledge that at last Europe's armistice had ended. . . .

But in the Belgian airport waiting-room full of British and American soldiers, the Brussels of my uncle, the city Christopher had such an affection for, seemed as remote as if I'd been munching the sandwich on La Guardia Field.

I first recognized Germany from a distant glimpse of the *Deutsche Eck,* that pointed promontory where the Rhine and Moselle meet. Sections of a shattered bridge stuck up out of the mud-colored water and a castle sat perched on top of the vine-terraced hills. Then the plane dropped, and we looked down into rows of burned-out houses—just shells of houses, without roofs or rooms. You looked down between their four walls to their ground floors, on which there lay either nothing or else a mound of smashed brick, smashed sticks of furniture, and garbage. From the clouds above and around us rain was falling into these shells, forming shining puddles on the useless floors. I thought of battered Brest, then of the aerial photographs I'd seen in the New York *Times* and *Life.*

Though I recognized nothing but the river, I knew we were over Frankfurt, a city once as familiar as any other in Europe. I made no great effort to see more of it from the air, for I imagined that within the hour, on our way to Headquarters at Bad Nauheim, we should be driving through its ruined streets.

This time the plane landed not at an airport, but in the middle of a large field. From it you could not even see a house. Standing there in the mud and rain with a view of green hedges and a line of empty American trucks, we might have been any place on earth where grass grows. No sign or word suggested that we were in Germany, or even in Europe, until finally I saw, on an embankment in the distance, an entire train that had been blown off its rails. Part on its back, with its little wheels in the air, part on its side, it lay there like a gigantic gray slug chopped into several equal chunks.

After half an hour two G.I.s drove on to the field. I was near enough to hear one of them say to the other: "Wonder if any of these guys want a lift to Nauheim?"

"Sure," I broke in, "we all do."

"Well," said the driver, "we've only room for one."

I asked Frank if he saw any reason why I shouldn't take the ride, and when he said no, I piled into the back with my baggage. The rain had begun to fall more heavily; a strong wind had risen, and despite the jeep's roof, we were all three wet and shivering within a few minutes.

By-passing Frankfurt, to my regret, we tore down an *Autobahn* at what seemed like more than fifty miles an hour. On the distant, rain-blurred horizon I recognized the rolling line of the Taunus mountains; then, rising from the flat green plain, the twin spires of the church of Bad Homburg. There, just eighteen years ago, I had spent my first night in Germany. In a room cluttered with heavy furniture, tasseled lampshades, cacti and an aspidistra or *Palme,* a doctor and his family of females had sat and stared at me as though I were an animal out of the Ark. During the meal of cold *Wurst* and potato salad, they all talked at once in a language not one word of which I could understand. It was only too clear, of course, that every remark they uttered was a personal comment upon the newly arrived paying guest.

I stayed four months in that house—not a wildly exciting summer; but for a young man born and brought up in the British Isles it was an eye-opener to some aspects of continental life. Punctually at two o'clock every afternoon the entire family retired to bed until four. During these hours no one was allowed to speak. Carefully disposing of that unbelievable object, the balloon-like *plumeau* on my bed, I lay on the mattress in the silent house and consumed most of the paper-bound novels, plays, and volumes of poetry published by Tauchnitz. As the weeks passed I grew very fond of the gentle, unassuming doctor who every evening studiously read two pages of H. G. Wells's *Outline of History,* and who neither encouraged nor frowned upon the inevitable relationship that formed between the foreigner and his elder daughter. With Maria I used to climb mountains, bathe in the town *Schwimmbad,* play bad tennis on good courts, and converse in a kind of private pidgin-English.

Sitting now in the jeep, racing down the *Autobahn* which in those days did not exist, I remembered my first visit to the Homburg springs—one of whose waters had tasted like rotten eggs and made me retch—and my astonishment at the first glimpse of German humor displayed on a picture postcard for sale at the kiosk. It showed, in color, a row of little toilet doors which *Männer* and *Frauen* were desperately trying to open. When nicked apart with a fingernail, these miniature paper doors revealed water-drinkers in various states of collapse on the toilet seats, their faces contorted in the agony of diarrhoea. . . .

I thought of the walks with Maria through the woods behind Homburg, and of my fury when, looking up from the floor of pine-needles on which we lay, I used to catch sight of a male head behind a nearby tree. I felt again the wild, youthful anger as I gave chase to the *voyeurs* who used to haunt these woods; and I remembered how, after the first such experience, I seldom set out in the company of the doctor's daughter without a heavy stick. . . . I was wondering what, after all these years, had become of this family and if I should ever get a chance to visit the house, when the jeep lurched off the highway, crashed down a narrow lane and drew up outside a large hotel in Bad Nauheim.

Since the middle of the last century, Nauheim—like Homburg—had flourished as one of the smaller German spas visited by the elderly and invalids, particularly by those suffering from diseases of the heart. The Park was a typical example of the hotel which used to house such visitors. It was not the kind of hotel that I prefer—too big, too clean, too expensive—but as a lover of hotels of any kind, a thrill went through me as I smelled the musty "hotel" smell, walked through the lounge of leather chairs and plush sofas, and approached a very amiable sergeant to "sign in" and book a bed. I expected difficulty, disappointment; I expected the discomfort and confusion that all armies seem obliged to create wherever they go. I was prepared for a dormitory, a line of cots jammed together in a small space, crowds of uniformed men cursing as they fell over baggage and one another in cluttered corridors. The sergeant, however, in that empty, silent, peaceful lounge, dispelled these fears with a question so bewildering that I had to ask him to repeat it before I could believe my ears.

"Yes, sir," he said, like the perfect receptionist at a Ritz, "now what kind of a room would you like?"

What kind of a room would I like? Room! A whole room!

"D'you mean to say?" I began; but, sensing my incredulity, he dashed to my assistance.

"Well, you see, we have outside rooms, inside rooms. There are rooms with two—"

"D'you mean to say," I interrupted in breathless disbelief, "that-I-can-have-a-room-to-myself?"

"Why, sure," came the unbelievable answer. "We are not at all full at the moment. Tonight we may be. You're lucky. You got here early."

"Well," I said, still in a dream of dismay, "I'd certainly prefer an outside room." And I felt like adding: "And let's have a private bathroom, a double bed, a sofa, and a writing table with a view over a garden, for I might like to start writing a story. It's so *peaceful* here in Germany!"

"Just sign here, sir," I heard the sergeant saying. "Room Number 88."

I found myself and my baggage in a small elevator with a plush seat. A corporal was conducting me slowly upwards to the third floor. Number 88 was in a corner, off a wide corridor. A key was already in the door; but the room had double doors. I pushed the second one open and stood still on the threshold with my mouth open . . . On my left were two beds covered in spotless linen and yellow eiderdowns; beyond them a writing table and chair, and on the floor a carpet of a rather beautiful faded pink. To the right stood a large wardrobe; beside it a sofa, an armchair with antimacassar, and a table with a white embroidered cloth. From the center of the ceiling hung a glass chandelier. Light flooded the room from three large windows, one of which was French. ... In a dream I walked through the room towards it, opened it, and stepped out on to a balcony, to find a round iron table and chair, painted sky blue. Leaning over the balcony railing, I looked down on two long, tidy beds of geraniums surrounded by mown grass. Opposite, under a huge flowering acacia tree in whose foliage birds were singing, a few German women and elderly men were filing soberly past an ugly pseudo-Gothic church. They wore clean, expensive-looking raincoats and they carried umbrellas. They looked as though they had just emerged for a constitutional after the rain; or they might, for all I knew, be on their way to the springs to "take the waters." In the church someone was playing *Abide with Me* on the organ.

In a dream I stepped back into the room, and noticed another door. I opened it carefully, expecting to be faced by an annoyed American officer in the next room. Instead, I found myself in a spacious white-tiled bathroom, which included that most continental object, a *bidet*. Another door led out of it, into the corridor. I turned the key in the lock, and then, returning to the bedroom, locked its door, too. Glancing up, a notice on the wall caught my eye. "Breakfast," I read in English, French, and German over a design of the Park Hotel and Gardens, "will be served from 8 to 9:30 in the dining-room. Service in rooms: 50 pfennigs extra." The notice concluded with a request to guests "to give their room keys to the receptionist before leaving the premises," and "to kindly refrain from bringing dogs into the dining-room."

On one more tour of the suite I found, on the small bedside table, a single book—a novel by P. G. Wodehouse which someone had carried off—when?—from the "Public Library, Alexandria!" Laying down the book, I stretched out on the sofa. "So this is Germany!" I said to myself. "What a place to write a novel!"

Then I fell asleep.

I was woken by a knock on the door. I thought—or I'd been dreaming—that I was in New York. Dazed, I staggered to the door, unlocked it. Outside stood a blond girl in an apron with a towel over her arm. She had her head lowered so that I couldn't see her face.

"*Gut'n Abend, Fräulein,*" I said. "Do you want anything?"

"The beds, the towel," muttered the girl, and she sidled round me, like a shy or sullen child, into the room.

Closing the door, I returned to the sofa, where I pretended to be absorbed in the Brussels newspaper. She was leaning over with her back to me and I watched her as she began turning down the bedclothes. She was a short, firm, sturdy-looking girl with long blond hair done up in plaits round her head. I wondered if in any country occupied by the Nazis, or even in Great Britain, there lived a girl today who looked as strong and healthy as this one. Because of her shy or sullen attitude I was determined to make her talk.

"Is your home here, Fräulein?" I asked. "Do you come from Nauheim?"

She glanced up for an instant, just long enough for me to catch a glimpse of the faultless pink-and-white skin, the round face, the clear light blue eyes.

"Near here," she snapped. "From Friedberg."

The words came clipped, like an answer to a military order. Here in this room they certainly sounded hostile. Was this the prevailing mood of the Germans? Was it resentment, hatred, fear?

"I used to live here," I said, "not far from Friedberg."

She promptly stood up straight, her eyes wide, hands on her hips. She stared straight at me, defiant, arrogant, in her disbelief.

"Where then?" she challenged.

"At Bad Homburg."

ARRIVAL IN GERMANY

A smile—despite herself, I felt—immediately transformed her face. At that moment she looked very handsome.

"Ach!" she breathed, in astonished acceptance of the statement. Then, after a pause: "Homburg *war schön*—Homburg was beautiful."

It is difficult to describe the exact tone of this trite, inoffensive remark. If ever I had forgotten or doubted the existence of a certain aspect of the German character, these three words as spoken by this girl were sufficient to remind me of it, to dispel my doubts, and to bring the years I had spent in this country rushing back as fast as would a familiar house or face. It was not, as I say, the remark itself, but the way she made it, the tone of voice. It was let fall with a sigh, in which the prevailing tone was undeniably a mixture of self-pity and sentimentality—characteristics I've learned to identify with cruelty—and it was accompanied by a slow wag of the head, as if by reminding me and herself that Homburg was beautiful, she was in reality saying: "Poor Homburg! Poor Germany! If you only knew!" This was the inflection of the voice I had heard so often in the past, was to hear so often in the immediate future, and which I could not help but associate with the German middle class.

"Isn't Homburg still *schön*?" I asked.

"Ach," she sighed, "it's different now. Everything's different. Nauheim's different."

"What do you mean, 'different'?"

"Na ja," she said, relaxed now, forgetful of my person, my uniform. *"Wissen Sie, damals*—formerly, you know, people used to come to Homburg, to Nauheim from all over the world."

"What kind of people?"

"Also, interesting people, *gel?* Foreigners, people with fine clothes, famous people, musicians, even royalty—people from all over."

"And now," I asked, trying to suppress a smile, "now they come only from . . . ?"

But she was not a girl to react quickly to humor, even if it were in slightly bad taste.

"Ach, now," she said with a grimace, "now no one comes. Nothing happens in Nauheim now."

"Well," I said, "there's been a war, you know."

"*Ja*," she sighed.

"Where were you in the war?"

"Here." She paused. "I'm always here," she added, sighing again.

"What was this hotel used for during the war?"

"Lazaret. Lazarets everywhere."

"May I ask how old you are?"

"*Ich?* Thirty-three," she said, blushing.

"You don't look it."

She glanced up, very red. "*Der Herr* is very kind," she said, then walked quickly into the bathroom and shut the door. As I lay back on the sofa I could hear her humming.

Later that evening some members of my group and a crowd of others arrived. The hotel was filling up. I quickly nabbed Frank to share my room.

Downstairs, divided from the dining-room by glass doors, we found a lounge, with a bar at one end. Scotch whisky was on sale for the equivalent of 20 cents a shot; also a young, light Rhine wine for 40 cents the bottle. In a corner of the dining-room four earnest Belgian males earned their supper by banging out ancient foxtrots and Strauss waltzes with a vehemence that dulled the senses and shattered any attempt at extended conversation. An obsequious-looking German maître d'hôtel in pince-nez hovered round the tables of the higher ranking officers, and a number of women of uncertain age, in black dresses and white aprons, either stood in line with their backs to the wall or dished out to us some very unappetizing food. It consisted mostly of American canned hash and vegetables warmed up. It wasn't until breakfast next morning, however, that we were introduced to what we soon christened "cushions." There were various kinds of cushions.

The commonest was a multi-colored circular mess, made, I believe, of a slice of stale bread, a woolly layer of powdered egg over which was dumped a thick slab of spam. The result reminded me of the caps we used to tie around horses' legs in icy weather, to prevent them from "breaking" their knees.

After our first experience of a Park Hotel cushion, I went for a walk with Frank through Nauheim. The town is built round a small park of huge elms and beech trees, some non-functioning fountains and a large *Kurhaus* which became a center of attraction because it was one of the few buildings in Nauheim to have received a direct hit. Rumor had it that Field Marshal von Rundstedt and his entire staff had once used this *Kurhaus* as their temporary headquarters. The allies, receiving wind of the fact, had bombed it—a remarkable example of precision bombing!—but the marshal and his staff had evacuated a few hours before.

While this building, now a shell half-hidden by scaffolding, may have acted as a magnet to newly arrived Americans, the natives of Nauheim were not interested. They were drawn elsewhere. We found them in small groups, standing in front of trees, before the town's proclamation board and the empty windows of closed shops. They stood there, silent, motionless for several minutes; then, shaking their heads, they walked slowly away. What they saw on these trees, boards and shop-windows, what faced them in some prominent spot in every street in every village and town, was a large notice from which glared a heading in immense black letters:

WHO IS GUILTY?

Under the heading were a number of enlarged, rather blurred photographs: hundreds of naked human skeletons were piled high on the open wagon of a goods train; what looked like a mountain of garbage was a mountain of ash and charred human bones; men in striped prison clothes hung from gallows, while children and babies lay on their backs on the ground, dead from starvation. Under each photograph a caption informed the observer where the picture had been taken.

Standing behind these groups of spectators, I never heard anyone utter a word. A woman would occasionally put a hand or a handkerchief to her mouth as though to stifle the moan or cry of horror; an elderly man with his mouth open would stare as though hypnotized for a few minutes; then one by one they would walk slowly, silently away.

I tried to put myself in the place of these people, to imagine what they were thinking. I followed them in my mind as they wandered slowly through the sunlit park, past the man whose spiked stick, in this murderous world, prodded at pieces of paper under benches and dropped them carefully, tidily into the wire basket; I watched them pass a line of wounded ex-soldiers of the Wehrmacht whose hands sprang to their peaked caps as they encountered American officers, who were not permitted to return the salute; I followed them through the *Sprudelhof* where wealthy invalids had once hoped to cure their ills in sulphur baths; I saw them shuffle by, unseeing, a photographer's window-display of ski scenes and close-ups of laughing German children and babies; and I came out with them into the streets of Victorian hotels and was close behind them as they slowly mounted the staircase to the stuffy, cluttered room where I imagined them to live. There, sitting invisible in their presence, I watched the trembling hand go out to the radio for relief, and I listened to the voice of accusation resounding through the room:

WHO IS GUILTY?

Who is guilty of the atrocities committed against humanity in your midst . . . ?

As the voice continued, minute after monotonous minute, describing in dreadful detail the endless list of crimes, I sat watching the dumb, expressionless face. And when the voice ended and started all over again with its "WHO IS GUILTY?" I watched the hand go out to the knob, saw the knob turned, and in the hollow silence that followed I tried to put myself in the place of this anonymous native of Nauheim; but no mental effort I ever made could have been more vain.

The native reaction seemed no different, one's efforts to penetrate the silent masks no less futile, when this notice was taken down and another put up in its stead. Asking no question, this placard stated a fact. Over clearer, more detailed photographs ran the bold black headline:

THIS TOWN IS GUILTY!
YOU ARE GUILTY!

Back in the hotel, during a discussion of German guilt and allied propaganda, an officer interrupted. "I think," he said, "that the manner in which we use the word 'allied' is a little loose. There are no guilt placards, such as we see here, in the Russian zone. And do you know what the Berlin radio is telling its listeners, what people in this zone who can tune in to Berlin are hearing? They hear details about the destruction of the city and what is being done to clear it up; about the water, gas, electricity and food situation and what is being done to increase rations; about housing, clothing, and other bare necessities of life. After this they are treated to a round-the-clock program of music, including the works of the Jewish composers, Mendelssohn and Offenbach—which have not been heard in this country for twelve years. The Germans, you know, are great music lovers. . . ."

This information did not, needless to say, end the discussion. But it set some of us thinking about the larger issues of propaganda and collective guilt.

Later that evening a civilian "leader," an anthropologist in private life, asked me if I'd like to join a "Documents Team."

"Sure," I told him. "What would I have to do?"

"Oh," he said, "track down and translate documents. You know."

I was afraid I did. I'd just translated five hundred pages of a German novel. The prospect of a desk and dictionary in Germany, instead of New York, was hardly appealing.

Then a most unexpected thing happened. I was wanted on the telephone. Telephone! Where could there be a telephone? Upstairs, in the colonel's quarters. The colonel stood holding the receiver. "Darmstadt," he said, and discreetly left the room.

"I've been trying to get on to you for days!" boomed a voice I recognized at once as Mervyn's. "What are you doing?" he shouted.

"Nothing. Absolutely nothing," I said. "But I may have to join a Documents Team."

"Oh, you poor fish!" he said. "Don't. You must come here at once and join our team as an interviewer."

That was what I did.

The following three days a group of us commuted, in a weapons-carrier, between Nauheim and Darmstadt, where we were handed out *Fragebogen* and, in the garden of a house belonging to a Nazi who had recently poisoned himself and his family, we were briefed in the art of interviewing.

On the road between the two towns the first thing that struck the Americanized eye was the absence of those advertisements for soap, chewing gum, Coca-Cola, automobiles and liquor. It seemed strange not to be half-blinded by the information that "Budweiser is something more than beer." Nor was there a sign on these peaceful rural roads or in the slumbering villages to remind you that this country had just been defeated in a World War. The contrast, therefore, on entering the ruins of Frankfurt was staggering. It was a weird experience to drive through a city you'd once known intimately and in order to get your bearings—to recognize even the section of the town you were in—have to base your calculations on the indestructible river or the tower of the gutted cathedral.

Since only one of the city's five bridges could be used, traffic converged in dense confusion on that battered bridge. Amidst the rumble of the American engines creeping over the precarious structure and the hundreds of men and women, like rats, swarming on and off it, I gazed round at the acres of corpse-like buildings with their black, hollow eyes, at the fallen roofs and collapsed ceilings, at curtain-rods and rusty bedsteads piled on mountains of brick, at a shattered marble mantel-piece perched on top of a chimney—amidst all this wreckage I could hear, above the rumble of the engines, the roar which until recently had not been heard in history: the crash of thousands of tons of exploding bombs, the blast of guns, the howl of fire sweeping from house to house in the wind, the howl of vengeance and the destruction of Germany. It was a roar which left you only when you were out of the shambles and in the country again. And even there, for hours afterwards, that silence did not seem like ordinary country silence, but silence a little sinister, like that between ear-splitting claps of thunder, or the stillness that falls in the streets of a city with the sudden falling of snow.

Destruction on such a scale takes the mind a long time to absorb. You have to live with it to believe it. You think of it at first not as destruction, as something done deliberately by man to man, but as an earthquake—The Earthquake, the phenomenon of our era. Nothing I saw in Frankfurt remained in so unharmed a state as to convince me I'd really been there before. The sensation was a little like that of returning to an apartment in which you have lived for years with your own furniture, to find that, filled with the possessions of a stranger, the only association with the past it has to offer you is the view from its windows. But here the view—all views—had changed.

I was reminded of the Frankfurt I'd once known by accident. On returning to the hotel one evening I found, lodged behind an invalid's weighing machine, a slim guidebook entitled *The Middle Rhine,* published in Mainz in 1929. Taking it upstairs, I began looking through the illustrations of the towns that used to lie along the banks of the rivers Rhine and

Main. Several pages were devoted to Frankfurt; and it was these, rather than any "reality" I had so far set eyes on, which brought back memory after memory of that past which seemed now to bear so little relation to the life I had since lived. One glance at what the Römer, the Kaiser Strasse, the Hauptwache, Goethe's birthplace once had looked like reminded me of places and people I had not thought of for years. It also made me realize, with a shock, the number of worlds an ignorant, unambitious but inquisitive youth lived in at once.

The picture of the tree-lined Kaiser Strasse alone evoked the memory of two of these worlds. Lying there on the bed in that sumptuous hotel room, staring at the photograph, I groaned with humiliation at the visions it recalled. I saw myself leaving a narrow, poky hotel bedroom, setting off dazed from lack of sleep, under those trees. It was early morning, for during the day I existed in an overheated bank, and German banks opened at the awful hour of eight. Behind the door of the bank's small airless lobby sat "Franz Joseph," the porter with the magnificent whiskers. He had been sitting there since 1880.

"*Gute MOR-je!*" he would boom in the Frankfurt dialect. "*Gute MOR-je!*" answered all the clerks and typists.

In my corner I stared at the commercial section of the *Frankfurter Zeitung*, pages I could not have understood in my own language. I doodled and I dreamed. Now and again I fell asleep. I read the story or serial *unter dem Strich* on the front page, and I began but never finished stories of my own. I planned tremendous novels. I made drawings of the vacant, sometimes vicious faces of the potential Nazis in the room. And I made drawings of the dark, sad, serious faces of the Jews. I listened to the conversations. The vacant and the vicious talked in low, lascivious voices and with lustful, guilty eyes about women and "houses of ill-fame"; and in loud voices about the prospects and prices of a vacation at some crowded resort on the North or Baltic Seas. The dark, sad faces, turning instinctively to one another, argued feverishly about domestic politics, about the horrors of the past inflation, about wages, the growing of vegetables, local musicians and concerts, even about banking. When the door opened and one of the directors passed through, everyone fell silent and pretended to be busy with papers on his desk. Punctually at eleven o'clock, out of table drawers appeared paper packages of bread, wurst, and ham. *Der verrückte Irländer*—the mad Irishman in the corner—was the only one without his thick midmorning *Brötchen*, his *zweite Frühstück*, his second breakfast.

During the lunch hour in the summer I used to try to wash away the atmosphere of this airless office by bathing from a dock in the muddy water of the Main. Sitting in the sun, eating frankfurters and potato salad from a cardboard plate, I tried in vain not to stare at the world's biggest bellies lying out on the boards. To this day I cannot understand how men could dare reveal such monstrous deformity to the human gaze. Surrounded by these inert, pallid, pig-like balloons of flesh, I used to look down at my own skinny bones and wonder if the balloons, perhaps, were as revolted by my appearance as I was by theirs. If they had shaved heads as well—or heads that had been shaved and begun to bristle—I didn't care or wonder what they thought.

At six o'clock, after nine hours of wasted life, I would go off in search of friends, or I might start on a slow pub-crawl. In the latter event I would begin the evening in the clean, expensive-hotel atmosphere of the Frankfurter Hof, amongst a number of young business men who bought their clothes in the West End of London and smoked Abdullah cigarettes. The only feature of interest in this dull place was the barman—a small, scraggy, yellow-skinned man with a face like a skull and mad, permanently wide-open eyes. He seldom talked, but when he did he had only one topic of conversation—The Revolution. He didn't—in those days, probably couldn't— specify what Revolution; and it wasn't until years later that I began to think of him as the most fanatical Nazi I'd ever known. Whenever I saw a picture of Goebbels with his mouth and eyes wide-open, screaming from a platform, I thought of that barman.

Once these pub-crawls got under way, they might last anywhere from two to ten hours. Having traversed half the city via a succession of bars and beer halls, I seldom failed to land up on a stool at the "Manhattan." A *Nachtlokal* opening at ten and closing at four in the morning, the Manhattan was the liveliest, most intimate spot in a not very lively town. Small, clean, dimly lit, an *echt* American bar with no dance floor, it was run by Tommy Fröhlich and his wife, Louise, who looked like a humorous version of Katherine Mansfield. Her husband was a sly, witty, sinister little man who'd lived in Detroit and was fond of poking his nose into other people's business and shooting risqué cracks in American slang out of one corner of his mouth. In German provincial towns anyone who had lived abroad, especially in England or the United States, commanded a peculiar prestige. He was considered a man of the world in a country where such men are rare, and where they are envied, respected, even feared more than anywhere else I know. Few Germans had the temerity to argue with the proprietor of this popular night-club. Even the rowdiest, most intoxicated client could be promptly silenced by a single stony stare from Tommy's sly little eyes. Working with Louise behind the bar, he employed one waiter, Fritz— a powerful, muscle-bound ex-prize-fighter who also acted as bouncer; George, a pale, fleshy individual who played the piano; and a swarthy, long-haired sentimental violinist who took dope and was known as Mark Antonio. My custom at the Manhattan was so regular, my visits so protracted, it was inevitable that Tommy, Louise, their employees, and I should become friends. It also seemed quite natural, when Tommy went off for the night or away on vacation, that I should take his place behind the bar. In this position, faced by an unusually complex clientele, in a small room invariably so packed that you had to shout to hear your own voice, I learned to speak an ungrammatical German with a German accent, how to mix a dozen different kinds of cocktails, how to drink without getting drunk, and how to behave towards others who had not learned that art.

On the nights when I worked, I used to remain in the bar until closing time. At this hour Fritz, George, and Mark Antonio, who lived by night, were just beginning to wake up. What little character I had developed was so undermined by my daytime existence that I could seldom resist their insistent appeals for my company over a "last beer." These last beers, of course, took as long to consume as last beers anywhere. My friends' favorite haunts for this early-morning indulgence were *Kneipen,* the lowest dives in the neighborhood of the *Hauptbahnhof,* or in some of the narrowest, rat-infested, sewer-smelling alleys of the Old Town. I have frequented some pretty queer spots in my time, but I don't remember breathing an atmosphere quite so sordid as that which pervaded these joints. The dives in port towns are, and the *schwulen boîtes* of Berlin after the First War were, God knows, sordid—but harbor taverns are peopled by sailors in uniform, girls, and pimps who create a certain tension, a crude, abandoned, juke-box gaiety reminiscent of the bal-musette. And in Berlin there was sometimes the excitement of seeing a face that still retained a faded beauty; there was the broad-shouldered body in skirts that made you stare and wonder, until you heard the over-heavy, tell-tale clump of the high-heeled shoe, which made you smile, then feel sad. It was the sadness rather than the sordidness of these *boîtes* that remained in the memory. The Frankfurt alleys catered to a different world. The people who haunted the *Kneipen* were not like people I've seen elsewhere. Long past their prime, they did not laugh and many did not look quite human. Not Hogarth, Rowlandson, or Daumier—not even Goya—ever drew such depths of degradation, dissolution, and despair as shone from the tiny, bestial eyes of these bloated, blotchy, beer-filled faces. The work of none of these artists shows the combination of the bald, bumpy cranium, the dribbling, sagging lower lip, the folds of slack skin over the once tight-packed rolls of neck, the receding or the loose, deflated double chin. Bosch knew such men, whom art historians of our day have described as grotesque monsters of his imagination, nightmare creatures from the folklore of the Middle Ages. The early George Grosz knew them even better. No artist dead or alive has reproduced so faithfully the female of this sub-human species: the vacant, leery, sodden eye, the white flabby flesh, the huge pendulous breasts, those shining gashes of scarlet, the lips that were never closed and always crooked; and finally the hands and the fingers—those lumps of cold lard from which hung the pink, permanently damp, nearly nailless sausages.

When the door of such places opened and we followed Fritz, still in his white waiter's tie and tails, into the dense cloud of smoke, through the stench of stale beer, cheap powder and perfume, mugs and glasses were banged on the table. Feet pounded the floor. The men revealed their gums in a toothless grin and the women who dared, stumbled—belching and blaspheming—to their tiny, swollen trotters. They sidled round us, their heads on one side, flashing a broken row of discolored stumps.

"*Der Fritz, der schöne Fritz!*" they whined. "*Der Georg! Mark Antonio, der berühmte Kapellmeister—spiel was schönes! Ach, und der Chimmie, der hübsche Engländer—wie goldig!*"

At the attempt to pronounce my first name I'd wince, and at the cold clammy touch of the sausage on my skin I could feel the heat mounting to my face.

"*Macht Platz!* Clear a table!" yelled the *Wirt*, whose bulk was so vast he could barely propel it round the room. Moving through the mêlée like some primeval pervert in leather shorts, he would shove the most sodden hulks from their chairs—or, if they were too far gone to move, he'd bang them on the backs of their snoring heads and, with a "'*Raus, Du besoffenes Schwein!*" pour the remains of their beer down their necks. By such an act, by a misdirected oath or accusation, because someone had detected a pocket picked, or because of some unbelievable jealousy between one wreck of a whore and another, a face would get slapped. Then there would be bedlam.

Lying back on the bed in the Nauheim hotel, the guidebook still in my hand, I closed my eyes and lived again, as though it were yesterday, a scene in which one slap of a woman's face had been the signal in one of these *Kneipen* for hell to break loose—for the still-smoldering memories of old furies, for the maddened rage of the impotent, for the aching pain of years of poverty and unemployment, the terror of insecurity, to rise into a flaming orgy of hatred, despair, and fear. The deformed creatures in men's clothes crawled to intoxicated life. Their glassy little eyes afire, they hurled their swollen bodies against the nearest wilting, beer-stained blouse. While the feverish little fingers began tearing it to shreds, the tow-haired head of the prostitute dived down, to sink her decaying stumps in the soft lump of lard. An inhuman howl shot through the uproar of the room. A fist flashed out, landing square and soundless on one of the flaccid breasts. Flashing back, flashing out, it pounded away like a piston at the human cushion. Then, blood oozing from the red-rimmed hole in her face, the bundle in feminine rags sank slowly backwards, the attacker on top of her. The falling bodies made no noise. Over them others reeled, and falling, formed a mass of struggling limbs. Tables overturned; glasses crashed and split in splintering pieces. . . .

Beside me as I rose and made for the door, Mark Antonio was on his feet. The violin was tucked under his chin, and with a benign expression in his watery sentimental eyes he drew the bow across the strings:

Trink . . . trink . . . Brüder-lein . . . trink!
Lasset die Sorgen zu Haus . . . !

Two hours later I was back in the bank.

DARMSTADT TO STUTTGART

4

WE left Darmstadt on the 29th of May. Our team consisted of seven men—a major, three civilians, and three enlisted men—and we were to travel over a certain area of Bavaria in two jeeps.

We were an oddly-assorted group. The major, the military "leader," whose functions were to find us food and billets and keep us out of trouble, was in civilian life a clinical psychologist. Mervyn, the civilian "leader," was a poet. John was a clergyman and Minister of the American Church in Munich until the outbreak of war. We four made up the first jeepload. The second jeep, pulling a trailer with all our belongings and a case of Rhine wine, contained Frank, a German-American sergeant recently out of college; the "Professor," a corporal and social scientist at a southwestern university; and Dudley, a six-foot, wise-cracking private whose civilian days had been spent on or near the San Francisco waterfront. If we had anything in common it was, with the exception of the major, the ability to speak a fairly fluent German.

As we moved away from the suicide's home, the major driving with his eyes into the sun, I looked back. The short avenue was filled with jeeps. On the grass, all round the rose beds, lay the usual khaki confusion—duffel bags, helmets, greatcoats, looted swords, swastikas, navigator's briefcases. And right in the center of it all, planted there by the inevitable G.I. spark, shone a small white marble nude, found among the possessions of the defunct family.

Darmstadt I remembered as a pink city, built of the local "red" sandstone. Its ruins were still pinker than those of any other city we saw. It had been undefended—that is, there'd been no important factories for war materials in the city proper. Despite this fact, it suffered one raid of the classical saturation type. And because of it, perhaps, the entire center of the built-up area was demolished. More than half of its eighty-four hundred dwellings were totally destroyed. The date was September 11, 1944; and the raid lasted fifty-one minutes. During these minutes 8,433 * human-beings were killed or burned to death and 2,439 * were seriously wounded. In the tremendous heat, witnesses told us, adult bodies turned brown and in a split second shrunk to the size of babies. After the raid more than 49,000 survivors (roughly half the population) fled to nearby towns and villages.

Natives of Darmstadt talked about that hour in voices quite unlike those of people in cities which had been bombed too often for the inhabitants to remember. They talked of it as perhaps the survivors of Hiroshima talked of their single experience of less than a year later, as The Nightmare that cannot be imagined by those who didn't experience it, nor ever be forgotten by those who did. Some—like the once-certified, who do not speak of insanity—could not be persuaded to talk of it at all. How many of us, the unbombed, the uninvaded—I've wondered since—do seriously consider sharing shattered Europe's sleep: the waking up every morning in some unlighted, unheated hovel to see all about us for miles the great graveyard, the permanent memorial of one short nightmare that had been real; a nightmare that would live with us and with our surviving children—unmentioned, unmentionable—to the end of our days?

Such thoughts, I repeat, have come seeping in since the day we left Darmstadt, because such thoughts, like the impact of concussion on the brain, are by nature delayed. They creep into the mind of a man after the initial shock, when he is alone and unprepared; they catch him unawares, but awake, in the lonely, silent hours of night, or when confronted by a

* Based on casualties reported to various police stations.

blank sheet of paper, armed only with his memories—memories he interprets according to his conscience, and which neither his anger nor compassion, nor even his forgiveness, can ever efface.

But in the reality of day, warmed by the summer sun, human companionship and the sound of our native tongue, we continue, particularly in the face of hardly comprehensible catastrophe, to think and speak in clichés. When you drive down the streets of Darmstadt you think, if it can be called thought, of the physical aspect of this particular ruined city— simply of what the eye sees. And what the eye sees everywhere is a high sea, a tempestuous ocean of pink rubble with jagged, perforated walls sticking up between the great waves. And gazing up at those tidal monsters, you wonder not what ruins mean to the ruined, nor even how long it will take them to rebuild, for these are the kind of thoughts at which the imagination balks. Instead, what seem at first more logical, more pressing problems present themselves—the problem, for instance, of how long it will take to dispose of the rubble, and where that rubble will go. You think of the thousands of tons of Bristol rubble that during the war was shipped as ballast to New York, where it was used by Mr. Moses to lay the foundation for Manhattan's East River Drive. You think of the plaque put up to commemorate the event, and you wonder, even if ballast were needed again, how the pink hills of Hessen could be transported as far as the distant sea.

The wind-screen was still afire before the major's eyes. Some military trucks, some civilians on bicycles were coming towards us. Our side of the road, however, seemed clear when suddenly a lone bicyclist swung right across our path. The major swerved to avoid him, jammed on his brakes. There was a tinny, toy-like collision, and the first thing I saw was a man impaled on his bicycle which was impaled on the hood and bumper of the jeep. A briefcase dropped from the man's hand, and the man, collapsing slowly as from a rearing horse, fell from the machine on to the cobbled street. I don't know what each of us did during the following instant. I only remember jumping automatically from the back seat and trying to lift the man to his feet. Someone beside me was doing the same. The man was young and blond, but he looked frail, ill, and he seemed stunned into speechlessness. While the two of us managed to hold him up, the major—assuming that since he seemed incapable of standing, some damage had been done to the victim's legs—began running his hands over his thighs. The young man, pale and trembling, hung like a corpse on our shoulders. Suddenly the major's hands stopped over one knee. He began to press it with his fingers. He scowled and finally pinched it hard. The victim took not the slightest notice. Then the major's hands traveled quickly down the leg, lifted the trouser.

"My God!" he exclaimed. "It's wood!"

We all let out a kind of suppressed guffaw, and Frank said: "Lucky swine!" This seemingly callous comment proved to be apt, for it soon transpired that had the leg been of the victim's flesh and blood, it would most certainly have been broken.

Since the young man still seemed unable to speak, the major searched his pockets. Their contents revealed that he lived on the outskirts of the city. "I'd better take him home," the major said.

Not until he had been driven away did we realize that quite a crowd had gathered. The spectators, of both sexes, were a wild-looking lot, wearing tattered, dirty clothes. The moment we seemed prepared to listen, they all began to talk at once, in a kind of pidgin-German difficult to understand. They were Poles, it appeared, who had been transported to Darmstadt, where for several years they had been doing slave-labor. In their various ways they were all attempting to express the same thought—their utter bewilderment at the way Americans had treated a German, to whom they referred as *"dieser Hund."* With weird gesticulations (punctuated by pouncing on our cigarette butts) they pantomimed how Nazi soldiers would have behaved under similar circumstances. They'd have crashed into man and bicycle, they explained, cursed him up and down from their cars, then raced on at breakneck speed, leaving the victim to his fate on the road. Our conduct seemed not only something they had never witnessed, but beyond their comprehension.

Before entering Heidelberg we stopped in the suburb of Neuenheim, at the house of Frau Dr. Else Jaffe, sister of Mrs. D. H. Lawrence, to pick up some documents. These documents had been prepared at Mervyn's request by two famous anti-Nazis, Professors Alfred Weber and Emil Henk. What they had written concerned exclusively the events leading up to the attempt on Hitler's life on July 20th of the previous year. When, later in Munich, we read these few pages we had proof at last to refute the charge that there had been no active opposition to the Nazis. We realized, too, that behind these few facts lay one of the strangest, most complex and tragic stories of the war. By its failure, the bulk of the remaining anti-Nazi brains of Germany had been wiped out. But a closer scrutiny of the documents revealed, both among the victims and the survivors of the Plot, a few names surprising to find on such a list. A glance at that of Johannes Popitz, that ultra-reactionary Prussian finance minister, who had personally received from the Führer the Party's golden badge; or at that of the former Nazi Police President of Berlin, Graf von Helldorff, as among those executed in September 1944, made one wonder what motives such men had for wanting to kill Hitler, and whether they had become active before they realized the game for Germany was up.

Heidelberg seemed to be a backwater the invading armies had by-passed. With the exception of its three blown bridges over the Neckar, the town offered nothing to remind you there'd been a war. The narrow Haupt-Strasse was packed with civilians. They were busy. They talked. I even saw people smile. But more remarkable was the look of health on most of their faces; their clean, unpatched, new-looking clothes.

The shirts and blouses of all but the aged were white and spotless, their faces, arms and legs tanned by the sun. They walked in and out of a few shops—open shops! Bookshops, with books in the window. Windows with unbroken panes of glass; scarlet geraniums and pink petunias in green boxes, and faces peering out over the flowers. After Frankfurt, after Darmstadt, Heidelberg was like a miracle or a very old dream. It recalled, even more than had the soot of London or the English landscape, the years when few of my contemporaries contemplated the possibility of another World War. Was it really twenty years since the day, during that Irresponsible Era, when I had come out here from Frankfurt in a fourth-class carriage with one of London's brightest of Bright Young Men? Perched up on those wooden, right-angled, back-breaking benches, squashed between gloomy middle-aged men with long pipes and bulging shiny-faced *Frauen* with bald-headed babies, he had suddenly turned to me as the train grunted into Heidelberg: "Christ, my dear, these *hide*ous people!" and thrust something hairy into my hand. Looking down, I saw a false beard, chocolate brown and very long. By the time I'd recovered from the shock and glanced up, he had transformed his pale, Greco-like appearance into that of a furious old gentleman in pince-nez and drooping black mustaches. . . . I wondered, smiling at the memory, if I were to walk into the Hotel zum Ritter after all these years, whether I should still find in its registry the entry of a guest describing himself as Dr. Whipplebottom—*Profession:* Murderer.

Now, in the same narrow street, not a hundred yards from that hotel, stood a long line of G.I.s carrying canteens, and beside them, like an elephant caught in a corridor, a two-ton truck. When the enlisted men had disappeared in the crowd, the major led us down a few steps into a large basement hall, which had once been a *Bierstube*. Americans were packed round every table but one. Here, in a corner, near a kind of stage under the only window, we sat down.

"Good God!" muttered the major, and following his eyes, we all stared at the stage. On it was an orchestra. And in that

Heidelberg hall of unrelieved dismalness, of khaki, smoke, and plates of messy food, where for centuries solid, scar-faced German students had swilled their beer, that orchestra—momentarily at ease—was composed of six skinny women of uncertain age. Four were peroxide blondes and two raven black; and they had glum, pinched, white, foxy faces that reflected like a mirror the gloom they stared so grimly out upon. One of the blondes sat before an open grand piano as though she were prepared to go on sitting there all her life. The others were seated on hard chairs, their arms crossed, their musical instruments resting on their laps or held between their bony knees. And each of them, in that dark undecorated cave, wore a black skirt of some shiny material and a kind of harlequin blouse of many brilliant colors. They sat there, rigid, silent, motionless, like waxen models for Carnival in the window of some nineteenth century provincial town, glaring discontentedly at the crowd of chattering, red-faced American men.

Then, all of a sudden, the ladies sprang to life. As though prodded by bayonets they rose together and crashed into a thumping version of *Valencia*. . . .

The girl who served us our soggy food was a short, fat little thing dressed in a khaki shirt and G.I. pants. When I asked her about the ladies in the orchestra I discovered she could understand only French.

"Les dames," I asked, "are they French, too?"

"Evidemment, Monsieur!" Did Monsieur imagine they were Boches? No. Boches they could never be. Those faces could have come only from France, and as they rose again and we watched them carving away at those instruments I had a feeling that with every stroke of the bow they were sawing off a German head and that they would not cease sawing until there were no heads left.

Outside, the sun still shone. The landscape of the Neckar valley surpassed even the most superlative descriptions I had heard of it. As the road followed the snake-like curves of that placid river and we passed under the shadow of the vine-terraced hills, between dark green clumps of Spanish chestnut, through the silent peaceful villages smelling of dung, the country began to grow slowly, strangely familiar. An optic memory made me more and more convinced I'd passed this way before. Suddenly I remembered. . . . Among my acquaintances who used to frequent the Frankfurter Hof bar, there'd been a tall dark young man who one evening sprang a surprise on me by suggesting that I accompany him on a trip to Southern France and Spain in his ancient Essex roadster. Without giving the prospect a second thought, I promptly rang up the bank and in a hoarse voice croaked that I was in bed with a fever.

We set off early one morning in Easter week, and I remembered only now, as we came upon the shambles of Heilbronn, that it was then that I'd seen the Bergstrasse in bloom, and that we'd stopped in Heidelberg for a second breakfast with my companion's sister, whom I found more attractive than her brother. One of his passions, which I had unfortunately known nothing about and did not share, was to rise soon after dawn and drive, in leather helmet, goggles, and a magnificent pair of fur gloves, as fast as the old car would carry us, as long as daylight lasted and sometimes longer. After leaving Heidelberg that day we had roared through this lovely landscape, shot through Stuttgart, and landed up that night, the engine seizing from heat and my hands stiff from cold, in Basel, Switzerland. And it was there, I recalled, as the sun went down this evening in the summer of 1945, that my traveling companion revealed to me the first of several peculiarities which were to lead to the final breach—at Barcelona, I believe—in a relationship which could never have stood much chance of harmony. He walked into the rather too grand Swiss hotel, and while conversing with the receptionist in English a little too loud (he had spent some time in the West End of London), he wrote on the register under his German name and my Anglo-Irish eyes a Piccadilly address. He then stalked upstairs, changed before my incredulous gaze into a stiff white shirt and immaculate evening clothes (a form of dress I had not dreamed of bringing with me), and marched out of the hotel in search of a female companion to dine and dance with.

As a full yellow moon began to rise over the gray countryside on the road to Stuttgart that evening, I fell to wondering what, during the intervening eighteen years, had happened to this acquaintance whose Anglomania I have since observed in many upper-class Rhinelanders and whose invitation, during some of the more depressing days of my youth, I had so rashly accepted. I determined to find out. And I succeeded. A month later, a mutual friend of ours, whom I had not seen in almost as many years and whom I managed to track down in a small country house near Munich, informed me that the man I'd once traveled with along this road was now dead. Recalling that his mother had been Jewish, I drew the tragic but natural conclusion. No, said my friend, this was not the case. True, both parents had been turned out of their home, and the mother, so my friend believed, had been thrown into a concentration camp; but such had been their son's ardent display of patriotism, such his ceaseless insistence on fighting for the *Vaterland* that finally, in the winter of 1942, this former Anglophile had been granted the privileges of wearing a Nazi officer's uniform and of fighting against Russia—where, a few weeks later, in the snow before Moscow, he had been killed.

Before we reached Stuttgart night had fallen, and with it a frost-like chilliness. The full moon bathed the land in a light so white that fields became sheets of luminous steel, hills silhouettes the color of coal. The voluminous foliage of an oak was carved from ebony, and a river, static in its bed beside the road, was a spotless street of silver.

From a shattered railroad bridge a pair of snapped iron rails, still held parallel by their sleepers, reared themselves perpendicular over our heads into the blinding face of the moon. On the summit of a mountain of broken brick, the skeleton of a roof had catapulted to rest. Looking up through its charred ribs, you could see the glittering ceiling of stars. On the other side of the road, its windows gaping holes, its doors in knife-like splinters, the entire front wall of a house leaned out towards us over the street; yet you felt little fear of its falling, for instead of a solid façade, behind which for years men had lived and died, you gazed in wonder at something as frail as a canvas backdrop that had been lifted from a stage-set representing a Night in Hell.

Presently we emerged into a great square, with the darkness of trees at one end and at the other a single tower as whole as on the day it had been built. In the center of the square, near a drunken lamp-post, the major stopped, turned off the engine. We listened. There wasn't a sound.

"Christ," muttered the major, "isn't there a soul in the whole damned place?"

"There are supposed to be one hundred thousand people left in Stuttgart," John said, and his voice seemed unnaturally loud.

"Look," Frank called from the jeep behind, "there's a light—in a window."

There was. Opposite the tower we could see a solid-looking building—that is, it seemed to have four walls and a roof— and amongst its rows of dead windows there was one, on the upper floor, that let out a light—a weak, golden, Rembrandt-like glow. The house, we discovered, was a hotel, and it bore the name of Zeppelin. Inside, fast asleep in a chair behind a glass window, lolled a little bald-headed man in his shirt sleeves. When woken, he informed us that the rooms were not for enlisted men, and that to get rooms the rest of us would have to obtain authorization from the billeting officer. He then wrote out for the major an address on a piece of paper. The enlisted men, he added, might find accommodation across the square, in a building which, we discovered next morning, had once been a wing of Stuttgart's modern *Hauptbahnhof*. It was now a gigantic, roofless shell, whose remaining walls were held together by a number of high connecting arches, like a Roman viaduct. Still nailed to these walls under the open sky I found clean, untouched billboards instructing travelers to which window they must go in order to buy tickets for one or another health resort.

With our slip of paper we moved away into the night. I was wondering how the major expected to find an address at such a time and in such a place, when there appeared in the blackness beyond our headlights a round white spot which seemed to move, to be swaying slowly to and fro. When caught by our beam of light, we saw that beneath the spot there staggered the uniformed figure of a man, but of a man, so it seemed, without a face. An instant later we realized that under the helmet of a French MP, the face was black.

Tall, thick-set, with a body suggesting gorilla-like strength, he came reeling towards the jeep and began, before we had time to speak, shouting at us in a language none of us could understand. Holding on to the wind-screen with one hand and waving a carbine wildly in the air with the other, he stood there shouting, while even from my back seat I caught waves of the unmistakable smell of brandy. The major jammed his foot on the gas and we bounded forward.

"Last week," he said, "these Senegalese caused a lot of trouble with the local women."

Looking back, I watched the MP standing unsteadily in the middle of the street, directing imaginary traffic with his rifle and yelling curses at a world in which our jeep seemed to be the only moving object.

Then, from one lighted window in a section of the city that still looked habitable, we heard a vague hum of male French voices. The major and Mervyn got out and banged on the door. A short pale man in his shirt sleeves stuck out his head. With the door ajar, I caught sight of a row of mattresses on the wooden floor within; on each mattress lay a half-dressed soldier. All the man in the doorway would tell us was that the city was occupied by French troops, that he knew nothing about a billeting officer, and that he was not interested in where Americans slept. To a question as to the whereabouts of his Commandant, he offered us some information which to this day I can only interpret as a paragon of cutting, surrealistic wit. Instantly, in a calm voice, as though this were Paris in peacetime and we had come to pay a passing call, he said: "Ah, *le Commandant,* he's gone to the theater!"

"The theater! Here! At nearly midnight!"

"*C'est ça, Messieurs,*" sighed the soldier. "*Je regrette.*" And withdrawing his head, he quietly closed the door.

The next stop we made was before a house to which we were drawn by a noise audible a couple of blocks away. This time the door, instead of being eased carefully ajar, burst open, and to the accompaniment of what sounded like an ancient piano and several accordions, out reeled half a dozen tipsy French soldiers. Above the racket of voices and raucous music, I overheard "*sales étrangers*" and other xenophobic epithets being leveled at our heads. A peremptory shout as to where transient American troops could find place to sleep brought immediate silence and a wagging of heads. Then one of the men disappeared inside and returned with a sharp-faced woman in an apron, who began talking at the top of a squeaky voice, waving her arms and gesticulating as only the French can. At the first sign of the tirade subsiding, we again put to her our simple question.

Billeting officer? *Merde, alors!* how could she know? To our dismay, however, she did. With a reluctance suggesting that she was being robbed of her last centime, she informed us that the officer lived at the end of the very street we were in.

Mervyn and the major vanished through a dark doorway and with the aid of a flashlight mounted a flight of rickety wooden stairs. They were gone for more than half an hour.

When they at last reappeared, their faces looked as white as the slips of paper they carried in their hands, and they were speechless. They had spent that half-hour arguing with three stubborn, disinterested little bureaucrats already half asleep with wine. The men had carefully examined, or pretended to, every paper in their possession and then insisted on them filling out a sheaf of forms. Only after these had been carefully read, checked, and rechecked were four Americans given permission to inhabit two rooms in Stuttgart for the night. Back we trundled to the Zeppelin.

We reached our rooms by means of a decrepit luggage elevator—one of those anachronisms typical of postwar Germany. The little man with the bald head led us down a grim, ill-lit corridor, unlocked two doors, threw them open without a word, and shuffled away.

We gathered in the room in which Mervyn and I were to sleep—the kind of room you find in any second-class hotel in an American town. With a bottle of wine each, we sat on the beds and chairs and drank out of tooth-mugs and for a long time said nothing. Darmstadt seemed further away than New York, and New York further than the nights at school when we used to sit up in the dormitory beds and start whispering in the dark. Remembering all those faces, I looked up and thought: we four have never sat together in a room before!

"What part of the States d'you come from, John?" I asked.

"Rhode Island," he said.

"Queer," the major muttered, "I've never been to Rhode Island."

Then we all began to talk at once, in a kind of feverish gaiety. Jumping from one subject to another, recalling a place, a country, a day, a friend, we unconsciously offered to one another snapshots of moments from our past. Of war, of Stuttgart, of the Nazis, even of the French we barely breathed a word.

When the bottles were empty I walked over to the long window, pulled it open, and stepped carefully out on to the balcony. Gazing down on that breath-taking panorama of moon-lit horror, I felt what I'd felt once as a child when I stood watching, through a hedge, women keening over a corpse at an Irish wake; I felt what I'd felt during "Easter Week," while listening to the bombardment of Dublin and watching the face of a friend, an old man, whose son had just been killed in an ambush; and I felt as I'd felt when I read the news, years ago in Berlin, that my eighteen-year-old sister had died suddenly of sleeping sickness. . . . I felt: if this is a necessary part of existence, then in God's name, what's the point of existing!

I turned my back on the view. And gazing round that room, I thought of all the hotel bedrooms I had worked and slept in over half the world; I thought of the unique impersonality, the inaccessibility, the anonymity of a room in an hotel. I recalled lying in bed at night, surrounded by unknown sleepers in a great city, wondering who had slept, or died, or made love—what drama had taken place in this bed, between these walls, before my arrival, and who would replace me when I was gone. I thought of the magic sensation of being alone and unlonely, of the wonder of walking into such a room in a foreign city and being able to say to oneself, aloud and unheard: "Think, no one on earth knows where you are!"

Mervyn was asleep. I walked over to the wash-basin and when no water appeared from the faucets I washed out my mouth in wine.

STUTTGART TO MUNICH

5

NEXT day we raced to Munich by *Autobahn*. I hadn't realized that the Nazis had used these highways as runways for the Luftwaffe. Every now and again, caught in its hideout on the edge of the carefully tended forest, we'd pass the wasp-like head of a small plane, its face smashed in or its entrails hanging from its green and brown body.

With us on the *Autobahn* traveled three types of traffic: American military vehicles, German bicycles and handcarts, and the ex-Wehrmacht soldier. The bicyclists—in baskets, grids, and trailers, on handlebars and on their backs—carried a maximum burden of the necessities of life. Perched on bedding and furniture in the handcarts, sprawled a couple of children, an aged man or woman, while the cart itself was pulled and pushed by from one to six surviving members of the family. The Wehrmacht soldier was immediately recognizable by his clothes and certain definite characteristics. For anyone entertaining a doubt about the German army's defeat, a glance at these individuals should have been sufficient to dispel it. Unshaven, their filthy *feldgrau* uniforms hanging from their gaunt limbs, their feet bound in bandages, these beaten men trudged the highways of Germany like outcasts. Moving about in pairs, they carried a bundle done up in a greatcoat. They walked in a special way, with their heads down, their eyes rarely raised from the ground. Their legs propelled their bodies along as though by conditioned reflex, as if, having carried their burdens so far—from Russia to Italy to France and back—they would cease to function not by degrees but suddenly, when at last the heart stopped beating. They gave the impression of being only half alive, of not knowing why they were here, or where they were heading. They greeted no one on the way and attracted from their compatriots seldom so much as a glance, for they were the symbol, they wore wherever they went the stigma of defeat. Their look of utter hopelessness reminded me of the look I once saw in the eye of an old horse, a look which said more certainly, more frantically than a human cry: "Oh, be kind, Man, and kill me, for that we animals cannot do!"

The remainder of the journey to Munich is memorable only for the sudden sight, in abnormally large letters on a signpost, of the word DACHAU. Whatever visions of atrocity this word had evoked in the past, the imagination had to reel once again at the irony of this death-camp having been laid by nature in surroundings so serene. Down this road fifty years ago, to these green meadows and the *Moos,* landscape painters had traveled from all over Bavaria to work and finally to form here a famous artists' colony. Dachau in those days was to Munich what Barbizon was to Paris.

The devastation of Munich was different again from that of other cities. The Bavarian capital seemed to have died in a peculiar way, like a handsome woman who has been shot to death many times, but whose skin, hair, eyes, and lips have left abundant evidence as to why she had been admired. The wounds suffered by the stately nineteenth century palaces looked grave but not mortal. One glance, however, through their gaping windows and you found their bodies burned out; little remained but the mockery of their outer frames. The verdigris dome and golden baroque tower of the Theatiner Kirche were still intact, but the church windows were missing, its columns cracked, its roof ripped off, its interior like a bashed-in courtyard. That day in May all the green tiles of the copper-capped Frauen Kirche were in place, but when we returned in July most of the tiles had fallen out.

Munich's most surprising sight was Das Haus der Deutschen Kunst, built by order of Hitler in the heart of the city. On this plain becolumned building, in which every year was exhibited all the bad German art the Führer considered good, hardly a bullet mark could be seen. When the bombings began, its near-white roof and walls were camouflaged under a canopy of small iron rings to which millions of leaf-like pieces of tin, painted green, had been attached. These gloomy drapes still hung like dead ivy in tatters from the roof. "Ah," sighed the Münchner, "only what Hitler built in Munich still stands. That's all the Allies consider we deserve as monuments to our past!"

As a more fitting monument to Germany's past, I'd like to see in a spot where none could miss it the bronze mask of a certain lion. This lion was one of four which for a century had been gazing down upon the world from atop the Victory Arch in the Leopold Strasse. Three of them now lay on their backs, their legs in the air, their wide-open jaws snarling at each other's genitals, as though in their final agony their one desire had been to rip one another to pieces. The fourth lion had managed to crawl away a few yards on his own, and there, cast on his side, gazing with terrified eyes at the fury descending from the skies, he unbends his elbow from the straightarm salute and, just before expiring, clenches the huge hand into a fist in the hope that if the world he is about to leave won't forgive him, the one to which he is going will.

Our journey ended in an ugly modern Schloss near Starnberg. In an enormous room with high shadeless windows overlooking the lake, we occupied five of nine white cots. All night Americans kept clumping in, dropping duffel bags, cursing, and going out again. At dawn the room was flooded in light. I opened an infuriated eye to glance at the snorer in the opposite cot. The round bald head looked familiar. Then I recognized it as that of a Hungarian economist who'd married an English cousin of mine. I'd last seen him in Hyde Park in 1935.

That day was a Sunday and we were free. I'd brought with me from New York a list of names and addresses of people who'd been prominent in the intellectual life of Munich before 1933. The list had been handed to me by Elizabeth M., who'd lived many years in this neighborhood and was also a good friend of Mervyn's. She didn't know if these friends were still alive or where they might be living, since all addresses were prewar. The nearest was that of Fräulein L. in Starnberg, about whom all we knew was that she'd been an intimate friend of the poet Rilke.

The address, with the house-number 7, would probably not have been honored with the name of Street in the States. Situated high up above the town, it was a narrow lane overhung with branches of bright green leaves. Immediately on the air along this sun-dappled path there rose the faint but unmistakable odor of dank shade, of moss, mold, and humus —a cool cellar-like smell which the woods and rivers of Ireland exude. What could have been more in keeping than that the gate of Number 7 was half-concealed in the folds of a gnarled yew-tree; that a tendril of traveler's-joy had pierced its lock as though to preserve its ancient chastity against the marauding key; that the gate itself was spotted brown with rust; and that paint of a faded, rain-washed blue, like fragments of a blackbird's egg, was peeling off its posts? The unwilling click of its latch, the creaking of its hinges was correct, as was the silver lichen on the stone wall, the golden-green moss on the path to the door, the long unkempt grass, and the ghost of a garden with its weed-ridden beds where you knew roses must once have grown. But here, before a heavy Victorian building of brick and stained-glass windows, a green front door in good repair, a row of bell-buttons with a German name under each, the analogy ended; and instead of the friendly welcome, the rush and the smell of dogs, of bread baking, and the kind voice bidding the animals "Whist, come here out o' that and lay down!" the door swung open and there stood on the threshold a severe-faced servant woman with a goitre, her sleeves rolled up, and in her tiny eyes a look in which defiance was fighting a losing battle with fear.

"I've come to inquire," I said, "if Fräulein L. still lives here."

Without a word, the woman disappeared into the gloom of the gaping house. I advanced a few steps into the empty porch. From there I could see into a large kitchen. A kettle sat steaming on a black oven, and a smell of frying fat pervaded the air. I heard a door open in the background and the whispering of female voices. Then another woman appeared—the owner of the house, I imagined—and politely informed me that yes, indeed, Fräulein L. did still live here; would the Herr Hauptmann please step this way? I called out to Mervyn, who had remained in the jeep, and together we mounted a creaking, carpetless staircase. On the threshold of a comfortable if somewhat over-furnished bed-sitting room we introduced ourselves, via our mutual friend Elizabeth M., to Fräulein L. After some stammered words of astonishment she asked us to sit down.

It is possible, at this early date, that we—or at least I—had not yet learned the subtle technique of self-introduction. I was inclined to ignore or underestimate the first natural reaction of the Occupied to the Occupier's uniform—a reaction which, at quarters as close as the door of the home, was almost invariably fear. It took considerable time to convince Germans that behind such a visit there was no motive other than curiosity and the desire to convey messages from friends who lived in a world they had never seen, a world about which, for years, they had been hearing little but lies.

Fräulein L., however, seemed at first less curious about her friends and the country from which we came than about her native land. She was a frail, ill-looking, somewhat lifeless lady who could have been described—in a phrase now defunct in Europe—as having seen better days. We mentioned that we had been in Frankfurt. Ach, *so was!* Frankfurt! And I had the impression that to Fräulein L. Frankfurt was a remote place, associated with some dim memory of the past. And Munich! Ach! Fräulein L., it appeared, had left her home in Munich for this *pension* during the fall of 1943, and she had not returned. What was our impression of "poor Munich" now? Terrible— must be terrible! It was quite a test for her imagination, because, although she had not been further than twenty miles from the city, Fräulein L. had never seen a bombed house. That, for a moment, was quite a test for our imagination. She had heard those dreadful planes—*Gott*, the noise!—as they flew over the lake night after night, and then the trembling of the earth a few minutes later. But Starnberg—nay, Starnbérg, she must say—had been very quiet; nothing had ever happened in Starnberg. Until the end, of course. That had been a nightmare. It was difficult, even now, for Fräulein L. to speak of her one close-up experience of war. Just a month ago, on the first of May, as the enemy drew near, some "suicidal" Nazis had decided to defend Starnberg. In the middle of the night two machine-gun squads had arrived at the house, commanded all the ladies (I understood there were no men) to go down to the cellar. Why? Because the Nazis were going to use the house and grounds as a machine-gun nest, and "fight to the last man!" All night long the ladies heard trenches being dug, trees felled, men cursing in fury, haste, and fear. Were the ladies, cowering under the house, to be shelled to death after all these years, in their cellar, on the last mad day of war? Then, at dawn, silence had fallen. But the ladies did not dare to move. One hour, two hours passed, and there wasn't a sound. Suddenly they were startled out of their semi-slumbers by the roar of engines and the trampling of heavy boots above their heads. At last the roar ceased; the trampling stopped. Once more silence fell over the house. Cautiously, during the afternoon, the ladies began to emerge from the cellar. They were curious, they were tired, and they were hungry. Fräulein L. crept up the stairs, carefully opened the door of her room. She stood gaping on the threshold. The floor, the chairs, the table were littered with the paraphernalia of battle. And here, on her bed, fully clothed, sleeping the sleep of exhaustion, lay two American officers!

"*So was!*" exclaimed Fräulein L., clasping her hands together. And then, breaking into English: "Ach, how they were tired! How glad I was to see them! And after so a night!"

The conversation then turned on personalities. Fräulein L.'s mother had died; her brother had disappeared. He was a painter who had lived in Paris; she'd last heard of him two years ago from Nice. Did we know him? (Oddly enough I did, but didn't realize it until months later. Back in New York I discovered that Fräulein L.'s brother, a painter of great talent but considered by his friends a hopeless alcoholic, had spent the first two years of the war in Gurs, one of the most frightful concentration camps in France. From there, after several vain attempts, he had finally made a miraculous escape and spent the remainder of the war hiding in the mountains. Today he is back in his studio in Paris.)

We asked Fräulein L. if she knew the whereabouts of any of the people on our list. She thought that one or two had died. She was acquainted with some of the others, but she had no idea where or if they lived. Then, just as we were about to take our leave, Fräulein L. remembered something. "A moment," she said, "there is upstairs a lady, Frau Professor von A. She might help you . . ."

"Frau Professor von A.," I interrupted. "That name rings a bell."

I racked my brains for the time and place where I felt sure I'd heard that name. But I couldn't remember.

"Poor Frau Professor von A.," Fräulein L. was saying. "Her husband, such a charming man, he was killed in Munich in an air-raid, while performing an operation."

As a last resort I looked at the list again. It was not among the names Elizabeth M. had typed. I was about to fold up the paper when I noticed, scribbled in pencil in my own handwriting at the bottom of the page: "Look for Emil S.'s first wife, Frau von A., probably in or near Munich, last heard of in 1941."

In a flash I remembered. A few hours before I left New York, Dr. Emil S. had rung me up. "I hear you are going to Germany." His voice was urgent. "Please, if you are ever anywhere near Munich, please try to inquire if a Frau von A.

and her children are still alive. She is my first wife, they are our children . . ."

"Was the Frau Professor once married to a Dr. Emil S.?" I asked Fräulein L.

"But naturally!" she cried, suddenly springing to life. "You know Emil?"

"Very well," I said.

Fräulein L. rushed from the room.

Mervyn and I exchanged smiles.

A moment later in walked a tall, handsome, well-dressed lady. Her pale skin was finely powdered and on her lips there was a just perceptible sign of rouge, the first I had seen on anyone in Germany. She shook hands gravely.

"Tell her," murmured Fräulein L.

"We understand, *gnädige Frau*," I said, "that your first husband was Dr. Emil S.?"

"*Ja*," she said, and slowly her eyes began to open wider. "You know him?" she asked quickly.

"Very well," I said. "He rang me up in New York a couple of weeks ago."

She took a step back, while her eyes and mouth opened and she lowered her head and her hands came up and covered her face. She slowly sat down, her head turned away. When she uncovered her face her eyes were glistening and she was smiling.

"Two weeks ago!" she said in almost perfect English. "You were in New York two weeks ago! You talked to Emil two weeks ago!" She gazed round the room in a daze. "How is it possible!"

"He asked me to try and find you," I said. "He has had no news of you and the children since—"

I noticed her eyelids drop ever so slightly and I realized once again that I had not yet learned the subtlety of restraint.

"How is Emil?" she asked urgently. "And Nora and the child?"

"They are all very well," I told her.

"He has work—patients in New York?"

"Yes, he has an excellent practice."

"Would it be possible," she asked hesitatingly, "could you possibly send him a message from me?"

"Certainly."

Then the Frau Professor began to talk. A spate of sentences poured from her.

"Excuse me," I interrupted. "I think you'd better let me jot down some notes. I'll never keep all that in my head."

She apologized, and while Mervyn talked to Fräulein L., I began to write:

Tell Emil I'm very well. Our house in Munich stands. Partly lazaret; eighteen of us live there—doctors, nurses, medical students. I've been working as nurse six years in lazaret. My husband was killed last year in raid; hospital went on fire. Our daughter, tell him, was living near Hamburg, but not heard of her for more than year. Her husband was killed in Russia. She had child, boy, 1942. Our son, aviator, last heard of in January, on Russian front. Pray he's a prisoner. Tell Emil his sister was very badly wounded in air raid. Her husband killed in Mannheim. Hope she has survived, but no news. Tell Emil his brother committed suicide in February. Don't know circumstances. Don't know anything about my sisters, all were in Berlin. I try not to think about that. Believe all nephews are alive. . . .

"Now that's quite enough," said the Frau Professor. "I'm so very grateful. I cannot take it all in yet—a breath of fresh air from the outside world, after all these years—it is hard to describe. I cannot thank you enough. . . ."

"You have nothing to thank us for," I said. "If you didn't happen to have been in this house . . ."

The same thought seemed to strike us both at the same time.

"Yes," she said, "I'm lucky—lucky to be in the Red Cross. I can get a little—how do you call it—benzine?"

"Gas," I said, and we rose to leave.

Back in the Schloss, the evening meal had already started. After Nauheim and its canned messes, the food was a joy.

The meat, the vegetables, the potato, cucumber, and tomato salads—of which there seemed to be an endless supply—were all fresh. Seated among officers and other civilians at three long tables, we were served by a tall, heavy, bald man with a big nose and shifty eyes. He was one of those obsequious Germans who, I felt, would have curried favor from any "master" with equal fervor. I took an instant dislike to him, and he knew it. Nevertheless, whenever he caught me alone he would always profess a passionate interest in the English language and, producing a small grammar from under his apron, ask me to "do him the honor" of explaining the differences between German and English tenses. At the same time he was a know-all, inclined to be patronizing if you were unwise enough to ask his advice. When you inquired, for instance, which was the quickest way to reach a certain place in the neighborhood, instead of telling you straight how to get there he'd throw out his chest and snort: "Ho! That is so easy!" implying that only a fool would ask such a question. When I went down to the kitchen to borrow a corkscrew (a trip I took every evening until we decided the corkscrew should be "liberated"), he first of all pretended he didn't know where it was, and then, on being told, he would hand it me with pompous reluctance, saying: "The Herr will return it soon, *nicht wahr;* it's the only one we have!" Which, of course, was a lie. My feelings for his wife were little warmer. A short, stout woman, she clearly wanted the world to know—while she silently, unsmilingly handed round dishes in a drawing-room dress—that the servant was far from the class into which she had been born. When a neighbor once informed us that the Schloss employed a fanatical Nazi kitchen-maid, I thought of this couple and did not feel surprised. That night, however, we paid little attention to them: we were tired and we had to get up at dawn.

"For God's sake let's go to bed early!" Mervyn said, eyeing John and me.

"For God's sake wake us up!" we replied.

Mervyn, who even in mid-winter seldom rises later than six, is as reliable and more insistent than any alarm-clock.

Baedeker says somewhere that Munich is liable to sudden changes of temperature. It warns visitors to be "on their guard, especially towards evening." The temperature must have dropped twenty degrees during the night. By dawn a high wind was howling round the Schloss. Rain blotted out the mountains, even the opposite shore: yesterday's placid lake was now an angry, inky sea. The weather continued this way for five days and nights.

At the grim hour of six-thirty, while the Schloss was still asleep, we met the enlisted men in the dining-room—breakfast being the only meal they were permitted to take in the "officers'" mess. Even at this time of day, over cushions and coffee, Frank, Dudley, and the Professor would begin—or rather continue—with their baiting of one another. It was a good-natured but somewhat one-sided affair, in which Frank and Dudley, both in their early twenties, always teamed up against the thirty-five-year-old corporal, casting excusable cracks at the number of different condiments he was capable of swallowing at once and the wolf-like sounds he made in the process of mastication. As an accompaniment to early morning cushions, the harmless tit-for-tat was a little depressing.

So was the twenty-mile drive into Munich. Icy rain whipped in from both sides of the jeep; sudden bursts of gale ballooned the canvas top from inside, then battered it up and down above our heads with a spanking, thumping noise.

Munich's ruins in pouring rain looked like a million overturned garbage carts multiplied in size as many times. The creatures crawling over the acres of filth were the shining rats emerging to gorge themselves on the decomposing graveyard when the last man on earth had been buried alive.

It was no effort for me to ignore the spectacle that morning. I had a sinking feeling in my stomach—due to preoccupation with the thought that I was about to interview a nameless

German civilian. I could not forget that, while the other members of the team had been interviewing for weeks, I had never in my life conducted an interview of any kind with anyone. I had read and reread the two set schedules, the *Fragebogen,* the questionnaires, which had been worded, it seemed to me, in the most peculiar German, and I'd put myself in the place of the interviewee and wondered how on earth I myself would answer some of these vague, some unintentionally humorous queries. We were to make notes of every answer, then fill in what was known as a "face-sheet"— a chart of details concerning the German's family, his occupation and address before and during the war; whether bombing had affected his health, his work, his sleep (!); what air-raid casualties there had been in his family; what damage his home had suffered; whether he had claimed indemnity after it had been bombed, how much he had claimed and how much received. After some further particulars about the sewage, drainage, and electric systems, we had to make a rating on the truthfulness of his answers, state whether he was hostile or friendly, unfriendly but reserved, or just plain friendly and talkative; and finally indicate the shade (black, gray, or white!) of his sympathies for or against the Nazi regime. Then, the moment the interview came to an end, we were to write out a full report on the four dozen answers.

What kind of people were these respondents and how were they chosen? They were supposed to be civilians of both sexes between the ages of 16 and 65. My youngest was a girl of 13, quite bright; and the oldest a man of 88, quite gaga. They were chosen *à la* Gallup poll and according to district. Every fiftieth name was drawn from the district's ration list and he or she received from the Military Government, a day or two in advance, typed on a scrap of paper, a summons to appear at a certain hour on the first floor of a house in the Planetta-Strasse.

This house had suffered only slight damage—a rare condition for a house in the center of Munich. It was a drafty, gloomy building most of whose windows were bunged up with cardboard. We each had a room to ourselves. Mine looked out on to a back-yard where the neighbors hung their washing and shouted to one another from opposite holes and windows. In one corner stood a tall green *Kachelofen;* near the shattered window a writing desk whose drawers were crammed with papers and photographs, many as old as the century. In another corner stood a glass cabinet full of useless china knick-knacks. Next door, the Professor was more fortunate: he discovered a top-hat, an early nineteenth century parasol and an ancient sword. Armed with these, during rare moments of relaxation, Frank and Dudley used to parade up and down the dark corridor, past chairs where the natives sat while waiting to be called in.

This first morning I hated the idea of going out into that corridor. I sat in my trenchcoat and shivered. At last, hearing the hum of interviews being conducted on all sides, my conscience got the better of me and I forced myself out of the room. There, huddled together on two chairs, sat a couple—a smallish woman and a middle-aged man wearing black glasses. When I asked which of them had been ordered to appear, my question was received with blank stares. I repeated the question, and finally the woman got up. Approaching me very close, she cocked her head to one side, cupped her hand round one ear. . . . My heart sank.

"Which of you," I shouted into the ear, "got the summons to appear?"

There was a moment of silence. Then a look of revelation spread across the woman's face.

"Ach, *so!*" she exclaimed. "He did. My husband got it!"

But it was she, not he, who produced the scrap of paper from her handbag.

"All right," I said, addressing the husband, "will you please come in?"

The man didn't move a muscle. As far as I could tell from the angle of his black glasses, he wasn't even looking at me. I leaned over and yelled at the woman that I wanted to interview her husband. She in turn leaned over him. She laid a hand on his arm. Only then did the man make a move. I was about to inform her that she would not be allowed to accompany her husband to the interview, when, to my horror, I saw that on his right sleeve the man wore a yellow arm-band with three large black circles, and that all this time beneath his overcoat he had been concealing a white cane.... This, I inwardly groaned, is Beginner's Luck with a vengeance.

But there was worse to come.

No sooner had I brought in an extra chair from the corridor, and got the couple seated close together close to me, when I discovered that not only was the woman very deaf, the man completely blind, but that he was almost stone-deaf as well! Nor was this all. Whenever I yelled a question at her and she turned and yelled it on to him, and he—after long deliberation—muttered his answer back to me (which the woman, unfortunately, lip-read), she immediately pounced upon him and accused him of talking nonsense.

"*Mein Mann*," she said, turning to me, "he doesn't mean that at all. He hasn't understood the question."

"What was that you said?" asked the man of his wife.

"Never you mind!" she yelled at him.

But the man seemed to mind very much.

"Don't pay any attention to her," he muttered, turning his blind eyes in my direction. "*Frauen*, they know nothing about politics. She's all confused."

Confused—though an understatement—is perhaps the best word to describe this interview. It did, however, suggest something which time was to prove a fact—that a striking number of Germans had been temporarily or permanently deafened by continual bombardment. The man had always been blind and up to the outbreak of war rather deaf, but explosion and concussion had rendered his deafness almost total. His wife's hearing, on the other hand, had been perfectly normal before the raids began. (The deaf, incidentally, never referred to their misfortune as such: the very deaf were invariably "hard of hearing," while the less deaf tried to make you feel that your German was even worse than you'd thought.)

The husband, despite his affliction, had worked in a munitions factory, to which he had traveled every morning by means of a number of trolley cars. Under normal conditions the journey, for him, took two hours. But on mornings after heavy night raids on Munich, he had never managed to reach his destination. He would start off in the first trolley (if it were running), change into the second, maybe into the third, but sooner or later one of the cars would be held up by the night's destruction, and he'd be compelled to tap his way home as best he could. Most such journeys he made all the way on foot, and very often they had taken him the remainder of the day.

The couple were Roman Catholics, and I understood that their professed dislike of the Nazi regime was due primarily to its persecution of their Church. They also voiced a second reason. "For us," said the man, "one of the worst features of the Nazi regime was the way the sick—the mentally deranged and the blind—were treated. These people were suddenly arrested and carted off God knows where. Some time afterwards their relatives received their ashes. I myself was arrested, but I suppose because I could still manage to do some work, they let me go."

It was significant and interesting, I thought, that when the blind man was asked whether he considered prices would rise in Germany during the next few years, he replied that in his opinion this very much depended on the Jews.

"The Jews?"

"*Ja*," he said, "I sincerely hope that when the Jews return, things will get cheaper."

Jews return? What Jews?

"The Jews who went to America, of course. They'll soon be coming back, *nicht wahr?*"

Then, as an afterthought—prompted, perhaps, by a sudden glimpse of the Good Old Days—he muttered a few words which have kept cropping up in my memory ever since.

"*Ja*," he sighed, "*unter den Juden*—under [sic] the Jews—we were always able to buy cheaper."

But the oddest remark I ever heard made by a deaf man came at the beginning of a description of the couple's behavior during air-raids.

"Ach," he said, while his wife for once smiled her approval. "Ach, when we heard the planes coming over at night, we just lay in bed and turned on the radio as loud as it would go!"

MUNICH AREA

6

SINCE the aim of our branch of the survey was to discover what effect aerial bombardment had on the morale of the German civilian, it may not be out of place to supply here some facts and figures concerning Munich's war-history.

Munich was attacked more often than any other Bavarian city. Between the first raid on September 19, 1942, and the last on April 23, 1945, the city was bombed 92 times by 9,493 planes, which dropped 24,454 tons of explosives.

The heaviest attacks came during the week of July 11 to 16, 1944—when 1,792 planes dropped 6,837 tons of bombs.

During the thirty months of Munich's bombardment, 6,242 Germans were killed and 13,000 severely wounded.

Before embarking on details of interviews with some of the survivors, I should make it clear, if I haven't already, that I do not consider my temperament suited to the Gallup poll type of interrogation. In fact, I doubt whether I could ever make an efficient interviewer. I became too interested in the character and personal history of the individual. I wasted time wondering how much he said was true, how much false. I found that the more intelligent Germans absorbed most time, not because they were cleverer liars or the most garrulous, but because I'd be tempted by their answers to ask off-the-record questions, whereupon they'd launch into a private "heart-to-heart" totally divorced from the subject of the *Fragebogen*. Even with the dullards, the DK's (those whose answer to every question was a Don't Know), the dismally ignorant *Hausfrau*, farmer's wife, washerwoman, the old grandmothers whose memories of their distant childhood were infinitely sharper than of anything that had happened to them since 1933—even with these people I wasted hours by relentless and often pointless "probing" for answers making some kind of sense. Actually, trying to bludgeon the inarticulate blockhead into speech was less infuriating than listening to those opportunists who, in order to sidestep some seamier side of their pasts, invariably shifted all responsibility on to others, rambled off on a self-pitying description of their deprivations, the horrors of "the terror" from the air, or what a terrible sight it was to see "poor little Germany" surrounded by enemies with all its beautiful cities in ruins. The prompt retort that I had recently seen the people of Paris, that the Germans were responsible for leveling most of the cities of Europe, for massacring six million Jews, and that they, the Germans, were the only healthy-looking people left on the Continent, never failed to make this class of person shut his mouth and look the other way. This was the first time, I often thought, that such people had considered the sufferings inflicted by their countrymen upon those of the nations they had bombed and occupied.

Nor could our experience refute the general impression the Germans managed to give to all Americans—that the only real Nazis in Germany had been members of the S.S. and S.A., none of whom we consciously saw. Of the Germans I myself interviewed, only one—a woman—admitted that she still considered National Socialism a "good idea"; and she was a Red Cross nurse who'd never been a member of the Party.

What we soon found preoccupying and dominating the minds of all Germans alike were two questions. Directly or indirectly, very often in a whispered aside at the close of an interview, we would be asked:

"What are the chances of Russia taking over the American zone?"

"When are we going to get more bread?"

So many thousands of Germans have been interviewed, so many thousand pages already written on the results that it is pointless at this date to generalize any further—even if one considered, as I don't, that generalizations serve a good purpose. One line of precise quotation from a German's lips (preferably in that language) can be more illuminating than a three-column "summary" by a foreign correspondent. For this reason I have extracted, from a great weight of notes, some sections of interviews in which a few Germans are briefly described and allowed to speak in the precise words they used during those first weeks after VE-Day. If the stupidity and ignorance revealed by some of their remarks sound incredible to American ears, the reader should remember, first, that many of the questions asked were vague, ill-worded and abstruse—in short, questions which few Americans, under similar circumstances, could have answered satisfactorily if turned on them and the United States; secondly, that the summons from the ex-enemy's Military Government took the individual German completely by surprise. Though he may have been told he had nothing to fear from the coming interrogation, this was the kind of story he had heard too often from his own government, and he had good reason to suspect the official word. Thirdly, at this date the Germans were still stunned by bombardment, fear, and defeat. Fourthly—and this, I'm afraid, is a generalization based on personal observation and one raising a highly debatable point—that the Germans have always been a people of unusual political ignorance. After twelve years of Hitlerian isolation, propaganda, lies, terror, and corruption, this ignorance has been reduced to a level as low, I'd say, as that of any other European country outside Russia.

There is, finally, one more subject which has provoked endless discussion, which in almost all these interviews is conspicuous by its absence, and on which Americans who were in Germany in the summer of 1945 are still being asked for opinions. This is the subject of German guilt. Did the Germans express any feeling of guilt? With the exception of such instances as those quoted in the interviews, the answer is definitely no. Our explanation of this phenomenon is simple: that the feeling of guilt among Germans is so colossal they simply cannot face it, much less give it expression.

TWO YOUNG MEN

I

Though young male civilians were naturally scarce, I happened to interview two during one week in Munich. The first was a working-class boy whose intelligence, judged by the standards of Hitler's Germany, was about average. The second was a shrewd, educated, unusually bright young man from the upper classes.

If this couple had anything in common it was not the fanaticism of the Nazi youth about which so much has been heard. While not convinced Nazis, they certainly were not anti-Nazis. Cynical, even fatalistic, they did not lack personal ambition. They seemed neither over-hopeful nor dulled by despair. The bright one was peculiarly detached; both were surprisingly unsentimental and calm. Also surprising was that even the less intelligent boy showed some individuality. And it must be said in their favor that, unlike so many of their elders, they revealed no servility, none of that all-too-familiar desire to please. I felt that, having seen and experienced human behavior at its most sinister, they had no illusions left, possibly no ability ever again to trust a soul. If this last be true, then I am ready to admit that they belonged to that lost and unteachable generation for which the pessimists insist there is no hope.

The face of young Gruber, to give him a name, the working-class youth, had the kind of expression I'd expected to see all over Nazi Germany—sullen, suspicious, bitter, with an attitude just short of hostile. He was pale, blond, and wore a white shirt and *Lederhosen*. After a passionate appeal to be allowed to bring his bicycle with him into the room, he sat down and informed me that he was a Rhinelander, that during the last occupation two of his aunts had married Americans and gone to live in the United States.

"So I feel some sympathy towards Americans," he said

rather grudgingly. Having lived more than half his life under the Nazi regime, he was clearly surprised to find that Americans did not behave like Nazis. "I didn't think we workers would be allowed so much freedom," he admitted. "I thought we'd be sent to slave in other countries—probably Russia."

A cutler by trade, young Gruber had been drafted into the Wehrmacht early in the war, then invalided out in 1942. The last two years he had spent working with his father in a hotel near Berchtesgaden. This hadn't suited him at all; he couldn't get on with the staff. "I was always having rows with them because I opened my mouth and said what I thought. The man who ran the place pretended to be a favored member of the Party; actually he was just an ordinary crook. . . ."

Gruber willingly admitted to having swallowed most of *Mein Kampf*—a book he of course hadn't read. "Yes, I really believed everything the Führer said—especially on the subject of *Lebensraum*. I used to look at the map, and it seemed to be as he said, that we were surrounded, and that Russia was far too big."

Young Gruber, needless to say, had not scanned the map purely out of passion for a Greater Reich. "According to our propaganda," he said, and one could hear how often he must have used just those words, "we would have gotten the Ukraine, and this would have been very good for my particular work, for we'd have 'settled' the Ukraine, and people like myself would have been badly needed there."

The fact that things hadn't turned out just that way didn't seem to worry Gruber too much. "As a cutler," he said calmly, "I think my talents will be more useful in peace than in war. I even have hopes of opening my own shop in Obersalzberg."

In the Nazi hierarchy Gruber had no use for anyone but Hitler. "The rest were all out for themselves; they all worked for their own pockets and stomachs. I used to see quite a lot of Dr. Ley at one time. He was drunk nearly every night. Hitler didn't drink!"

There were times when I felt that the advertisement lavished on Hitler's abstinence helped as much as any other propaganda to keep him in power.

Gruber had no doubts about why Germany lost the war. "Sabotage by the leading political men," was his prompt answer. "At the beginning of the war there were many younger men in the political leadership. But they were soon taken out, sent to the front, and killed. Only the old lot remained, and they didn't give a damn for anyone but themselves."

Partly owing to poor health, but also because he seemed to have had an unusual gift of the gab, young Gruber had led an extraordinarily unharassed life after quitting the army. He was one of the very few Germans who was not speechless with astonishment at being asked how much time he had taken off from his work.

"I really don't know how often I was absent," he said, without the ghost of a smile. "I guess a few hours a week. I just used to stand in front of my boss and go on talking till he couldn't stand it any longer. 'Oh, get out!' he used to say. And I went."

Gruber never listened to a radio and never read a newspaper. "They always said the same thing." Maybe for this reason he had always felt confident of German victory. But this was not the reason he gave. "I believed what Goebbels said about the power of the V-weapons," he said. So great was this faith or wish-dream that Gruber began to *doubt* Germany could win the war only when a friend managed to convince him that "American troops had crossed the Rhine at Mainz. This was the first time," he added, "that I said to myself: *Da stimmt 'was nicht!*—Something's gone wrong!"

Gruber seemed fascinated, like millions of others all over the world, by the most dramatic episode of the war—Rudolf Hess's flight to Scotland. Gruber's angle on one immediate result of the flight, however, was new to me. "It is true, isn't it," he asked, "that the moment Hess's peace efforts failed, there was a *putsch* by leading British Nazis in England?"

This led him to ask another, less uncommon question:

"How are German-Americans being treated in the United States?"

"With extraordinary fairness," I told him.

He shook his head slowly in disbelief.

"After what Americans have learned about your concentration camps," I said, "I can well imagine you find this hard to believe. By the way," I added, "what is your opinion of these places?"

I expected young Gruber to shrug his shoulders and dismiss the subject as part of the Allied propaganda. Instead, he for once lost his calm. He grew red in the face as he almost shouted: "If what we hear is true, then it's the *grösste Schweinerei die es gibt!*—the biggest foulness ever perpetrated!" If this was an act, then young Gruber shouldn't have been a cutler.

And what about Hitler? Did Gruber suppose *he* knew nothing about these camps?

Near to tears, Gruber expressed the conviction that "the other leaders must have kept the horrors of concentration camps secret from Hitler."

When he saw my mocking smile, he added through clenched teeth: "But if Hitler *did* know, then he was no better than the rest!"

He then got up and strode towards his bicycle. In his rage he got it stuck in the door.

II

The other young man, though of a very different class and character, also showed the suspicion, the sullen semihostile attitude I had expected to find in Germany. For fully twenty minutes I was able to extract from him little more than a few negative grunts in answer to the set questionnaire. I slowly managed to break down his reserve and gain his confidence ("establish rapport," in official parlance) first by offering him a cigarette (a temptation I could see he longed to resist), then asking him personal questions about his family; and I finally thawed him out by grunting encouragement at some of his more thoughtful answers.

He was twenty-four years old and a Catholic. Dark, good-looking, well-dressed, he could have come from almost any country in Western Europe. His father was a gynecologist, and he himself had passed his final medical examinations and become a full-fledged doctor only a week before the Americans had entered Munich. From the outbreak of the war until early in 1941 he had been allowed to continue studying medicine in Munich. He had then been drafted and sent to Russia as a private in the artillery. In 1942, still in the Wehrmacht, he had returned to Munich to continue his studies.

"For the past three years," he said, "I have been a medical student by day and a fire-fighter by night." Despite this latter activity, he was one of the very rare Germans who professed an indifference to air-raids. "I can't say they affected me one way or the other," he said, calmly.

His attitude towards military occupation and the collective human excess that follows in the wake of battle was equally calm. "I knew what to expect," he said. "I saw and experienced military occupation when we took Kharkov. The Germans behaved there just as the Americans have here. And the population of Kharkov behaved just as the Münchners did. The way both plundered and looted was practically identical. I witnessed all this, of course, with the eyes and from the point of view of a soldier. *Bitte?* The German soldier? No, in my experience he behaved neither worse nor better than any other soldier."

Only when, with some reluctance, the young doctor had to admit that his father had been a member of the Nazi Party since 1937, did he look a bit sheepish. He lowered his eyes as he added: "I don't know whether he will be able to continue his practice or not. As for me, I'm only a voluntary assistant at the *Poliklinik* and financially dependent on my parents. I won't be able to earn my living for years. I'm very young, and there are so many older physicians."

Contrary to the usual formula that "things would have been

terrible . . . we'd have all been sent to concentration camps had Germany won the war," the young doctor considered that a German victory "for me, personally, would have been pretty good—much the same as before 1939," as opposed, of course, to before 1933. Between these years "things went much quicker for us students and doctors. To get started in a full practice didn't take so long. But what's the good of thinking about that? Germany hasn't won the war!"

He had very definite opinions as to why she had lost it. "If it were necessary to wage a war at all," he said, and it was here that his tongue began to loosen, "we shouldn't have treated the Jews as we did. We shouldn't have treated the Catholics as we did." I noticed that he was honest enough to use the first instead of the third person plural. "Our behavior towards the Jews," he went on, "was a *Kulturschande*. Here were we calling Germany the Land of Culture, and then we go and behave like that towards some of the most cultured people in the world. I am referring particularly to the treatment of Jews *before* the war. I do think that during the war it would have been all right to have had German Jews interned. Otherwise, considering the treatment they had received before 1939, they would naturally have hindered the war effort."

He was also of the opinion that many political blunders had been made before the war. "Our foreign policy was all wrong," he said. "We should have made a pact not with Russia, but with England. But once having made one with Russia, we should have stood by it. We should have made a pact with England at the time of 'Munich,' and stood by that." He was particularly bitter about corruption—"corruption within the Party, within the Wehrmacht. This began in France as early as 1940 and continued throughout the war. There was also corruption among the officers at home—but the worst of all in this respect were the paymasters."

Inevitably, like the great majority of Germans, he considered the military leadership had been good at the beginning. He referred to the attack on Poland, France and the Low

Countries not as the *Blitzkrieg,* but as the "process of expansion" which, while "well-handled," was conducted "too fast. They wanted too much too quickly. They should have used the result of this expansion as a protective boundary, and been content."

His remarks concerning the political leadership, however, were most unusual. I don't remember any other German who revealed such cool objectivity, nor any other—not excluding one fanatical Nazi woman—who dared to maintain that the Nazi political leadership had been good. "Yes," said the young doctor thoughtfully, "it was good—that is, you understand, *an und für sich*—(considered) in itself, apart from the rest. But for it, Germany would have been defeated three years earlier. The National Socialists knew and understood the power of coercion. They used it to its fullest extent, but they overdid it and they underestimated the enemy's power of production. The Russians—now, they exploited the power of coercion better than we did. *Bitte?* Do I consider coercion good for a nation? *Lieber Gott, nein*—I wasn't talking about *das Volk.* Your question concerned the political leadership! And I have to insist that that, as such, was very good—good for the 'system,' for the State; but not good enough—not, as I've said, as good as that of the Russians. The proof of the pudding, you know . . . Stalin is the only man alive who knows how to keep a nation geared to modern war for a long time. . . . The trouble was that we knew the meaning of 'battle,' but not of total war. Now we know, because the war has been fought on German soil, and the enemy is with us. The last war—ha, that was just a *Feldzug*—a campaign!"

When the interview was over the young doctor leaned across the table towards me. "You know," he said in a low voice and with a grim smile, "you know, our trouble is going to be that the Americans don't properly understand the German mentality."

Hm, I thought, it probably takes a Hitler or a Goebbels to do that.

A LAWYER

He was a dark, swarthy man of forty who in 1934 had lost a highly paid job as legal adviser to the Government because his wife had one Jewish grandparent. From then until 1942, when he was drafted into the army, he had managed with the help of a partner to continue practicing law—a profession he had soon grown to hate because, as he put it, "throughout the whole country there was no such thing as justice. In Nazi Germany there was no possibility of enforcing decent laws. The punishments were appalling and out of all proportion to the crimes committed."

In October, 1943, while he was in barracks, his apartment had been badly damaged, and in April of the following year totally destroyed. "The conditions of evacuation were so awful," he said, "that our little girl of two-and-half caught pneumonia and died a few days later."

He was now living with his wife and surviving daughter in one small room in a suburb eight miles from the center of Munich. He was obsessed by two fears—armed foreigners (DPs)—and the possibility of the Americans moving out and the Russians moving in.

The former fear seemed well founded. During the last month he'd had three bicycles stolen by DPs—"one by a Pole who fired at me here in town." A few days ago one of his neighbors in the street where he lived had been shot and killed for refusing to give up his bicycle. The following evening, in the next block, a married couple had been attacked by two armed men—"they were Russians, I believe"—who killed the husband, seriously wounded his wife and went off on their victims' bicycles.

"What adds insult to injury," he said, "is that I know where my machines are! I have seen them on the black market at the Sendlinger Tor, priced at 20,000 marks each! The difficulty for the occupation forces," he added, "is that so many of these gangsters are dressed in American uniforms. . . ."

What he considered an even more difficult, more serious problem for the Americans was that of denazification. "There are thousands of Party members, you see, who were not Nazis (he inferred, of course, that he fitted into this category!); on the other hand, there are any number of real Nazis in good positions. They are still in their same apartments in the city, while we live in one room in a suburb. We must take care that these people go—for we fear Communism—and the difference is very slight. That's our great danger. . . ."

After Communism, the lawyer considered the next greatest danger to be the German youth. "Most intelligent men of my age, you see, knew from its beginning that the war was lost. We realized that almost the whole world would be against us. From my experience in the Wehrmacht, I saw that the older soldiers were not for Hitler, but the youth—especially the young men of the Hitler Jugend—they were all convinced by Goebbels' propaganda. I myself was astonished at the extent to which the youth was taken in. Goebbels succeeded primarily by appealing to their lowest instincts. This is going to be a terrible problem in the future."

Though the lawyer himself may not have been deceived by this propaganda, he seemed to have had an odd respect for the man who made it. "Goebbels was not only by far the cleverest of the lot," he maintained, "he was also the most courageous. While Hitler was never seen in public in any German city after the bombing started, Goebbels was constantly showing himself in the streets—with the result that on at least one occasion, in the Rhineland, he was stoned."

For Hitler's military strategy the lawyer had nothing but contempt. "It was Hitler who gave the double command to take Stalingrad at any cost and at the same time for Rommel to capture the Suez Canal. Any fool could see that one of these efforts was bound to fail. As it turned out, both did. After Stalingrad, every intelligent German prayed that Hitler would sue for peace. We knew then there was no possible hope." (Even some of the most moronic Germans agreed on the hopelessness of the situation after Stalingrad.) Nor had he seen any hope in the 20th of July Plot. "I still think it was a bluff," he said. "Simply an attempt—unfortunately successful—to liquidate certain generals and other influential anti-Nazis." An interesting commentary on the effects of Nazi propaganda.

As he wheeled his "fourth" bicycle down the corridor, the lawyer turned. "During the war," he said grimly, "every day I got out of bed I wondered if it would be my last. Now I think the same thought every time I get on one of these machines!"

THE FOREMAN'S WIFE

The overwhelming majority of Germans were not necessarily sycophants when they gave answers which sounded a little too pleasant to American ears. When asked how they were getting along under the Occupation, nine out of ten maintained they had "nothing to complain about." Often they would add a statement to illustrate how *anständig*—how decent they found American behavior. The remark of a frowsy, middle-aged woman—wife of an ex-foreman in a factory which produced locomotives—was typical. "When American soldiers see me waiting in line for my daily beer," she said, "they often come and give it me themselves." (The politest G.I. description for this beer, incidentally, was "ninety-seven per cent yellow water.") When asked if the Occupation were better or worse than she had expected, she answered: "Ach, much better!" It is not always fair to judge these reactions as examples of "bootlicking." For the most part such answers were genuine, for Goebbels' propaganda had sunk in. "We heard," said the foreman's wife, "that we wouldn't be allowed out on the streets, that we women would be raped by Negroes, that we'd be separated from our husbands and our children deported. Of course," she added with an unctuous smile, quite unaware of her flat contradiction, "we never believed what Hitler and Goebbels said about Americans. We are free people now—*nicht wahr?*"

Whether she believed it nor not, she—like so many women—

was constantly quoting what she'd heard. She seldom compromised herself by divulging what she herself had seen or thought—if, that is, she'd done any thinking. Instead, she invariably invoked her husband, laying the responsibility for her statements on the absent foreman.

"My husband, he always said we should leave Germany and go to the United States."

Supposing Germany had won the war? "Oh, *weh!* My husband always said we wouldn't have been allowed on the *trottoir!* (A favorite Munich expression.) He said we wouldn't have been allowed to breathe—that those of us not in the Party would have been sent to Dachau!"

She told me, with a certain pride, that it had been her business to collect money for the Red Cross, and then, with a suffering sigh, how she was expected to denounce those who didn't contribute. "My husband, of course, he always said the money went to the Party funds, anyway."

The main reason why Germany lost the war? *Ach Gott!* how could she know that—a simple woman like her, who had never "broken her head over politics"? Shrugging her shoulders, gazing up at the ceiling, she finally came out with what at first seemed a surprising answer. "Hitler's wanting to be a combination of Napoleon and Frederick the Great and conquer the world—*nicht wahr?*"

I didn't bother to ask where she'd heard that one.

The discrepancy between what she'd heard, then seen contradicted by events didn't seem to have taught her much. "I'd always heard," she said, "that the German army was very unwilling to continue the war, that when America came in they'd give up. That was the moment I said, 'The war is lost!' *Bitte?* The Germans went on fighting for three and a half years? *Na ja, lieber Herr,* they had to—didn't they!"

Like many Germans of both sexes, her chief grudge against the Nazi hierarchy was that they overindulged in alcohol. "We heard," she said bitterly, "that even the generals were *besoffen*. Here in Munich everyone said Gauleiter Wagner was a drunkard. As for Giesler,* when the Americans had come as near as Dachau, he got so drunk he smashed up the city's radio station!"

Maybe it was on account of his reputation as a teetotaler that she was quick to try and whitewash Rudolf Hess. "Ah," she sighed, like a woman reminiscing about her favorite son, "when der Hess flew to England, we said *he* at least is doing his best for us!"

Of the Hess flight she had a peculiar notion. "There was a big row, you know, between der Hess and the other leaders. He couldn't agree to what they said, so off he flew on his own. The only one who agreed with him was Captain Ernst Roehm—and he was caught and shot as a traitor! That's what I *heard,* mind you. . . ."

When reminded that Ernst Roehm had been killed in the 1934 "Bloodbath," she wagged her head. *"Na,"* she muttered, "all these names—one always forgets who's who!"

What she'd heard about the purpose behind the Allied bombings was perhaps odder still. "I heard some people say," she said, "that the British and Americans bombed our cities so as to land parachute troops behind our lines! I even heard that on the radio. *Bitte?* Yes, it's the only reason I can think of!"

Had she ever listened to the Allied radio?

This was a question which made every German blush with embarrassment. It had evidently been a subject of endless clandestine conversation, an unlawful act which very few had not committed. Germans answered this particular question like guilty children who've lied to their teacher and who, on learning at home that the lie has been discovered, pray it will be forgiven by an indulgent mother. Their behavior revealed, I thought, the depth to which the need for discipline and authority is rooted in the German character.

After a silence and a bashful smirk, the foreman's wife

* Who succeeded Wagner as Gauleiter of Munich and committed suicide in May, 1945.

finally admitted having listened to Switzerland and Luxembourg. . . .

When had she begun listening?

"*Na ja,* when Hitler went into Austria, Denmark, and all those other countries . . . !"

AN ENGINEER

He was a short, stocky, healthy-looking man with a large jutting jaw and an irritating habit of attempting to tell long irrelevant stories—whose chief purpose, I gathered, was to show his superior knowledge and intelligence. I was soon convinced that war or no war, *under* the Nazis or *under* the Americans he was equally determined to serve and to shine.

"I had always hoped the Americans would take Bavaria," he said. "The only other alternative would have been the French, and the French, you know, they are bad administrators. They would have been full of hate and reprisals—though, of course, I admire the French as a people, and I can speak their language."

Sly enough not to pile on the flattery too thick, he threw in some remarks criticizing the occupation—remarks which again were meant to serve a double purpose. "What I can't understand," he said, "is why communications and transportation are made so difficult. My family, for instance, is still in the Bayerischer Wald, but I can't see them. I can't leave town. I can't get a pass. I find this law too strict—although I know," he added with a wink, "that Münchners do get through the patrols. Many Americans are very decent and close an eye to people who are cut off from their wives and children. But take my case in the professional sense. I'm a construction engineer with assignments and connections all over the American zone. Now the Military Government has given orders for a private railroad bridge to be repaired, forty kilometers out of town. Until the repairs are made, three badly-needed engines will be held up. Though I am employed by the Military Government to supervise this work, I cannot get a pass to go and visit either the bridge or the men who would do the job. Until such passes are granted, none of these all-important jobs can even be started; nor can any of the decent, hard-working engineers make sufficient money to support their families. Actually, I am working at the moment on a number of small projects here in the city—helping to repair the electrical works, and finding out how much weight the floors of the Führerbau and Verwaltungsbau can stand. This is where all the art treasures that were found in Czechoslovakia are to be stored."

Had Germany won the war, the engineer was certain he would have been in a bad way, "because I was not a member of the Party." Nor, in his opinion, would victory have benefited his trade. "The National Socialist Party," he said, "had tremendous plans for postwar building—not for the reconstruction of cities, but for the erection of vast buildings in all large towns. Munich, for instance, was to have had a new railroad station of colossal proportions, Berlin an arch of triumph double the size of any other on earth, while the capital's Grosse Halle was to have cost no less than a milliard marks. There would have been money enough, just as there is now; but where would we all have lived—and on what?—while all these grandiose schemes were being carried out? As I say, there's money enough in Germany today, but there's no merchandise. This is dangerous, because no matter how well men are paid, if they can't buy anything with their money their interest and will to work quickly evaporate."

For Germany's defeat the engineer put all the blame on the Nazi leaders. "I thought from the very beginning," he said, "that Germany, and the whole of Europe with her, was heading straight for the abyss. I do think, however, that Germany did stand a chance of success and of righting some old wrongs if only she had called a halt in 1940. The problems of Danzig and the Polish Corridor would have been settled. Germany could have returned the Occupied Countries their independence (*sic*), regained much lost prestige and found herself in a very strong position as a nation. . . . But to have taken on so many other countries at once was madness. The leaders should never have declared war on Russia or the U. S. Militarily, their worst fault was their insistence on trying out "Wonder Weapons" instead of producing enough tanks, planes, and guns whose efficiency had already been proved. But after all, what could you expect of a man like Hitler? What could you expect of a man who never had a profession? *Lieber Gott,* that man couldn't even ride a bike or swim!"

The engineer was one of numerous Germans who could not understand why the Allies—"especially the British," whom he considered responsible for most of the damage—had bombed the *centers* of so many German cities. "If they thought," he said, "that this would make the civilian population revolt, they were terribly mistaken. In fact, I would like to say this: if they *hadn't* destroyed such vast numbers of homes I really believe they might have stood a good chance of seeing an anti-Nazi uprising. Actually, what they did by their destruction was to disperse the population all over the country, and so prevent these anti-Nazi men and women from meeting and forming an effective opposition. [An interesting point.] If they thought, on the other hand, that the only way to prevent heavy industry from producing was to demoralize the workers by incessant bombardment, then again I think they were mistaken, because the bombardment of the factories alone was so terrific and so successful that the Germans never had a chance to move enough of them underground or into mountain hideouts, which was what they were trying so hard to do.

"If only Unconditional Surrender had been accepted after ths '20th of July,'" he concluded, "Germany would have looked very different today. Himmler would have tried to grab power, but only some of the more fanatical S.S. and the Gestapo would have been behind him. The situation facing us now would have been comparatively simple. I might add that I was very nearly thrown into a concentration camp after the 20th of July for having dared to remark in public: 'There goes our last chance!'"

VETERANS OF THE HOME FRONT

Although ex-soldiers were not supposed to fall into our orbit, they did turn up for interviews every now and again. In Munich I had two in one day. They were both in their fifties; neither had seen combat. Since we never asked Germans for their names, I'll call them Herr Schwarz and Herr Braun.

Herr Schwarz—a shifty-looking customer who retained about him a dilapidated continental air and insisted on speaking pidgin-English until I asked him to stop—had been a hotel manager for many years. Starting in England before 1914, he had continued in this profession during the Twenties at Madrid, Barcelona, and Toledo. Returning to Germany in 1933, he had become a member of the NSDAP three years later. In 1944, of his own accord, he had joined the army, landing a cushy job as interpreter for prisoners-of-war.

Herr Braun's history was less colorful. He looked like a deflated bank clerk, which is precisely what he was. Having spent all his adult years in that most soul-destroying of institutions, Braun had had his body and what remained of his soul inducted into the army in 1943, at the age of fifty-two. He was rather riled because American troops had turned him out of his Munich apartment, leaving himself and his wife one room.

"The Americans said they would go away in twenty days," he complained. "Yesterday was the twentieth day." He raised an eyebrow as if to imply that no such irregularity would ever be countenanced in a bank, and that I might take the hint.

Both men showed the prevailing mood of the middle-aged—to please. "Through my job as interpreter at an international PW camp," said Schwarz, "I learned that Americans are more human, more decent than most Germans, many of whom are characterless. Of course, there are reasons for this," he was quick to add. *"Ja,* Germans have never been taught to be individuals. Our propaganda," he continued, "had warned us that Americans would behave like Communists...."

Communists?

"*Ja,* because they were allies of Russia, and therefore had the same system of government!"

When Schwarz had asked American prisoners about this, "they laughed—*sehr anständige Leute,* very decent people!"

Braun, even less bright a specimen, said he was "very glad to be occupied by the Americans, who are more *sympathisch* than other people." (In the American zone "other people," of course, were always the Russians and the French—to whose populations and countries the Germans had done the most damage!)

Asked how he thought he'd make out during the next three or four years, Schwarz seemed enthusiastic. "Well," he said, "I have three sisters. Two run a market-garden in the United States, and the other does the same thing over here, near Bamberg. I hope to be able to join the latter, and go into business. In time—who knows?—the family might do some international trading, *nicht?*"

Braun had no such hopes. "Ach," he said, leaning back with a sigh, "I have no children. And I'm of an age when I do little but think and wonder and wait for what will come." That, I thought, was just how I'd pictured myself twenty years ago, if I'd remained in the bank!

Supposing Germany had won the war, what effect did they think victory would have had on prices at home? (For the life of me, I could never understand the point of this question.) Schwarz had little doubt that things would have been better had Germany won, "at any rate in the long run. After all, Germany would have been able to feed on other countries, and she could have imported from Africa. People shouldn't get the impression that Germany was ever self-supporting."

Braun's picture of a victorious Germany was different. "Ach," he groaned, "we'd have had nothing. There'd have been no *Bürgertum* left (by which he meant no bourgeoisie).

There'd have been no point in saving, because all of us would have been on the same level. . . ."

Like Russia?

"Ja," he muttered, "like Russia." But then, with what I perhaps imagined to be a slight shudder, he added, "almost."

Despite his being an ex-soldier, or maybe just for that reason, Braun showed little interest in military affairs.

Of the German army's leadership he could think of nothing to say. He scratched his head and looked like a child who has been asked to solve an intricate mathematical problem. Finally, pushed and probed for an answer, he grunted: "Na! The military leadership? *Ich hab' mich wirklich damit wenig befasst!*—I really didn't think much about it!"

Schwarz, however, was scornful of both the military and the political leaders. *"Der Führer,* you know . . . *Bitte? Ja, der Hitler,* of course—he and his generals were never united. The good men in the army were liquidated. Germany could have won only a short war. After the defeat of France, I knew the war would go on for years."

The army was clearly an institution neither veteran enjoyed being reminded of. Had there been a moment during the war when Braun felt like throwing up the sponge? *"Aber selbstverständlich!*—But naturally!" he snorted, suddenly coming to life. "What a question! The day I was drafted, of course!"

Evading the question, Schwarz's answer revealed, I think, something more characteristically German. "Ach!" he exclaimed. "If only I'd been a farmer! They were the ones who had all the food. A poor devil like me, sitting in the barracks all day, what chance had I to get out into the country? Even if I'd had a relative in a provision store, I'd have been better off. But there—I hadn't!"

7

WHILE we were still interviewing in Munich, word came from Headquarters that instead of a year or even six months the Survey had to wind up its work in the European theater within a few weeks. "You'll probably all have to be off the Continent by the first of August," we were told.

"Lucky damned bastards!" growled Dudley, echoing the sentiment of the enlisted men towards the civilians. The cause of their resentment was understandable and threefold: first, they were receiving but a fraction of the pay civilians were getting for doing the same job; second, as army men they never disguised the fact that they were having a hell of a good time on the Survey, which they hoped would continue indefinitely; and third, while to civilians the end of the Survey meant Going Home, to enlisted men it meant returning to the boredom of army life in England until such time as they had enough points to get discharged.

I personally received the news with mixed feelings. Interviewing German civilians was a job like any other; sometimes interesting, more often monotonous; but it was taking up almost every hour of the day, and some of the night. If our stay in Germany was to be cut so short, I wanted to make as much use as possible of the limited time. The one thing I did not want to do was to leave Germany without having met a soul I'd known in the past. If any of these people were alive I wanted to find them. But how? Even if we were fortunate enough to have some free time in the Frankfurt area, where most of my friends had lived, how could they be located after twelve long years of Hitlerism, in the midst of such devastation?

Even though I'd not known a soul with a home in this part of Bavaria, I was all the time conscious of the possibility that one day, in the street, in the ruins, on the road, I might run into a familiar face. I never did. I eventually found those faces only as I would have expected to find them in more normal days—by looking for them in the places I associated with their names. I never met a German friend by chance, unless the manner in which I met Florence Strauss can be called chance.

One early Sunday morning, during our second week in Starnberg, I unearthed from my duffel bag, as a final resort, an address book in which for two decades I had jotted down at random the names and addresses of friends. I opened the book and began fingering its worn pages with a feeling of utter futility. Faces and places confronted me from all over the globe. Under the letter A alone I saw myself sitting with a large blond Russian woman at the Café du Dôme in Paris, and on the next line I was having a meal in the house of a Japanese family in a village on the island of Oahu. By the time I'd reached the sixth letter of the alphabet I'd grown tired of traveling. With little hope left, I turned one more faded page. Howard, B.—in twenty years this friend's wanderings covered as many lines and half-a-dozen European countries. Hannay, Cannon J., Kensington. Before he had married us, my wife and I'd had to leave two suitcases in his vestry as "proof" that we were residents of his London parish, where neither of us had ever resided! Hart, Erich . . . Hart? Who was Hart? Seldau, Oberbayern. Seldau? I'd never been there, never heard of it. Yet this was my handwriting. F. and E. Hart. . . . Then, in a flash, I remembered. F. was Florence— Florence Strauss of Frankfurt. She had married Erich Hart. . . . Athlete . . . decorated by Hindenburg. . . . "I'd no idea Hindenburg was so huge!" . . . Florence . . . golf champion . . . her charming Irish mother . . . "my best friend" we used to call one another. . . . Max, Papa Strauss, he was Jewish. . . . What had happened to him? Florence was half-Jewish—a *Mischling*. What had happened to Florence?

Where was Seldau? I stared at the word in the address book, at the names above and below it, in search of time and place. It came. I got it. 1935. The lobby of the Berkeley Hotel in London. Louise Jameson, the wife of the Englishman who made bathtubs in Frankfurt, friend of the Strauss's. The conversation in the lobby about Frankfurt friends. "Florence and Erich have left Frankfurt and gone to live in Bavaria. . . . They've bought a charming farmhouse near a lake." And in 1935 I had taken the address, copied it out in the little red book. Why? Had I expected to see them again? No. Not unless Florence had fled. Not so long as they lived in Germany. It had depended on Hitler. What had not depended on Hitler? The lives of tens of millions of men had depended on one madman. A curtain had come down between that country and my world. All that remained to me of the Harts after thirteen years was a ten-year-old Bavarian address. Now, here, was that address. And here was I—in Bavaria. And slowly the curtain rose. Back the past came creeping, in an endless reel of colored pictures.

All the pictures were shot in the open air, for this was the Weekend World—a world confined to well-to-do people who owned automobiles and on Saturdays and Sundays motored a few miles out of town to the *Wald*—a forest of beech, oak, and pine. One summer in the Twenties a few of the best-to-do had employed a couple of Englishmen to come over and lay out for them in the forest the most beautiful playground in all Germany. Vast numbers of trees were uprooted, and in their place wide lanes of sun and shade were sown with grass seed. Within a year workmen were mowing and rolling eighteen patches of superb velvet green, like undulating billiard tables. Into these a small round hole was sunk, and into the hole went an iron rod with a scarlet flag attached. Near each velvet patch workmen placed a red box full of sand, and a bench where the weary well-to-do could rest before once more picking up the wooden club, balancing the little white ball atop a pinch of sand, and then hitting it with all their might down the splendid fairway or into the gloom of the silent forest. The fame of the playground spread. The *sportifs,* English-aping well-to-do of other cities, even other countries, converged upon the Frankfurt forest. With long brown leather bags slung over their shoulders, these cautious capitalists met on the geranium-trimmed terrace of the "modern" Club House. Here, under multi-colored sun-shades, over the late afternoon bridge table when cocktails were served by waiters in short white coats, *Grafen* and lesser Gentiles bowed to families of German Jews; sleek, sophisticated ladies from Berlin invited tweedy, whisky-drinking Englishmen to the Wannsee; young and middle-aged Americans giggled with the girls; and—from a lower rung in the social ladder—occasional natives with shiny pink heads, stout disapproving wives, large collections of clubs and little knowledge of the Game, stalked off to the first sandbox, looking as much at home as boiled lobsters on a lawn.

It was a small, dull, formal, unnatural, and therefore unnaturally serious world from which, as an unattached foreign observer, I derived a certain amusement. Golf was a game I had ceased to take seriously at the age of twelve, when the headmaster of a snobbish prep school presented me with a silver cup as the most proficient player. No one on the Frankfurt links, I'm sure, ever believed that story—least of all the Strauss family, with whom I spent many summer weekends. I had no clubs with which to play the Game, and I refused to buy any. Instead I used to borrow an instrument known as an "iron," and with this smack my way with Florence, her parents, brothers, or anyone else with sufficient sense of the ridiculous (there were mighty few) round the miles of green. An iron is a useful weapon. I could drive with it, putt with it, hit a long shot on the fairway, even use it instead of a mashie, simply by not attempting to lift the ball, but hitting it hard and square, croquet-wise, along the ground. The only spot where the iron and I had to admit defeat was in a bunker.

Here I just picked up the ball and tossed it over my shoulder. The Strausses and their friends were among the few who did not condemn such unorthodox conduct, even secretly, as a violation of bourgeois behavior and the sacred rules of the ancient Game. Fortunately, Florence—a girl blessed with a beautiful figure and a most un-Germanic humor inherited from her parents—was a champion player, even more expert than her brothers Walter (killed later in a plane crash) and Patrick, who worked in a bank in Cologne. On account of her proficiency she was chosen to represent the city, to play in inter-city, even international tournaments. On such occasions her brothers and one or two "scratch" players would form a team, and—possibly out of fear that the competitive spirit might render the Game too grim and sober—they would take me along as a kind of comic relief, armed with my iron, which I wielded as a weapon or a walking stick. We would set off in automobiles, to Bad Ems, to Kissingen, and Wiesbaden. Sometimes we drove as far as Cologne, where Patrick, a woolly-haired counterpart of his sister, formed a team to compete with that of his home town. On these trips we spent the nights en route in *Gasthäusern* along the Rhine, drinking ourselves from a mellow mood through spasms of uproarious gaiety to a dreamless sleep on the local wines. On our return the Strausses would give me dinner in the book-lined, cultured comfort of their Irish-German home—where, by their natural, unostentatious friendliness and hospitality I was made to feel almost a member of the family.

In this family I found a wit and a *joie de vivre* conspicuously lacking in the Weekend community—lacking, for that matter, in so many strata of German society. The Strausses did not take themselves over-seriously; unpretentious, they did not strive to be what they were not. Speaking English and French, with a knowledge of both countries, their literature and their histories, Papa Strauss was one of the best-informed Germans I knew. Yet even he, with all his worldliness, seems in retrospect to have shared, though in a lesser degree, a denominator common to nearly all Germans: he did not apply his knowledge of history and politics to the times he lived in. I never heard contemporary politics discussed so little as in Germany. Small wonder, perhaps, that when the first "Brown Shirts" began to appear on the streets of Frankfurt, people looked out of the windows and laughed. "Nazi" was a term provoking ridicule and humor, and in those days I don't remember meeting a soul who took it seriously. Four years later Hitler had the entire country in his power.

I cannot recall how Erich first appeared upon this scene, but I do remember feeling jealous of a man who, picking up a golf club for the first time, could manage in a few weeks to outdrive me with an iron! Starting to play the Game more or less as a joke, within a year he had lowered his handicap to a single figure; he had also been elected secretary of the club, and he had married Florence. Tall, broad, with a fine head, oval face and thinning hair, Erich was one of those rare individuals who combined the physical strength of a giant with the gentleness of a serious child. An Olympic Games champion and winner of innumerable prizes for athletics, he had been personally honored by the President of the Reich. "I'd no idea old Hindenburg was so huge!" was all Erich's modesty allowed him to say of that occasion. . . . Only as I closed the address book and began to concentrate on this half-forgotten world did I remember having been told that when, a year or two later, a similar honor was to have been bestowed upon him by Hitler, Erich refused to accept the decoration. Erich having compromised himself at this date, Florence being a *Mischling*, what chance was there, after ten years, that they still lived in "the charming farmhouse near a lake?" What chance was there that they still lived . . . ?

Common sense and the fate of others in a like position should have made me realize how remote the chances were. Yet on that Sunday I acted as though some inner conviction were urging me to believe not only that the Harts were alive, but that during all those awful years the impossible had happened—they had never moved from the address I had been given in the London hotel. The moment I decided to make the trip I refused to consider it might be in vain. Having found out from the know-all majordomo downstairs that Seldau was less than an hour's jeep-ride from the Schloss, I went unhesitatingly to the PX and bought two weeks of rations I had not used. I filled my musette bag with cigarettes, Hershey bars, candy, toothpaste, and chewing gum. I even threw in a few cigars.

I set off with a map and a strange sensation of expectancy. I drove slowly, concentrating on the pictures of the past, drawing that past up to the present in a barely conscious effort to erase the years, to force the unnatural gulf of time to disappear, to make the act seem perfectly natural, to create, in short, sense out of chaos. Driving north through Starnberg, I then turned west across a green romantic tongue of land dividing two lakes, without conscious awareness of my surroundings. All of a sudden my attention was attracted by something which seemed at first as natural as it would have been at any other time, but which then—it took me minutes to realize—was as unlikely a sight as I'd yet seen in postwar Germany. A few hundred yards on my right two charabancs packed with people were snorting slowly up a hill. . . . On top of the hill sat perched an enormous monastery, its red-tiled roof and copper tower glistening in the sun. From it, across the acres of green meadow, came the sound of pealing bells. The world was suddenly very Sunday, very "normal," very long ago.

Drawing up on the side of the road I looked at the map, to find that I was facing the Pilgrimage Church of Andechs. I followed the charabancs up the steep incline. When they came to a palpitating halt outside a Gasthaus at the top of the hill, I stopped under a tree and watched the passengers descend—oldish men with long brown mustaches, farmers in their Sunday best, middle-aged women with bony red faces and black dresses, young girls and children carrying wilting bouquets of wild flowers. Some families promptly sat down on the steps of the closed Gasthaus and began eating hunks of dark bread. Others walked slowly up the shady path to the church. I locked the jeep and followed them. The children stopped in their stride and stared at the lonely American uniform with wide, curious eyes. But the grown-ups took so little interest that I didn't feel self-conscious. Outside the entrance to the church rose a huge flowering acacia, and in its shade, on patches of grass between ancient tombstones, sat a bevy of healthy-looking girls, laughing and eating *Brötchen*. From within came the musty smell of incense. Then, crossing the dark threshold of the porch, I stood still, caught my breath and blinked. With one step I had walked into a fairy palace of gold and multi-colored gems—a palace erected, one felt, for the purpose not so much of worship as of dispelling gloom. It was like a child's dream of paradise, a storm of luxurious color where the season is always summer and everyone is gay. What effect, I wondered, would it have on a man's life if, instead of having been dragged every Sunday of his childhood to the grim, unadorned, puritanical drabness of a Protestant church to listen to a wrinkled old ogre droning on and on about the flames of Hell and the fury of God, he had been brought to such a place as this, to sit and feast his eyes on some of the most spectacular, most sumptuous rococo art created by man?

All the pews were occupied and the greater part of the congregation stood silently in rows at the back and along the pillared nave. Worming my way through the crowd so as to get a better view of the service, I paused at last behind a one-legged man on crutches. Staring over his shoulder, I discovered that there were two altars, one on the ground level, set in surroundings of jeweled magnificence, and another, suspended on a white-and-gold spiral-banistered balcony, above it. Here, behind a wrought-iron gate embroidered in golden filigree, a gray cloud of incense was floating up to the roof, and a broad, slow-moving figure clad in white and purple vestments was conducting the service in a booming voice. The narrow altar before which he stood was balanced at such precarious eminence under the painted ceiling that the sea of faces below were all turned upwards, their mouths open.

Glancing back at them from the door, I was reminded of a crowd watching, in breathless fascination, a trapeze demonstration in a circus.

Outside, the sunlight seemed to have lost its intensity. I had a feeling that by emerging from the church into the open air, I was actually leaving the sun behind me and walking into a landscape of shade.

I drove south, cutting across the unhealthy-looking marshes of the Ammersee, then north, where the narrow road skirts the lake, runs through the village of Fliessen and into Seldau.

The noon sun was now hot, the countryside prematurely heavy with summer. Driving slowly up the clean, deserted, tree-lined street, thinking vaguely of the people in the charabancs and wondering how many of them had been able to enjoy the miraculous light of that church during the last few years, it occurred to me, with a shock, that not even in America had I felt further removed from the atmosphere of war. I was almost through the village before I at last caught sight of human beings, a man and a boy. They were walking along the roadside with Sunday sedateness, yet with an air of people who didn't quite belong. I passed them, slowing down, and as the man saw I was about to stop he quickened his pace, seemingly as intent as I on hearing another voice in the country silence. Without a word of introduction he came straight up and, gripping the side of the jeep with both hands, began shooting at me half-finished questions which I felt he'd asked, in vain, a hundred times before. By now I'd grown so accustomed to these verbal assaults, both while interviewing and on the road, that my head was shaking him negative replies before he'd taken out time to draw his first breath. No, I had no idea what was happening in the Russian zone. No, I could not tell him when he would be able to travel, neither when trains or buses would begin to run, nor how his wife would be able to hear of her son's and husband's whereabouts. Seeing my lack of interest in him, he promptly lost his in me. His hands dropped from the jeep's side and he shrugged his shoulders hopelessly, like a child whose mother has refused him candy.

"Now," I said, "maybe you can tell me something. Do you happen to know anyone here by the name of Hart?"

He glanced up and in his small, mean eyes I could see a gleam for which only the German language has the perfect word: *Schadenfreude*—"malicious joy at the misfortune of others," as the dictionary describes it.

"*Ich?*" he said, drawing up his shoulders with a barely perceptible smile of triumph. "I'm no Bavarian. I'm a refugee— from the Russians. I know only strangers in these parts."

"Where's the *Bürgermeister* live?" I demanded with all the authority I could muster.

Before he had time to reply the boy moved suddenly out from behind his father. "*Da!*" he piped, pointing to a house some fifty yards back from the road.

"*I* will ask him," said the man, pushing the child aside and moving off. The boy, however, ran ahead of him towards the house. In a couple of minutes they returned, accompanied by a short man with shifty eyes and a Hitler-mustache under a red-veined pointed nose. He, too, was followed by a boy of about ten, with an open, surprisingly pleasant face. The little man stepped swiftly up to the jeep, then stopped with a violent jerk, as though he had suddenly decided not to jump over it. Instead, snatching his hat from his head, he clicked his heels and bent himself double in a quick, preposterous bow. While the two boys stared with fascinated eyes at the jeep, the little man proudly informed me that *he* was the burgomaster, and by his tone and manner gave me the impression that the whole village was at my disposal for the asking.

"*Der Herr Hart? Aber freilich*—the family Hart, they live quite near. . . ."

If the Herr Hauptmann would do him the honor, he would accompany the Herr Hauptmann and guide him to the house. The Herr Hauptmann could not easily find it alone. . . . He began to bow again. *"Bitte schön. . . ."* Placing his hat back on his head, he prepared to get into the seat beside me.

"Thanks," I said, with an imperious gesture of my arm which I hoped didn't look as false as it felt. "Thanks. What about your boy? Does he know the way?"

"Ja! Yess!" shouted the youth in delight, and he vaulted into the back of the jeep just as his father's hand sprang once more to his hat. As the jeep jumped forward I saw in my mind's eye the boots snapping together and the body bending itself, robot-like and too late, into a right angle.

It was typical of the child's unthinking desire to please the person who happened to be the source of his momentary pleasure that, as he guided me off the road and down a twisting, high-hedged lane, his excited treble voice should use the monosyllabic foreign words his ear had managed to snatch delightedly since his country's doom. . . .

"Here—right!" he piped, and turning promptly in that direction I realized, too late, he had meant the opposite, but had still to learn the English for *links.* As I informed him, choosing words and voice with care, of his error, and watched the unembarrassed eagerness with which he listened to it rectified, I was struck once again by the overwhelmingly important part that even a meager knowledge of languages plays in the modern world.

At a dead-end in the lane he said, in a voice low with unconcealed regret, "Here—family Hart!" and he had vaulted from the jeep before I'd switched off the engine. When I thanked him for his assistance he dropped his head, then looked up, his eyes earnest with entreaty, one hand reaching out towards the jeep.

"I—here—all right?" he dared himself to whisper.

"It's up to you," I told him. "I may be here some time."

Opening the gate, I was vaguely aware of voices, of figures beyond the foliage of some intervening trees. I passed under the branches and emerged on to a slope of lawn. And there, against the background of an ancient, orange-colored house flanked by a lush border of sky-blue delphiniums, stood—

all alone and facing me on the mown grass—the familiar figure I'd been seeing ever since I'd come upon the name of Hart in the address book.

"*Du!*" she gasped as I approached, and the syllable sounded at once strange and intimate, until she broke into English, "My God, it's been a long time, Jim!" and then all was as familiar as before.

"Thirteen years," I muttered, and for fully two minutes, after nearly a third of our lives, we argued as to whether it was twelve, thirteen or fourteen years.

"There isn't much to say, is there!"

"Too little and too much, I guess."

"Can you stay with us?"

"Just an hour or two."

"Where on earth have you come from?"

"New York."

"How on earth did you find us?"

"Tell you later," I said.

"You *would* be the first to turn up! Would you like a drink?"

"A drink?" The suggestion suddenly sounded so odd, just because it was so in keeping with the past, so familiar, that I burst out laughing. She burst out laughing. And we stood there, our hands over our faces, shaking with uncontrollable laughter.

"Oh, dear—however many the years—they haven't changed you!"

"Nor you," I said, and looking at her for the first time, I saw only that the once perceptible lines about the mouth, across the forehead, had grown deeper.

Suddenly a girl-child with a lovely freckled face appeared as though from nowhere, stood on one leg, holding on to Florence's hand. She was wearing a white, blue-spotted summer frock and she stared up at me out of blue, inquisitive eyes.

"Oh, this is Bobbie," said her mother.

"Hullo, Bobbie—how old are you?"

"Ten."

I took the limp, down-turned hand and clamped my mouth shut as the question came rushing so naturally to be asked. But promptly and miraculously Florence, as though divining my thought, turned and answered it for me.

"Erich!" she shouted towards the orange, creeper-covered house. "Erich!"

In a white shirt and old, stained *Lederhosen* he came out of the dark of the door and down the steps. On the last step he stood still, and from that distance he had not altered. Only after the gasp of astonishment which brought him fast across the lawn, did I see the shrunken body, the sunk-in face, the gray pallor which sunburn could not cover, the deep grooves of suffering round the mouth, the dark circles under the prematurely aging eyes.

"*So was,* Jim!"

"*So was,* Erich!"

Slowly a mischievous gleam came into his eyes; the creases of his face broke into a star of lines, converging on the mouth, as he said, "And your iron, Jim? You still have it?"

Immediately the spell was broken. Back rolled the years; out crept the ghosts of the Weekend World—the dispersed, the displaced, the disappeared, the dead.

"Yes, we heard of him last in Bombay—but that was some years ago."

"They were all killed in one raid on Hamburg in '43."

"No, never heard anything of them after '39."

"They managed to get out to Stockholm—don't know what happened to them then."

"We heard they were in Cairo—but that was years ago."

"Oh, they're in New York. Didn't you know? I'll give you their address. I imagine they're still there."

"Penniless in Brussels, hiding—when we last heard. I can't believe he's still alive, poor old man. His wife vanished. He must be over seventy."

"They came for her. Never heard of her again."

"We think he died in Dachau. . . ."

Florence left us for a moment and Erich said, "Do you remember your 'best friend'?"

"Florence's mother? I hadn't dared. . . ."

"She died—of cancer—in '43—in Munich."

"Did she suffer for long?"

"I'm afraid so. We couldn't get a decent doctor. There weren't any left."

"And Papa Strauss?"

"He got out in '39. To London. He's still there—as far as we know. Florence had a letter through the Red Cross about a year ago. He must be terribly poor. No work. No income. He's just seventy. . . ."

"Erich," I asked, as we started walking slowly towards the house, "what have you been doing all these years?"

"I was a medic all through the war. Almost never out of the hospital. Only towards the end I was put on to defense duty during the raids. We've been pretty lucky."

"And Florence? How were things for her?"

"They never actually came for her. There was only the constant dread, the everlasting fear. But they didn't come. . . . It was almost as if they forgot about this valley. People on the run took refuge here with Florence. But you never knew, from one day, one hour to another. . . . Ironically enough, Florence got her biggest shock when the war was over—about a month ago. The French . . ."

"French?"

"Yes, the Americans got in first, of course. But after a while they left, and in came the Moroccans, who systematically plundered the whole valley. They came here. I was still in Munich in the hospital. Florence was alone with the kids. By some miracle they didn't touch her. She's pretty tough and sensible, you know. . . . But they looted the entire place, smashed up things in the house, killed all the livestock, and went away with everything they could carry. Still, we were pretty lucky."

In the living-room I recognized the English sofas and chairs, the complete Voltaire, the line of Trollopes, Papa Strauss's favorites. Erich produced some wine glasses and began pouring vermouth from a decanter. As I was about to ask him how he came to have the vermouth, Florence came downstairs with a blond child in her arms.

"This is John," she said. "He's two-and-a-half." Then, as though the child had reminded her of another, she turned to Erich. "Have you told Jim about Patrick?"

"Patrick?" Her brother's name was one more I hadn't dared mention.

I noticed that they were both smiling, as Florence said, "Yes, he was here, you know."

"Here? Where did he come from?"

"From Cologne, of course. You don't mean to say you've forgotten the weekends in Cologne?"

"Of course I haven't. But—well, it's so long ago, so many things have happened since. Besides, Patrick . . ."

"Well, wait and I'll tell you," Florence said. "Most of the war Patrick worked in a factory, which was blown sky-high in the first raid in '42. For four years he lived more or less permanently in cellars and shelters, and worked at night twice a week as a fire-fighter. They didn't come for him, until suddenly in September, '44, they made a final round-up of *Mischlings*. Patrick knew they were coming. His girl-friend had been tipped off. So a few days before they were to come, she joined him in his hole under the ruins. All winter he never came out. They had no ration cards. Friends and his girl got him food. But almost immediately she became pregnant, and at the end of February her baby was born. A boy. A week later, a couple of days before Cologne was taken, the Americans launched their final monster raid. Their hideout received a direct hit and they were buried for hours in the rubble. They dug their way out. Forty-eight hours afterwards they were liberated. And at the end of the following week they were married by an American army chaplain. . . .

"Then, last Sunday, we heard the rare sound of a car at the gate. I rushed out of the house, just as I did this morning, and who should I see coming through the trees—Patrick! He was terribly thin. It was just three years since we'd seen him. . . ."

"How did he manage to get down here?"

"The Americans had allowed him a car. They gave cars and a limited amount of gas to the few so-called Non-Aryans who had survived in Cologne and were well enough to travel."

"That," I said, "is the first piece of good news I've heard in a long time."

"Now come," said Florence, "we must have something to eat."

"I'm not going to eat your food," I said. "I've got my own. I've also brought some little odds and ends for you."

"Don't be silly. We don't want anything. Anyway, you'd better come and meet our friends first."

We moved out of the house on to the balcony. From there, for the first time, I noticed a small group of people seated round a table at the far end of the lawn.

"Some of them have been staying with us a long time," Florence said, as we walked across the grass. "Hiding from the Gestapo. Refugees from the East. The bombed-out from Munich. None have any homes."

There were several women and a couple of men sitting round the table. I caught none of their names, but I remember some of their faces—a black-haired, pale-faced girl with beautiful brown eyes, who was picking red currants from their stalks and dropping them in a basket; a handsome, aristocratic-looking man who had lost an arm on the Russian front; and a heavy, Jewish-looking younger man sitting next to an enormous woman at whom I took one look and went on shamelessly staring. Every feature under the brown straw, flowery-crowned hat was larger than life. She might have been taken for the Fat Woman out of a circus—with her bulging, sagging cheeks and rolls of chins, the full-lipped mouth and bulk of body—had it not been for the bold, unflinching eyes above the great arched nose which gave her the dignity, haughtiness, and quiet power of some biblical giant upon whom a madman has had the temerity to throw a woman's hat. Her speech was in keeping with her figure. Employing none of the so-called niceties of civilized conversation, she boomed across the group at me with the fearless directness of an empress whose word is law.

"Well, young man," she said, and I noticed that everyone stopped speaking when she spoke, "where have you come from? New York? How's New York? It's a long time since I saw that little old town. I guess it's much the same. They had Prohibition when I was there. That was no place for the likes of me." She let out a boom of a laugh, and when I laughed she laughed again and looked me over with an appraising eye. "Still, no doubt I'd have been better off if I'd stayed over there. . . . Say, now that you're here, what are you going to do? If you don't bump off the swine pretty quick, you'll find the going tough. The rats! They've nothing to lose, they're trained in murder, and when they get hungry . . . Ah, I wish we had some of your food—takes a lot to fill this old battleship!"

As she patted her body with a huge hand, I took the opportunity to open the musette bag. Standing up, I emptied its contents onto the grass. At sight of the cigarettes, the candy, the chocolate bars, the chewing-gum, a loud gasp went up from the group; the girl Bobbie let out an excited scream, and John was down on his hands and knees with his mother after him. As Florence was picking him up from the ground at my feet, I managed to whisper in her ear, "Who on earth is *she?*"

"One of the wonders of the world," Florence whispered back.

The next instant I heard the booming voice again. "Say, what's that you've got there, young man? Do I see cigars? *Gott,* I haven't had a cigar since I was in Dachau!"

I stared at her. Then I picked up a cigar, and as I handed it to her I shot her a dubious look—which she did not miss.

"Come and sit down, young man," she said, in answer to my silent challenge. "I'm sorry, I guess I'm just a little peculiar. I'm no heroine. Don't you get that idea. To be a hero you must know the meaning of fear. I'm funny that way; I don't remember ever having been afraid of anyone. I didn't suffer much in that stinking hole. In fact, they kept me there only three weeks. When those swines of guards started pushing me around, I turned on 'em and gave 'em a bit of my mind. I'm not accustomed to being treated like this, I said, and I threatened to report them. Oh, I can be a bit of a bully, too—when I want. The only people bullies respect, you know, are bullies. Sure, I got my cigars all right—and I even ate what could just be called food. The rats! My family used to be in the wine business. What did the rats do? They carted the whole cellar off to Austria, and smashed up the house, the furniture, everything. What for? Because the rats saw that it was *good!* How can you Americans understand that? This is organized Evil on mass production scale. There are tens of thousands who are no longer human. They are infectious, carriers of Hate. They act from the depth of despair, from ungovernable fear. They will always destroy the good, the poor, the weak . . . because the poor, the old, the weak, the flowers in the field, my friend, are what they fear most, and most want to destroy!"

The woman took a pull at her cigar and got up. *"Kinder!"* she boomed. "I must be off. *"Mein Lieber,"* turning to the heavy young man at her side, "let us show our American friend what we have to thank his Military Government for."

I followed them across the garden and round behind the house. There, to my amazement, stood a sleek and shining *feldgrau* automobile—a low, powerful Mercedes Benz.

"Ja," she said, opening the door while the heavy man got into the driver's seat, *"Ja,* I happen to know to whom this little toy once belonged. What's more, I know where he is. When the Military Government is kind enough to let me have a little more gas, I'm going to save those good boys some trouble. I'm going into Munich and," she cocked her cigar revolverwise, "bang! that'll be the end of that one. Well, s'long, young man—thanks for the smoke and give my love to l'il old New York!"

Later, as we sat round the table, eating thin lentil soup and chopped frankfurters—which my hosts insisted on my sharing—I conveyed to them my astonishment that such a woman should have managed to live through, unscathed, the last few years in Germany. They saw at once how difficult I found it to believe even what I'd heard, for both the Harts said immediately, "You must believe. If ever there was a woman who did not lie, who deserves a Mercedes and more, it is she. What she did not tell you was that the only time she felt in real danger was when a Dachau guard caught her slipping bits of her food to some poor devil who was starving. She was caught. But that didn't stop her doing it. She did it every day."

"Who was the big man with her?" I asked.

"Her son," Florence said. "He was three years on the Russian front, like a lot more *Mischlings*. Most of them were killed. And their 'Aryan' parents, instead of being notified that their sons had fallen at the front, were sent the ashes with a note saying he had been shot while trying to escape."

I have since told the little I know of this woman's story to many people. All who had never lived in Nazi Germany were incredulous; but some of those who had, who had suffered and come through, have said, "Yes. I believe it. I knew one such person. They did exist. But only for a handful did such behavior prove enough."

When I took leave of the Harts, the boy I had picked up on the road was sitting in my seat in the jeep.

"Sorry I was so long," I said, as he guided me back to the village. "Were you very bored?"

"*Garnicht!*—Not at all!" he said emphatically.

"What have you been thinking about all the time?"

"I wasn't thinking much," he said. "I was driving the *Auto*."

"Where to?"

"*Nach Amerika!*" he said, and he laughed at the passing landscape as though he were already on his way.

Over supper in the Schloss that night I told John and Mervyn about my day in the country. I'd begun to describe the church at Andechs when John said he knew it well. "You should see the Pilgrimage Church at Wies," he added. "That's the last word in German baroque." Then he turned to Mervyn. "By the way," he said, "in my search for material on the church situation here, I managed to get this," and he handed us a document. It was an account of the students' uprising in Munich in January, 1943.

The rebellion, we read, was no local or sudden flaring-up. Groups of anti-Nazi students had been working underground in Munich ever since '37. Assisted by the churches, the secret organization spread to other universities, particularly to Bonn and Vienna. The leading spirit behind the movement was Professor Kurt Huber. When war broke out and dispersed the groups, three students—Schurik Schmorell, Hans Scholl, and his sister, Sophie—joined forces with Huber. While the Professor drafted pamphlets, the students wrote an anti-Nazi manifesto (now famous) and undertook the more dangerous work of distributing this inflammatory literature. They also designed posters which they pasted at night on the university walls. They daubed the houses of Nazi professors with huge red swastikas, then slashed them over with black paint. They staged demonstrations which caused tremendous excitement among the students, but which finally led to indiscretions on the part of the leaders. . . . Another group, led by the student Hans Leipelt, of the University Institute for Chemistry, passed on news they picked up from foreign broadcasts. They tried to check Nazi propaganda by distributing banned histories of pre-Hitler Germany. They prepared dynamite for blowing up the Nazi faculty. One day, the account concluded—after Huber, the Scholls, and Schmorell had been caught and executed—Leipelt heard that Huber's widow and children were destitute. He immediately started a collection for them in the Institute. But someone denounced him to the Gestapo. . . .

"Those who condemn the Germans for their lack of opposition," muttered Mervyn, when we'd finished reading the document, "should have spent six months here during the war."

"Would there be a chance," I asked John, "of talking to any of the relatives?"

"That," he said, "is what I was going to suggest. This afternoon I ran into an old friend of mine, Miss McCaig, an Englishwoman who was stranded here during the war. She happens to be living with the Schmorell family a few miles from here. She said she'd arrange for us to visit them tomorrow afternoon."

Next day turned very warm; the lake looked like glass as we set out from the Schloss.

"D'you know anything about the Schmorells?" I asked John.

"Only what Miss McCaig told me," he said. "The father's a well-known doctor. Came originally from the Baltic, I think; and I believe the mother's partly Russian. They have one daughter."

"I wonder," said Mervyn, "if they'll feel like talking of the son."

"Miss McCaig thought they would," John said, "so long as she's present."

We drew up in the shadow of a flowering privet hedge. The street was in a suburb—green, silent, empty. The combined perfumes of chestnut, privet and honeysuckle filled the air. On a gate cut out of the hedge, I noticed a board with the name Schmorell. John lifted the latch and we walked through.

Two middle-aged women, in summer frocks, were sitting on the lawn. We shook hands with Miss McCaig, who then introduced us to the Frau Doktor—a pale, thin, still beautiful woman with a quiet, gentle voice.

"I'll just run in and tell the Doctor you're here," Miss McCaig said.

While the others talked, I looked up at the bright, parchment-colored villa. Flowerbeds were carved out of the grass under the walls, and a young bush of wistaria had begun to creep up between the large windows. The house and garden might have been anywhere in Europe where houses still stand and gardens grow.

Then Miss McCaig reappeared, followed by a tall, gaunt, good-looking man and a young, blond, husky girl. She wore spectacles with thick lenses. The Doctor's tweed coat hung from his slightly stooped shoulders, and I noticed that he had strong lean hands that were never still. After a few minutes his wife suggested we go indoors and have some tea.

In the dining-room we met our hostess's sister and another lady, a friend of the family. In a bright, clean, airy room we sat around a circular table, drinking tea. The conversation continued hesitant, spasmodic, vague, until at last John chose a moment of silence in which to make his bold inquiry.

"We were wondering," he said, addressing himself to the Doctor on my side of the table, "we were wondering if you'd care to tell us of your son—unless, of course, talking of him still upsets you."

For a moment no one spoke. The Doctor leaned back, raised his eyes, clasped his hands together. "I would be very glad to tell you of our boy," he said, in a quiet, composed voice.

Only his wife did not look at him. Her elbows on the table, hands framing her pale face, eyes averted, she stared straight before her, as the Doctor began to speak.

"Schurik was by nature a studious boy," he said. "But for a long time, all through the summer and fall of '43 he—"

"'42, Papa," the daughter corrected.

"'42, dear? Of course, Natasha, '42."

"*Ja,*" the mother murmured, "'42." Then, still without addressing anyone and in a dreamlike voice, she said: "I think Schurik was more than simply studious. He was by nature religious. He was so absorbed in spiritual problems, in devotional literature that he would visit pastors and theologians and talk to them for hours. He had great faith. Professor Huber had a powerful influence on him. . . ."

"That's true," agreed the Doctor quietly. "But, so as not to give a false impression, we must remember that at this time he was also concentrating on his exams. All through that summer and fall he seemed to be studying unusually hard. He would come home from the university in the evening, play the piano for a little while, then eat his supper and go straight upstairs. He didn't talk much, and appeared preoccupied. When we went to bed we used to see his light under the door. On account of the exams we didn't disturb him. But even when he'd passed them, he didn't relax. Once I had to come downstairs in the middle of the night, and I saw his light still on. I didn't say anything. But soon we thought he was beginning to look pale and nervous."

"He was losing his appetite," the mother murmured. "And now and again, in the very early mornings, we'd hear him playing the piano. . . ."

"Always Tschaikowsky," Natasha said.

"So we suggested he take a day off," the father went on, "and not work so late. It wasn't good for him, we told him. But he said he had some very important work to do, that he must finish it. He hoped it wouldn't take him much longer. Then, towards Christmas, he started ringing up in the afternoon to say he'd been kept at the university and wouldn't be home for dinner. He had to work with some other students, he said. We saw less and less of him, and we began to wonder what he was doing. We showed our curiosity in various ways, but he always passed it off, saying he would tell us later. 'I can't tell you just now,' he would say. Once or twice he stayed out all night. We tried not to worry too much, because we trusted him implicitly. We knew he'd never do anything we considered wrong. Christmas and New Year passed and still he went on working late into the night. Then came January and the riots in the Deutsches Museum. The occasion was the anniversary of the Foundation of the University, and in the course of a speech to the girl students, Gauleiter Giesler made some particularly crude remarks. Schurik was—"

"He said, Papa," Natasha interrupted, "he said it was not their business to marry, but to propagate the German race!"

"Yes, dear, I know," the father said. "The girls began walking out of the auditorium. Others banged their feet. The students made such a noise, it seems Giesler could barely finish his speech. Afterwards, there was a great demonstration in the Square outside. It was dispersed only after a long time, by the *Überfallkommando* of the police."

"All night," Natasha said, "the students sang songs of freedom in the streets. There were soldiers among them, too."

"*Ja*," the Doctor went on, "these demonstrations had a remarkable effect on Schurik. He seemed very excited. Though he continued to work as hard as ever and often rang up to say he'd not be home till late, he looked more lively, less pale."

"His appetite improved," the mother murmured.

"Then one afternoon in the early spring," the Doctor said, "the doorbell rang. There were three men outside, in plain clothes. I had never seen them before, but I knew what they were—I knew they were the Gestapo. They asked for Schurik. He was out, of course. When I said I didn't know where he was, they came in. 'We'll wait!' one of them said."

The Doctor paused, and I noticed that he was pressing his hands against his knees to stop them shaking.

"It was four o'clock," he started again.

"Five, Papa," Natasha interrupted, "because the telephone—"

"No, darling," the mother said, and I noticed the veins standing out on her white arms as she held her face between her now rigid hands. "No, darling, it was just after four. I remember, because I was just preparing tea."

"*Ja, Ja*," agreed her sister, "it must have been just about four—"

"*Aber Tante Toni!*" Natasha insisted, smiling, almost laughing now in her excitement, "Schurik telephoned at five—"

"But dear child," the father said, raising his trembling fingers. "I haven't got there yet. You forget that the men stayed here for more than half an hour. You forget that your mother, guessing that Schurik was still in the university, asked if she might make a phone call, and that the man said 'No!' and stood there in front of the phone, with his hands in the pockets of his coat. It was five, as you say, when the phone rang, and the man picked up the receiver before we could make a move."

Here the mother pressed her fingers into her eyes and, rising from the table, left the room with the teapot.

"We knew it would be Schurik; it was the hour he always phoned; and we prayed that he would immediately recognize the voice as none of ours. 'Dr. and Frau Dr. Schmorell are urgently waiting their son's return,' we listened to the man saying into the phone. 'Hullo?' said the man. *'Hullo?'* he shouted. Then we knew Schurik had rung off. The man swore terribly and began trying to trace the call.

"The other two went on waiting. They told us we were under guard. Then one of them went upstairs. We could hear him searching the house, opening and slamming drawers. He seemed to stay an awfully long time in Schurik's room. Then he came down and stood with the other man, waiting. They waited all that evening and when night came two of them brought each one of us, alone, in here, and questioned us about Schurik's life—"

"They asked us who his friends were—their names," Natasha said, and she suddenly got up and left the room. An instant later she returned with her mother, carrying some papers in one hand and the teapot in the other.

"Yes, dear," the father said. "And we said we didn't know. Luckily we all said we didn't know. We said he'd been working hard for months, and always came home late and alone. I can't imagine, I told them, how it's possible for our son to be wanted by the police. 'He is reported to have been in bad company,' said one of the men. That was all any of them said about Schurik.

"They stayed all night, downstairs, while we were allowed upstairs. We looked out of the window and saw that there was a guard around the house. We made no effort to sleep. We lay there praying we might not hear the click of the garden gate. We didn't hear it, and the men were still there in the morning. Then we were taken away in a car—"

"They first questioned us all over again, Papa," the girl said, and from the papers in her hand she passed round the table a snapshot of a dark, unusually handsome youth.

"It's very good of him," the mother said. Her face was still between her hands, her light blue eyes staring straight ahead of her, as her husband continued his story.

"We were held for two nights, in separate cells," he said, his voice growing louder now. "And questioned and questioned all over again. On the second day they told each of us that they had managed to extract confessions from the other two, that now they knew the names of Schurik's friends. . . . We asked where Schurik was, and they told us he'd been arrested. He was to stand trial for his life, they said. We asked what he had done, but they would not tell us. We asked to see him, but they would not let us. And once more, despite the confessions they had boasted of, they demanded the names of Schurik's friends. It was easier for his mother and me, for we knew only one or two, but Natasha—" the Doctor hesitated, his voice shaking—"she knew them, though we didn't know she did. It was harder for her, and when she went on shaking her head and refusing to speak, they began—to torture. . . ." The voice trailed off again, and a shaking hand went out and gripped the table-edge.

"Herr Doktor," said John, breaking the intense silence, "please don't let this upset you too much. If you would rather not continue . . ."

"They blinded her in one eye!" the Doctor said, his voice a little choked with the effort to control it. "They kept him in jail," he continued quietly after a pause, "waiting for his trial, for weeks. We knew and he knew he might have to die. We also knew his 'crime,' and we felt proud. We were allowed to see him only twice. We never saw him happier. I doubt if I ever saw a happier human being. . . . Then we learned he'd been convicted and condemned to death, and that we could not see him again, unless the plea for mercy were granted.

"We had one last desperate hope—to find a friend or friends

who might use their influence to save him. But who? We searched high and low. The willing ones were powerless. So we swallowed our pride and confronted men in high positions whom we didn't know. It was all in vain. And all that time, all through May and June and half of July, right until the end, the boy never lost his courage. On the contrary, his great faith increased. It was *he* who kept up *our* spirits, by letter—for he was allowed to write to us twice a month. In every letter he kept reminding us how much harder it was for us to bear, than for him. . . ."

From the papers in her hand Natasha produced a small sheet on which were written a few lines in type.

"That was his last letter," the father said, handing it on to me, "after the plea for mercy had been refused."

One by one, in silence, we read the brief, extraordinary document.

"After the refusal," the father went on, passing a shaking hand over his eyes, "we made one last plea to the lawyer. 'If our boy must die,' I said, 'could you not use your influence and beg that he be shot?' "

" 'Ha!' said the lawyer, 'don't let that worry you, *Herr Doktor*. Beheading's much quicker. They're so practiced at it!' "

As though to relieve the shocked silence, he added quickly: "They told us when it was over. But—but they wouldn't let us see him. They wouldn't let us see him. . . ."

"And the newspapers," the mother's faint voice suddenly broke in, "the newspapers called him the—the criminal, Schurik Schmorell. . . ."

"You didn't mention the guard, Papa," Natasha said.

"What, dear? Oh, the guard. *Ja,* the last time we saw our boy, I'd had a few words with one of the prison guards. He seemed a decent sort and spoke highly of Schurik. I met him once again, weeks later. 'Your son,' he said to me, 'he went out of the door with his head in the air. He looked up at the sky, then at a tree over the wall. Then he walked forward, singing something. It sounded like a hymn,' he said. But he wouldn't tell me any more. They wouldn't let us see him. If only they'd let us see him!"

Months later, while trying to recapture in my mind the story of Schurik Schmorell as we had heard it from his family, I wrote to John, asking him to check me on certain points. In his reply, he said, "you remember the wonderful letter he wrote his parents after the trial. It was a masterpiece of Christian faith. I only wish I had a copy of it. . . ."

I've tried in these pages to let living characters speak for themselves. Thinking of this letter from a boy who can no longer speak, I felt I'd sooner omit his tragic story than attempt to write it without including the last words he wrote.

Fortunately John had kept the Schmorells' Munich address, and luckily again a friend of a friend was working there in the American censorship. I wrote to her at once. The following, in part, is her reply:

Munich 23.6.46

I was fortunate enough to reach the Schmorells two days before they were forced to leave their home . . . which has been requisitioned by the Army of Occupation for American personnel and their families. So that added to their sad history were the throes of moving and the sorrow of leaving a home of long standing.

It will undoubtedly interest you and the Rev. John Haynes that the man who denounced the Scholls, and was responsible for the death of young Schmorell as well, has just been sentenced to a five-year term in an *Arbeitslager* by one of the newly-created German courts to purge the country of Nazism. He proved to be a very poor, inferior minor official and certainly a strange instrument to lead to the death of three such splendid young people.

In the meantime I have discovered through a newspaper item the Schmorells' new address. I am sure they would be pleased to hear from you and Mr. Haynes. Our meeting was such that I would like to do anything I can to give them a little cheer.

Enclosed in this letter were copies of no less than seven letters from Schurik Schmorell to his family, all written from prison. There follow the first, the fifth, and the last.

Munich 30.5.43

My dear Parents

I have nothing new to tell you from here—everything goes on as usual. But a few things I want to mention, so that your grief may be a little easier to bear. In case the plea for mercy should be refused, please bear in mind that "Death" does not mean the end of life, but rather the contrary—birth, transition to a new life, a divine and everlasting life. Thus there is nothing terrible about death. It's separation which is hard and difficult. But it will be less hard and difficult in the thought that we are not separating for ever, but *only for a while*—as during a journey—so as to meet later *for ever and ever* in a life infinitely more beautiful than the present, where there will be *no end* to our being together. Bear all this in mind; for it will surely make your burden easier. Be embraced and kissed by your

Schurik

Munich 2.7.43

My dear, dear Natasha

You will surely have read the letters I've written our parents, and so be pretty well informed. You may be surprised when I write you that day by day I grow inwardly calmer—yes, even gay and happy—that I'm generally in better spirits than I used to be in the days of Freedom. How has this happened? I'll tell you at once. This whole grievous "misfortune" was necessary to put me on the right path—and so in reality it was no misfortune. I am, in fact, glad and thank God that it was given me to understand this sign from God, and through it to find the right path. For what until now did I know of Faith, of real deep Faith, of Truth, the last and only one—God's Truth? Very little. . . . Yet now I have come so far—even in my present situation—as to be gay, calm, and confident, no matter what the future may bring. I hope that all of you, too, will have gone through a similar development, and that after the deep grief of separation you have reached with me the point of thanking God for *everything*. . . . This whole disaster was necessary for me, that my eyes might be opened; not only for me, but for all who have been touched by it, including our family. Hoping that you have all properly understood God's sign. Love to all, but especially to you, from your

Schurik

Munich 13.7.43

My dear Father and Mother

Now it seems that it was not meant to be otherwise and that today, according to God's will, I shall terminate my earthly life in order to pass into another, which will never end and in which we shall all meet again. Let this reunion be your comfort and your hope. This blow is harder for you than for me, for I am passing on in the knowledge that I have acted according to my deepest conviction and the Truth. All this enables me to face, *with a calm conscience,* the approaching hour of death. Think of the many millions of young men who are losing their lives out there on the field of battle: their fate is also mine. Give my love to all our dear friends. . . . In a few hours I shall be in a better life, and I shall not forget you. I shall ask God to give you comfort and peace, and I shall be waiting for you. One thing above all I want you to keep nearest to your heart: Don't forget God!

Your Schurik

Prof. Huber, who sends you his best wishes, is going with me.

KEMPTEN AREA

8

BEFORE leaving Starnberg for Kempten, a crisis arose. Everything went wrong. The major was called back to Washington. John had to fly to Paris to see his Bishop. The Professor, who had already visited Kempten to requisition us a house, was also summoned to Paris in order, it was rumored, to be examined for promotion. Finally, Mervyn had to stay in Munich for some "Background" reports. As a result, the leaderless team consisted—temporarily at least—of Frank, Dudley, and myself. And here the trouble began. Two jeeps and a trailerful of baggage, cots, rations, and wine had to be driven to Kempten—and of the three of us only I could drive! Dudley had attempted to procure an army license in Darmstadt, but on his first outing in a jeep he'd run slap into a tree, since when the subject in his presence had been taboo. Now Frank, when the crisis began to loom, had been persuaded to take a test. Unknown to him, I'd watched some of his valiant efforts. They were like the first attempts a child makes to ride a bicycle. However wide and straight the road, he just didn't seem able to steer straight. When the Major, the Professor, John, and finally Mervyn all prayed me in their various, well-meaning ways to "for God's sake go slow and look after Frank and Dudley," I promptly had a vision of a convoy of two-ton trucks roaring towards us round a hair-pin bend in a narrow mountain gorge. As for Frank and Dudley, I didn't dare ask for a description of their visions. Judging by the pallor of the former's face as we set off, and Dudley's mock-heroic speech beginning, "Into thy hands, dear Frank . . . !" I gathered they were no happier than mine.

Fortunately, since the weather was perfect and we had all day for the journey, there was no need for haste. Driving at beginner's speed, I soon got a crick in my neck from constantly looking round to see if the other jeep were still on the road. By noon it still was. Frank was surpassing my most optimistic expectations. Now and again I thought of stopping to congratulate him, but I dared not tempt providence and run the risk of his crashing into the back of the trailer. But I had another reason for wanting to stop. Ever since John had mentioned it in such glowing terms, I'd been wondering how we might wangle a visit to the church at Wies. I'd found it marked in tiny letters on a large-scale map, and though the detour would add some fifty miles to our journey, I could see only one good reason for not making it. The reason was Frank, to whom I hadn't dared mention the idea for fear of prolonging a drive which for him might prove a nightmare. But when we finally did stop—to eat our K rations on a wide, empty stretch of road—and I saw Frank's beaming face, I divulged my secret and asked him if he'd mind.

"Mind!" he cried. "Wonderful! My girl back home is studying architecture. I can write her pages about it tomorrow. How about you, Dudley?"

"Anything you say, Frank! What am I but a poor and lonely passenger—at your beck, your call and—don't forget!—your mercy, Frank!" Dudley then staggered to his feet and with a ration-box raised above his head, a chunk of biscuit wedged under his nose, he clicked his heels. "To the wheel, *mein Führer*," he roared, "and let us hence! Who knows, in the gloom of yonder crypt, I may utter a blessing 'pon thy soul! T'will give thee courage, O fearful friend, to circumvent crashing convoys, corners—!"

"Halt, blasphemer!" howled Frank, stampeding to the jeep. "Thou un-nervest me!"

Taking the lead again, I heard behind me, echoing across the countryside, bursts of their stentorian song.

At Peissenberg, instead of turning west towards Schongau, I took a narrow road, direct south, which led us above the deep ravine of the Ammer-Tal into the village of Rottenbuch. Outside a Gasthaus I stopped to pick up a lone corporal who was thumbing a ride back to his barracks in Füssen. I warned him that though we expected to pass through that town on our way to Kempten, we were at the moment making a detour to try and find a famous church at Wies. "It's near Steingaden," I added. "Maybe you know the way."

"Ain't no famous church in these parts," the corporal said. "I bin travelin' this God-damned road for three weeks—never saw no church."

"I hope you're wrong," I said. "I guess it's off the road and you didn't see it."

"Hi, Jim!" Dudley said, as Frank moved up alongside. "You missed seeing us nearly go into the ditch!"

"What happened?"

"At that sign post," said Frank, "where it said: Bad Tölz—Dudley screamed, 'Look out, Frank! Bad curve!'"

"Ha! Ha! Ha!" squealed Dudley.

The church of Wies, of course, was not on the road the corporal had traveled so many times. It was a couple of miles off it, up a steep lane that wound through a wood of firs and emerged suddenly among rolling green meadows. Here, in startling solitude, against a theatrical background of snow-capped mountains, stood a plain white octagonal building with a black slate roof and a clock-tower at one end. On the door a notice in large Gothic letters informed us that cameras were *streng verboten.*

The four of us (with a couple of cameras) were grouped together on the threshold when I pushed open the door; and once more, as at Andechs, it was like looking in on a child's idea of Heaven. The dazzling effect of light, the sense of space and unified color after the green meadows and the building's prosaic exterior, were so unexpected that we stood stock still. Then the corporal uttered a half-suppressed "Golly!" and—despite the silent, utterly deserted church—we crept in, like deer-stalkers, on the toes of our combat boots.

Through the long unstained windows came shafts of white

incandescent light, bathing the whole building in a brilliance that made us blink. The painted ceiling—where Christ, at a seemingly unreachable height, sat balanced on a rainbow against a heaven of blue—shone brighter than any sky. Even the tall rectangular columns, the white undecorated walls gave off a glitter, as though they had been cast yesterday out of frozen snow. The organ's façade, trimmed in gold, might have been chiseled from pure, unblemished ivory; and the two pulpits of pink marble, crowned with cherubs and overlaid with an ornamental crust of gilt, looked so small, so fragile as they hung without visible support from between pairs of pilasters, that you could not imagine a man—however light of bone—climbing up into them to preach.

The orgy of rococo culminated in the high altar of the sanctuary. In its center, under glass, reclined a wooden figure draped in linen, with natural hair and beard, before a scourging pillar. It was round this symbol of the Saviour, pieced together by two Premonstratensians in the early 18th century, that the church had been built and its fame as a place of pilgrimage begun. The pillars guarding it were of coral-pink and pale green marble with cornices of gold, and above the altar hung a huge gilt-framed painting of St. Joseph, the church's patron Saint. Round the picture clung bevies of winged angels, small sugary white statues, scintillating stars, golden crowns, splashes of pale blue paint, turquoise marble—a deep jungle of decoration merging to form a perfect harmony of color.

"The only thing I miss," Frank remarked, as we walked reluctantly towards the door, "is not being able to hear that organ."

"Gosh!" exclaimed the corporal. "Look at all those crutches!"

"I'll know where to come," Dudley said, "when I get to be an old, old guy."

Outside, as at Andechs, the sky seemed overcast, the green of the meadows and the mountains to be unnaturally dark, as though under some great shadow; yet from horizon to horizon there wasn't a cloud and the sun shone as brilliantly as at noon.

Somewhere between Steingaden and Füssen the road makes a bend and you see in the distance a kind of phosphorescent splash on the side of a high green cliff. As you approach, the color turns a mellow buff and takes on a peculiar shape: pale yellow pencil-points rise out of the mass, in which dark dots and slits appear. All of a sudden there emerges the complicated outline of a castle, resting on air, like a mirage. It's not like any castle you can imagine made by man, rather an artist's phantasy of a king's palace in a fairy tale. Though I wasn't prepared for it and had never seen it (in my mind I'd always placed it nearer Munich), I'd heard of it for so many years I knew what it must be. I knew, too, that no one but that particular Ludwig could have ordered anything quite so flamboyant as Neuschwanstein.

Once the eye has convinced you you're not dreaming, and you've begun to absorb the surrounding country—the abbeys, castles, fortresses, the gorges, the motionless glassy lakes, the waterfalls, the grottoes, the tree-covered hills; above all, the sudden overpowering nearness of the mountain-peaks—the Schloss of Neuschwanstein, the madman's dream, seems perfectly in place. For this landscape—at once the most majestic and most melancholy I know—seems as supremely fit a spot for the grotesque in architecture as it does for madmen, and giant madmen at that, to inhabit. If ever the human voice were to be heard echoing from these summits and valleys, I could think of none more appropriate than the bellow of Brunhilde, or that of Adolf Hitler howling annihilation from the crow's nest he built, a few miles away, at Berchtesgaden.

Even in the air of the mountain- and monastery-dominated town of Füssen, with its dark slumbering alleys which cannot have altered in half a thousand years, I felt something sinister, something not quite sane.

"Has this town any industry?" I asked the corporal as we

stopped to let him out in the main square. "Does it produce anything in particular?"

The corporal seemed uncertain. Then he said: "Oh, sure. There's one big factory near our place. Ropes."

Ropes? At first it sounded ludicrous. But what could be more ludicrous than Füssen, meaning feet? Ropes? Yes, ropes was right—and I thought of one particular purpose to which the Nazis were practiced at putting ropes.

Climbing northwest out of Füssen, away from those claustrophobic valleys, out of the gloom of the deserted lakes, the country grew more sane and civilized, the air less heavy. But on the steeply rising ground the road became a ribbon snaking into twists, blind curves, and hairpin bends. Once, glancing over an undefended precipice, I saw in a field hundreds of feet below the white American star on the roof of a khaki automobile. A mile further on, turning a corner, I heard the roar of an approaching convoy, Frank's dread. I wrenched out the handbrake, raised my arm, sounded the useless grunt of a horn, hugged the bank and thanked God that we were on the inside of the road and that it had a bank to hug. Frank appeared round the bend behind me at the same moment as the convoy's leading jeep rounded the corner in front. For an instant I saw myself being squished between jeep and jeep and then the two-tonners telescoping into one another on top of us all. Frank's front wheels were wobbling, but at the crucial moment his nerve held. With his teeth clenched, he drew up just in time behind the trailer, and with our off-wheels lodged in the grassy bank, we sat and waited while truck after truck—engines hissing and the great wheels spraying clouds of dust in our faces—went whoosh-whooshing by.

After this experience we drove with greater caution, until the road straightened out and down in a valley we saw the terra-cotta roofs of Kempten.

The house the major had requisitioned was a typical interbellum German villa, in the Park Strasse, a street high up above the town with a magnificent view of the Alps and the surrounding country. The house, of three stories, was built into the hill, with a garden on three sides and under it a garage for a couple of cars.

To make room for us two families had been turned out, and in their place we found waiting a tall young man and a middle-aged woman. At first they eyed us in silent awe. Then, the moment we began to speak they opened their mouths and gaped. Three Americans speaking German! The woman started asking questions. When would the *Herren* like supper? What did we want to eat? Could she unpack for us? Would we like to see over the house, choose our rooms? When was the nice *Herr Major* coming back, the one who couldn't speak German? To whom should she give the keys?

In the midst of this torrent of questions two more women appeared, one carrying a bunch of roses, the other a bowl full of red currants. They stood on the doorstep, like well-dressed beggars, bowing over the fruit and flowers as though they expected something in exchange. Dudley and Frank promptly got a fit of the giggles and disappeared.

"I am the owner of the house, and this lady is my daughter," the older woman said, still bowing over her bowl.

I was about to take the bowl and ask her in, when she said, "It is forbidden to enter our home."

"Do you think, *Herr Hauptmann*," the daughter asked, with a sly smile, "do you think we could keep our rabbits in the cellar? They'll get stolen if we—"

She was interrupted by a whirlwind invasion of children, half a dozen healthy-looking blond boys all much the same age. When they saw me they fell silent and stood there, gaping.

"Where do these children come from?" I asked.

"How well the *Herr Hauptmann* speaks German!" exclaimed the mother with an unctuous grin.

"One child is mine," the daughter said. "His name is Toni. He's a very good boy. His photograph is on the wall in the study. His father took it. There's another one in the dining-room. If the *Herr Hauptmann*—"

"Would you please tell all the children, including Toni," I said, "to go away and stay away?"

"Weg!" cried the older woman, waving the bowl and spilling some currants. "Shoosh! *Na,* see what you made me do!"

The children ran giggling down the steps and continued gaping from the gate.

"Would the *Herr Hauptmann* care to see the garden?" the older woman asked. *"Er ist so schön. . . . Wissen Sie—"*

"No, I wouldn't," I said, and all of a sudden there rose in me a feeling of such contempt for these two fawning females and what they stood for, that I longed to knock the fruit and flowers from their hands. Instead, I took them quickly from their outstretched arms.

"Thanks," I muttered.

"Bitte, bitte, Herr Hauptmann!" said the older woman.

"Nichts zu danken!" said her daughter, and they moved off, bowing backwards up the garden steps.

In the kitchen I found Dudley, Frank, the woman, and the young man in fits of laughter.

"Hedwig says she doesn't like men!" Dudley said in English as I came in.

"I never said such a thing!" the woman retorted in German, laughing. "I said I never wanted to marry."

"How d'you understand English?" I asked.

"She lived seven years in New Joisey!" Dudley said. "Can you imagine!"

"And she has an aunt in California!" Frank said.

"What are they going to do here?" I asked.

"Hans is a cook," Frank said, "a professional cook."

"Yum! Yum!" muttered Dudley.

Hedwig bent down and slapping her knee, burst into roars of laughter. Hans laughed, then Dudley and Frank. The kitchen echoed with laughter.

"Hedwig," George said, "she says she can do anything."

"Except marry," I said in German.

Roars of mirth. *"Los! Kinder!"* said Hedwig, with sudden activity. "The *Herren* must be tired. They must eat. They must unpack. Come, Hans, get the baggage up!"

Hedwig, I thought to myself, is going to be what the English call "a treasure" and the Germans "a pearl."

With the assistance of six giggling children, Hans and Hedwig, the jeeps were unloaded and garaged, the duffel bags, rations, cases of wine and cots heaved up the steps and distributed—all in a few minutes.

I unpacked in the only bedroom on the second floor. The room contained twin beds, two large wardrobes, a dresser and a view from its window of a maternity home across the street, the unbombed roofs of Kempten, and the distant Alps. From habit or curiosity—probably from having spent so many years in hotels—I began opening the wardrobes and all the drawers. They were empty. No, not quite. On the top shelf of one of the wardrobes the ex-occupants had done just what I myself had often done when sub-letting an apartment: they had stored up there all the odds-and-ends—the photographs, cards, letters, a pair of shoes, an old hat, a curtain-rod, paper, pins—which you invariably discover at the last moment, that moment when you're sure you're through with the boring business of packing to get out for someone else, strangers maybe, to come in. The shelf containing the odds-and-ends was high up, just about the height I'd stored my own odds-and-ends in the New York apartment; and as I looked at the pathetic jumble of German relics I saw my own, but instead of me looking up at them—at odd photographs of my childhood, my family, my wife, some private correspondence I couldn't persuade myself to destroy—instead of me, instead of the American stranger to whom I had sublet the apartment, I saw staring up at them a German in a Nazi uniform, with an evil grin on his red, tipsy face. Then I watched him walk away and start opening all the other drawers....

Which I did. And the drawer in the bedside table, the ex-occupant had forgotten in his or her hurry to empty. Like mine, it was packed with letters and small diaries, faded snapshots of intimate friends. And as my hands were over the papers and diaries, I saw again beside me the evil grin of the Nazi soldier, his fat fingers thumbing through my life, and

I closed the drawer (and never opened it again) and walked away into the room next door, a sitting-room.

There I removed from the inevitable piano (I have never stayed in a German house that lacked a piano—O God, I thought, what would the Germans be like without music!) a mourning-framed photograph of a pudgy German soldier in a Nazi uniform and a vapid studio smile on his face; and as I took it down I saw the other Nazi, the one with the evil grin, marching with huge mud-caked boots across the drawing-room of my parents' English home, pulling from the wall the painting of my brother and kicking it under the sofa.

I placed the pudgy soldier in a drawer of the big glass bookcase and settled down to look at the books. They suggested that the tenant was a teacher, who had tried to conceal his interest in literature by dressing the better books in jackets of brown paper—thereby making them more conspicuous! The teacher, if indeed that were his profession, had made a better, but not good enough job, of hiding something else. Dropped at the back of a shelf, invisible until the books had been dislodged, I found a four-foot roll of paper which I imagined at first to be an architect's blueprint. It was a blueprint, all right, but of far more interest than that of any building. It was a campaign poster to raise funds for the erection of a local rural school, and on it were fifteen pencil portraits of the leading lights, from the bearded *Oberbürgermeister* down to the Hitler-Jugend *Pimpf,* in Kempten's educational hierarchy. The portraits were not caricatures. They were drawn from life, and dated 1937. After consideration of this fact, the reasons for the poster and a careful study of each face, I came to the conclusion that this was one of the most revealing documents I had ever seen of the Nazi character and mentality.

I flattened out the poster on a table in the dining-room downstairs, and while Dudley and Frank studied it I gazed at a rubber tree which, planted in a pot in one corner of the room, rose as far as the ceiling and from there spread its one massive branch of shining fleshy leaves clear across the room.

I had already forgotten the grinning Nazi soldier; I saw him again only occasionally, and only when I was alone.

A few minutes later Hedwig called *"Zu Tisch! Bitte,"* and started serving us a meal which began with tomato-and-onion salad, followed by veal cutlets and a mountain of *Bratkartoffeln,* and ending with coffee and a bowl of raspberries-and-cream.

Having eaten ourselves into a stupor, we staggered into the kitchen to congratulate Hans, who was now dressed in a long white apron and a chef's tall hat. At our expressions of admiration for his cooking, he smiled modestly and waved a shattered arm and hand, on which two of the fingers were paralyzed. He'd been wounded, he told us later, at the end of three years fighting in Russia.

"Hans," said Hedwig, "is accustomed to praise. He used to be chef at one of the best restaurants in Munich. His mother ran a restaurant here in Kempten until a few weeks ago."

"If you have some more coffee and some sugar and some fat," Hans said, "I will be able to exchange it for other food you may want. . . . I know my way around," he added, with a faint smile.

"How about milk and eggs?" I asked.

"Eggs are scarce," he said. "It's hard to get them in from the country. But there's plenty of milk and cheese. The factories are working, and the Allgäu is the best dairy country in Bavaria. Some consider Kempten Camembert as good as the French. . . ."

"Pfui!" snorted Dudley, holding his nose. "Don't gimme any of that stuff!"

I left them in fits of giggles in the kitchen and went upstairs. In my room I found the bedclothes turned down and my pajamas laid out across the pillow. It was the first time I'd slept alone in a room since leaving London. I tried to keep awake to enjoy the luxury. I lay back with the map of Bavaria and tried to figure out the best way to reach a place called Kirchheim where, the following day, I was to interview Fürst Fugger von Glött, one of the few survivors of the 20th

July plot. But before I'd found Kirchheim the sun was shining through the window onto the map which hours ago had slipped from my hand.

I wanted to stay in bed to enjoy the luxury of being able to and of being alone, but the sun and the silence of summer were too tempting. I began dressing before the open window. On the horizon a spotless blue sky merged imperceptibly into the misty mauve peaks of the Alps. Under the pale purple haze lay the green valley. Nearer, the fields were cut sharply by the terra-cotta roofs of the town. In the maternity home across the street an infant screamed. A young mother in a red dressing-gown stepped out onto a balcony, squinted up at the sun, caught sight of my uniformed figure in the window and turned in again.

During a breakfast of powdered eggs (only Hans knew how to make them taste like a fresh omelet), I saw through the windows several women, a man and a child staring in my direction from the balcony of the house on the other side of the garden. The man's face was invisible behind a pair of binoculars, but the child I identified as Toni, the blond boy whose photograph hung above me on the wall. For an instant I felt my fingers tightening their grip over the knife and fork. . . .

Having polished off the "eggs," I smoked a cigarette on the slope of rock-garden behind the house. I sat on a flagstone in the midst of flowers and listened to the chiming of church bells down in the town. I climbed up through the vegetable garden, snatching an odd strawberry or raspberry as I went along. Then I returned to my room, collected a box of K rations, the map, a bottle of wine, and walked down the steps to the garage.

Kirchheim, I had discovered, was a remote village in the neighborhood of Memmingen, only an hour short of Augsburg—a long drive, but I had the whole perfect Sunday ahead of me. As I swung the jeep out into the street, doors burst open and children came clattering, chattering along the sidewalks. They were blond, well-fed, well-washed, well-dressed, healthy-looking children of the well-to-do middle-class, and the sound of a jeep filled them with an almost hysterical excitement.

"Herr Hauptmann! Herr Hauptmann! Bitte, bitte! Vun kilometer? Yess? No? Tank you!"

Then, above their treble piping, I heard an adult female cry, and looking up I saw Hedwig racing down the steps.

"Herr Stern!" she was shouting, and breathlessly she pressed a small soft package into my hand and quickly darted away. Through the wax-paper I could see a fat veal sandwich.

I drove slowly through the clean, seemingly unblemished town. Crowds of darkly clothed people were climbing up the steps of the twin-towered baroque cathedral. The occasional groups of G.I.s playing ball looked out of place—or rather, their voices sounded incongruous. I stopped and picked up a six-foot sergeant, whose billets were three miles out of town. He was from Kansas and I gathered he was bored: the beer was "pure piss"; he was not allowed to fraternize; there was nothing for a guy to do. He didn't know whether we were on the road to Memmingen. How could he know? He'd never been anywhere, and anyway all these villages looked much the same. Yes, sir, the country sure was beautiful, but he knew a God-damned more beautiful country, and he wouldn't be happy till he was back there. I let him out. He said, "Thanks, bud," and I drove on.

I had traveled some twenty miles on a gratifyingly empty road; I'd passed mournful-looking natives wending their way to Mass in the sleepy, cow-smelling villages; I'd watched and waited while a laborer herded some cattle across the road to be milked; I'd taken off my cap, my jacket, loosened my tie and was away in Heaven knows what peaceful daydream, when suddenly some children I'd just passed broke the country silence with a concert of breath-taking screams. I pulled the handbrake right out. The tires screeched. For a split second I wondered how I could possibly have hit a child without knowing it. Then I looked up. . . . Ten measured yards in front of the jeep there had been a bridge. Now there was none. Instead, I gazed down a precipice of several hundred feet into a torrent of green mountain water.

It's a shame that shocks give rise to anger. I owed my life to these children. I hope I thanked them accordingly, but when I asked them where I could cross the river and they opened their mouths and gaped and shook their heads, I could have spanked each one of them with pleasure. And when a local farmer informed me that every bridge for seventy-five miles had been blown up, that there was nothing for it but to drive all the way back to Kempten, I wiped out in my mind every remaining member of the S.S. In reality, I drove that jeep back to Kempten at a speed that sent the Sunday church-goers scuttling like chickens into the ditches.

I found Kempten's one remaining bridge, crossed it, passed the skeleton of what had once been a huge S.S. barracks (the only ruined building I saw that day), and relaxed only when I knew I was on the Memmingen road and that there were no more rivers to cross. Then I shifted in my seat, leaned back, and purred along at a civilized speed. The road was a driver's dream—a cement surface under a cool tunnel of sweet-smelling linden; it went into curves and see-sawed over low hills just often enough to prevent any possibility of boredom. At occasional cross-roads I would slow down and gaze at a wooden shrine of Christ on the Cross and wonder how long it had been there, who had erected it, then why it had not been desecrated. Once in awhile, all by itself in the open valley, I saw the inevitable, motionless, already rusty train, abandoned in its tracks; and again I wondered on what day and for what reason it had come to rest just there. At sight of the *Gasthaus* in the village square I dreamed of cold beer and delivered a hearty curse at a vision of Hitler's face. This, and the lack of traffic, the loneliness of the road, were the only reminders of mankind's most frightful slaughter.

Even pedestrian traffic was sparse that morning. But for this fact, I probably never would have noticed that single girl. There was nothing remarkable about her, except that during that summer in Germany it was unusual to see a girl walking all alone, carrying nothing, on a deserted country road. I had a fleeting glimpse of her in a light green dress, striding along the edge of the grass, swinging her arms. I passed her and didn't look back. Half a mile further on I came to a fork in the road and, not positive of my way, stopped the jeep. I got out, stretched my legs, and with the bottle of wine and a cigarette, settled down on the side of the road. The world of summer was utterly without sound. I sat smoking and drinking. I remember thinking of my apartment in New York, wondering if my wife were there and what she was doing at this moment in America, when I heard footsteps behind me. I looked up. Above me, one hand resting on the jeep, stood the girl in the green dress. Her legs were bare and she wore sandals. She was so heavy with child that several seconds passed before my eyes reached her face. It was a pallid, rather nondescript face, with sad gray eyes. Strands of longish blond hair, pinned up in a loose bun, hung down her neck and over her forehead. She kept brushing back these wisps of hair with a hand that was hardened and coarse. The fingernails were black and broken.

"Excuse me," she was saying as I got to my feet, "but do you think you could possibly take me a few kilometers?"

Her voice was pleasant, perfectly calm.

"I'm sorry," I said. "It's *streng verboten*. You must know that."

She smiled—sensing, I thought, that she shouldn't.

"You speak German?" she asked, unable to suppress her surprise and delight.

"Yes," I said. "I used to live in Germany—years ago."

Her eyes opened wide. "Ach!" she exclaimed. Then her face fell. "It's hard," she said, "traveling in Germany now."

"It certainly is," I agreed. "Where have you come from?"

"Rome."

"What? Rome?"

"Yes," she said. "I was getting on all right until a couple of days ago. In Italy things are different. . . . *Lieber Herr,* don't you think you could take me a little way, just a few kilometers?"

A hundred thoughts came rushing into my head at once.

"How long have you been in Italy?" I found myself asking without knowing why.

"Four years."

"Where are you heading for now?"

"Frankfurt."

"Frankfurt?" My eyes dropped from her face to her body. "Frankfurt's hundreds of kilometers from here," I said, "even as the crow flies."

"I know," she said. "But Frankfurt's my home."

"I used to look upon it as mine, once," I heard myself saying.

"Was?" she cried. "You know Frankfurt?"

In her excitement her hand went out to me. Then she quickly withdrew it. I found myself turning away. I leaned against the jeep and stared at my feet.

"Have you been in Frankfurt lately?" she was asking.

"No," I lied. "No, not for years."

"It's such a lovely city. . . . Do you know the Old Town, do you know the Kattgasse?"

"Yes," I said, "I knew the Old Town very well."

"And the Römer . . . ?"

"Yes, I used to drink *Apfelwein* at the *Schwarze Stern*. . . ."

"Ach, der Schwarze Stern—so was! How is it possible! We always stopped there when we came back from our climbs in the Taunus. Now I know you know Frankfurt. Ach, if only I were there again! *Lieber Herr,* could you really not take me just a little way?"

"What good would that do?" I asked her, looking her straight in the face.

"Just that much good," she said calmly. "Just that much nearer home."

"You realize that it's forbidden," I said. "No exceptions are made. If we are picked up, which sooner or later is certain, you or I or both of us may land in jail. All roads are patrolled. You understand?"

"I understand," she said.

"Get in," I said.

As we drove off, I noticed with annoyance that my hand was shaking on the wheel and that there was a faint smile on her pale lips. I drove slowly, feeling slightly sick, and prayed for an empty road.

"D'you mean you've been walking all the way from Rome?" I asked.

"Oh, no, I set off on a bicycle."

"When did you leave?"

"I . . . I don't know. I've forgotten. Perhaps three weeks, perhaps a month. It seems longer."

"Where's your husband?"

"He's dead," she said. "He was shot by the Fascisti. . . ."

I wanted to ask why, but it was hard—hard to break that silence.

"He was Italian," she said at last. "He took me to Rome. I didn't like it. I was homesick all the time. I couldn't make friends. My husband spoke German. I could never learn Italian. I tried hard to stay on after he went. He would have wanted me to. But then the baby, it began to grow, and I thought and dreamed of home, and one day I thought it might be too late. . . . So I packed two little suitcases and my husband's rucksack and I rode away. . . . In Italy I got lifts. Things are different there."

"And where's your bicycle now, and all your luggage?"

"All stolen."

"Stolen? Who stole them?"

She hesitated, and during that short silence we turned a corner, and round the corner I saw a convoy—tractors, four-ton trucks, tanks, half-tracks, jeeps—coming rumbling in a thundering unending line towards us.

"See that!" I muttered, half to myself.

"Yes, I see," I heard her say.

Before the first truck was upon us I saw two officers leap

to their feet in the front seat. As it thundered by, they shook their fists at me and yelled. The men behind, hearing the yells, yelled louder, howled together in a chorus that rose above the deafening roar of the engines. I wanted to step on the gas, but instead I changed into second, crept along at snail's pace, in an attempt to give the impression I had every right to do what I was doing and that I was not running the gauntlet I felt I was running. Like all convoys, it seemed to have no end. From behind every engine the screams and raucous cries of derision and shaking fists continued. Only one thought encouraged me: They can't stop!

When at last it was over, it was I who stopped. My mouth was parched. I uncorked the bottle and handed it to the girl. *"Prost!"* she said, glancing at me. *"Prost!"* I answered.

"This is the most comfortable ride I've had in a long time," she said.

I put the bottle away and drove on.

"You were telling me how all your belongings were stolen," I said. "Who stole them?"

"An American soldier," she said.

"An American? How d'you know? Where?"

"On the other side of Kempten. He wore the American uniform, like yours."

"What did he say? What language—?"

"He didn't say anything, only shouted. I was alone, and there was no one in sight. Suddenly he jumped from behind a tree, knocked me off the bicycle, pulled the rucksack off my shoulders, grabbed my handbag, and rode away on the bicycle. I screamed and hit him, but there was no one to hear and he was big. I've been walking ever since."

"It's very unlikely he was an American," I told her. "Americans don't need to steal bicycles. Most probably he had stolen an American uniform. Where have you been sleeping?"

"Anywhere. Sometimes people are kind. My condition helps, I think. Sometimes people prod me to make sure. When people aren't kind, or doors don't open, I sleep in barns. It's summer. That's a good thing. I was always a bit of a *Wandervogel*. And I'm pretty strong."

"What about food?"

"*Ja*, people on the whole are kind. Usually they spare me something. But it's different now. I have to beg. I have nothing to offer. I'm not used to that. Still, so long as I get home . . . My mother will look after me when my time comes. . . ."

"When's that?" I asked.

"Six more weeks. I'll make it, if I'm lucky. I've been pretty lucky so far. Except for my clothes. It's so hard to keep clean. And my bicycle. If only I had my bicycle. . . . I often rode seventy-five kilometers in a day. I could have been home in under a week. I know it's silly to be talking about home all the time, but I've been away so long. . . ."

"How long is it since you heard from your mother?"

"*Ja*, it must be more than a year now."

"Have you been reading the papers much?"

She laughed, almost gaily. "The papers! *Ach, nein*. They tell nothing but lies."

"I'll have to stop here," I said. Some way ahead I could see a stationary truck and a line of G.I.s sitting on the side of the road. "Don't you say anything," I said. "I'll do the talking."

As I came to a halt, all the G.I.s looked up and gasped, "Jeez!" I heard one of them mutter. A sergeant came up and I asked if there were an officer around. No, the captain had gone on ahead. I explained briefly why the girl was in the jeep, and he kept looking at the girl, then looking away. When I finished, he said: "Christ, that's certainly a tough one!" Then he informed me there was a garrisoned village not far along the road. "Try the C.O. there," he suggested. "Are you sure she's on the level?" he asked, smiling.

"Pretty sure," I said, thanked him and drove on.

In the village the jeep was immediately surrounded. A young, handsome captain broke through the staring crowd. I showed him my two impressive-looking passes, told him my story. He was extremely sympathetic, but apparently not sure what should be done. Finally he went off and conferred with another officer. In a couple of minutes he was back.

"You'd better take her into Memmingen," he said. "But be sure you turn her over to the AMG there. You say she has no pass?"

"No," I said. "She has nothing."

"How did she manage to get by the patrol posts?"

I repeated the question to the girl.

"Ach," she said, "they just looked at me. Most of them were very kind."

I translated for the captain. He smiled. "Guess it's hard not to be soft sometimes," he said. "You'll find the AMG in the middle of the square, can't miss it."

I thanked him, and as we moved on I remember hearing someone in the crowd shout out: "Why the hell did you pick on that one?"

I felt such relief at the humane manner in which we had been treated that I immediately passed on the news to the girl. Her reaction was more than surprising; it was positively frightening. She let out a gasp and grabbed my arm.

"Turn me over to the Military Government?" she cried. "But *lieber Herr,* please—I know you'd never do that. You who've been so kind—!"

"But listen," I said. "The American Military Government is not the Gestapo. What d'you think's going to happen to you? You'll be properly looked after. You'll be taken to a maternity home. Memmingen, so far as I know, is not like Frankfurt, it's not been—"

"But *lieber Herr!*" she shouted. "Frankfurt's my home! You don't understand. Please stop. Please let me out. The Military Government would keep me. As you say, they would put me in a home. I would have to have my baby in Memmingen. In Frankfurt, at home, I . . . *Ach, lieber Herr,* I implore you. . . ."

Her cries had become hysterical. I stopped the jeep. Tears were flowing down her pale, unpowdered cheeks, and in her sad gray eyes there was a look of awful fear.

I took her trembling hand. "Listen," I said, "are you sure you're doing the right thing for yourself, for your baby? Supposing, in Frankfurt, you found . . ."

"Ach, in Frankfurt," she murmured, closing her eyes. "In Frankfurt I know people. I have friends. I am home."

"Perhaps you are right," I said. "Perhaps you know best. Do you really want to get out here?"

"If I may."

She was out of the jeep and on her feet as though they had no extra burden to carry.

"Memmingen is an hour's walk," I said.

"Ach, that's fine," she said. She wiped her eyes with her wrist and smiled. The look of fear had gone.

I stretched out my hand. "Good luck," I said. "You deserve some."

"Thank you for your kindness," she said.

I didn't look back, but drove straight ahead, and probably very fast. I don't remember. I remember only seeing—as I passed under the arches in and out of Memmingen—what I had seen a month before: the battered remains of the few houses left standing in the Old Town of Frankfurt.

North of Memmingen the country spreads out into a pale green plain; the earth grows a lighter brown, the roads turn the shade of sand, dry and dusty, and the sky seems as immense as over an African desert. At the top of a hill overlooking the small town of Mindelheim, I stopped and ate Hedwig's sandwich on a bench under an apple tree. Beneath me, the orange-tiled roofs and the church spire lay packed in cushions of green trees. Beyond, an ocean of flat fields continued as far as the straight line of horizon. Somewhere on the other side of that peaceful plain lay the village of Kirchheim.

But crossing it was not a peaceful journey. The jeep was soon having every bolt in its body jolted loose on the worst road I've ever encountered outside Spain. Narrow and pitted with a million holes, it was covered, like the Roman road from Pamplona to Saragossa, in a blanket of white dust so thick that when I glanced back I could see neither land nor sky behind me. In about eight miles I passed only one human being, a woman leading a horse with a load of sweet-smelling clover—and when she saw the jeep approaching she dropped the rein, flopped into the ditch, and covered her head with her apron. Not having passed a signpost in a long time, I pulled up beyond the cart and asked her where and how far was Kirchheim.

"*Daw!*" she muttered, and pointed to a single white tower rising from a hill a couple of miles away.

Looking back from the crest of the hill, I could see the rippling rope of dust curling up behind the cart, and I could follow the white thread of road all the way across the plain to the spot above Mindelheim, where an hour ago I'd been sitting eating my sandwich.

On the edge of the village a patrol post had rigged up a pole across the road, a sentry-box beside it, and painted over them a design of black-and-white stripes.

"Wouldn't need a moon to see that!" I said to the corporal who took my pass.

"Gotta find something to do," he muttered, "in this Godforsaken hole!"

"D'you know," I asked him, "where a family called Fugger lives?"

"Mean the guy they call a First or Prince or something?"

"That's right. Prince Fugger."

"Boy, you wouldn't want no moon, either," the corporal said, "to see that little shack. Our officer's mess there's as big as Times Square. God-damned castle—right under the tower."

I knew something about the Fugger family because I'd worked in banks and I've always been interested in painting. Once, years ago, on a short visit from Frankfurt to Augsburg, to see the Holbeins and Cranachs and Burgkmairs, the masters who had lived and worked there, I'd found the name of Fugger all over the city. There was a *Fuggerei,* a name which made me laugh until I discovered it was a Roman Catholic Settlement founded by the Fuggers in the 16th century; there was a Fugger Haus, a prominent Fugger Strasse, and a Fugger Museum installed in a sumptuously decorated Italian Renaissance palace which went by the name of the Fugger Bath Rooms and which was full, not of baths or water, but of ancient Fugger furniture, coins, and medals cast by Fuggers with metal from their mines. On my return to Frankfurt, I commented on all this "Fuggerei" to a strange little bearded banker I knew, who promptly threw up his tiny white hands in horror at my ignorance.

"Aber, lieber Freund!" he exclaimed, "don't you know that the Fuggers were the Rothschilds of the 16th century!"

"You mean they were bankers?" I said, somewhat mortified.

"Aber selbstverständlich! They were the first international bankers, the wealthiest merchants in the world! And," he added, "they were not Jews!" He, a Jew, evidently found this an uproarious joke, for he let out an odd little cackle, like a pea-hen: "He! He! He! No, not Jews! He! He!"

From the village street you couldn't see anything of what the corporal described as "a God-damned castle," but once inside the arched gate, I realized he hadn't been exaggerating. The Schloss was like a gleaming white fortress, with tiny attic windows jutting out of a dark-orange roof which continued on and on until it lost itself in a forest of trees. At the end of a short gravel path flanked by lemon trees in tubs and a circular pool cream-white with water-lilies, gaped a doorway as grim and ghostly as the entrance to a cave. Confronted by the size and nearness of the Schloss, I felt suddenly very small and struck with much the same sense of awe as when, in the salad days of the seventh Edward, my brother and I used to be invited to Christmas parties at Dunsany Castle in the County Meath. The awful array of tall footmen in blue velvet, silver buttons and knee-breeches hovering about with expressionless faces and the silent stealth of cats; the terrifying holes for eyes and slits for mouths of the men-in-armor holding shields and swords in motionless steel fingers; the cathedral height and historical gloom of the halls and rooms and corridors with the thin-lipped, parchment-faced ancestors glaring down from the walls; the wonder of the tremendous glittering tree, the thousand candles in the ballroom and the blue-and-silver sentinels keeping grim guard with tiny ridiculous sponges tied to long thin poles of bamboo; and finally the giant Lord himself, the teller of gentle Tales, in bulging pink coat with Eton-blue facings, tie askew, mustache bristling, squinting through his thick pince-nez as he boomed orders like a monarch at Her Ladyship or a lackey in a dark chamber where illuminated masks of slit-eyed Orientals made by his own huge hands turned the child's stomach into a balloon and his sleep into a nightmare for weeks. . . .

Not since those days, I think, had I approached human habitation of such proportions with intent to enter. As though my associations with such a world had been divined, two boys—of a type I've seldom seen outside Britain—emerged from the cavernous door into the sun, and coming up to me, in their clean navy-blue gentleman's Sunday suits, with that dignified, innocent self-assurance I've noticed in our day only among Andalusian peasants and the dying class to which the boys so clearly belonged, they smiled with such magnificent, outrageous flirtatiousness in my face that I had to grit my teeth to stop myself laughing.

"Is Fürst Fugger in?" I asked the elder boy who might have been seven or eight or nine.

"Jawohl," he snapped as though my arrival had been expected; and raising his short right arm, he dropped his head towards it in an ushering-in gesture I presumed he had taken from the statuesque flunkeys I expected at any moment to see.

In the cool gloom of the great porch we passed, instead of flunkeys, a couple of particularly disreputable-looking G.I.s, sitting hunched, with rifles slung over their shoulders, on beer barrels, playing cards. Raising their heads, they gazed at me for an instant, started to rise, then—seeming to think better of it—they flumped down and went on with their game. I followed the boys round a corner, where they stopped suddenly in front of a great door and iron grill. Here the elder one, with a grin of unconcealed delight, pounced with all his weight on a thick rope, whereupon a loud ringing broke out and seemed to go on echoing all over the countryside until the door parted in the middle and an old man with white hair, black bow tie, and starched shirt placed a heavy key in the grill and pushed it open.

The elder boy repeated his ushering-in gesture and we stepped into a cave-like corridor which, from floor to vaulted ceiling and for fully a hundred yards, was crammed with wooden crates.

"What's in all these boxes?" I asked the boy, the miniature prince, the Fuggerling or whatever he was.

"Treasure!" he breathed, with a sense of mystery and pride. "Treasure from the churches and museums of Augsburg, Würzburg—all over."

Passing through another door, we began to climb a wide, green-carpeted staircase, round and round and round. It was light and airy here and on the whitewashed walls above every couple of stairs hung a simply-framed water-color of a Schloss —Schloss after Schloss after Schloss—and all the way up the stairs the elder boy kept looking round and staring me up and down and smiling that outrageous smile. I might, I remember thinking, chase the two little princelings up the stairs to the top of the castle, along some of its ghost-ridden landings and round and round the circular steps into the belfry of the white tower, and there I might put them to bed and slowly, surely smother them with—with whatever the Princes in the Tower were smothered with. . . .

But I didn't chase them. I didn't even speak until at last, a little breathless from his climb, the freckled rose-like skin of his cheeks a trifle flushed, the boy asked, smiling still, "What name shall I say?"

It's difficult not to answer that question truthfully (even if it should occur to you not to), when it's thrown at you that way. And so—as we finally ceased climbing and started walking down a wide, street-like corridor where Fugger after Fugger after Fugger followed me with his ancient eyes from the walls—I told him. I told him as he stopped abruptly in front of a door which—with his hand on the knob and his head on one side and the smile more mischievous, more outrageous than ever—he suddenly flung open, and into what at first seemed empty darkness he threw back his head and howled at the top of his lungs: "Herr S T E R N !"

I have no doubt that, had the blinds not been drawn in that room against the sun and heat, I should have seen six or seven people jump from their seats in surprise, fear or maybe even terror. But during the few seconds I stood there blinking with blindness and embarrassment on the threshold, all I could see were the human forms and vague white faces turned up in my direction. Then a man rose quickly to his feet, came marching towards me and, bowing slightly, took my hand in a firm grip.

"Fugger," he said simply.

"May I see you for a moment?" I asked.

"With pleasure. Please come into another room."

I don't know what I'd expected a Fugger to look like, but I was surprised by the fine head, the high intellectual brow, the smile and quiet voice of immediate and indefinable charm. With his dark spectacles, small gray-black mustache, bow tie, the sparse hair brushed back from the forehead and falling thicker over the ears and neck, he looked so unlike my conception of a descendant of German bankers, so unlike a man who'd recently been condemned to death for plotting against a ruthless dictatorship; and so like, on the other hand, a man of letters, so near in feature, voice and manner to my memories of James Joyce during his last months in Paris, that— as he led me into another dark room and we sat on an ornate, threadbare sofa—it was on the tip of my tongue to remark upon the resemblance.

I refrained, needless to say, and instead embarked somewhat hesitatingly upon the nature and purpose of my visit, hinting as best I could, without revealing all, that we had in our possession some of the bare facts about the attempt to kill Hitler just a year ago. Could he, as participator in that plot, shed any light on its tragic failure?

"Ja," he said gravely, clasping his hands and leaning over towards me so that I noticed for the first time the deep lines of suffering round the mouth, *"ja,* a tragic failure—that's just what it was. Germany had not many men of brains and decency left. But today, you know—as a result of that tragedy—I wouldn't know where to look for a combination of the two. In nine months after last July thousands went . . . and *how* they went! The best brains we had. I often think," he said, suddenly smiling sadly and pointing a finger to his forehead, "that I was spared because I didn't have enough! But I would prefer that to the other theory—that I am here just because of my title! Can you think of anything more fantastic, more base? But it would be just like them. . . ."

"Could you tell me," I asked, as I offered him a cigarette, "something of the part you played in the Plot?"

"Nun," he sighed, opening his hands. "It never amounted to much, and now it amounts to nothing."

Settling back in the sofa, he leaned his head against a worn cushion and seemed to contemplate the dark ceiling. Then he bent forward with some energy. "I take it I can talk freely," he said, smiling. "It's not a habit easy to regain, but I'll try. . . . I don't know whether you know it, but I belong to an old, old family. They had enormous wealth, owned great tracts of land all over Germany and Austria. I'm not sure how many castles belonged to them, but I do know that those of us who remain—the few dregs left—now own two. And I also know that that—" he paused and smiled as though he sincerely enjoyed saying: "is two too many! Well, you may wonder what this has to do with your question. Perhaps it hasn't a great deal, but the point I'm trying to make is that families such as mine have certain traditions which go very deep, too deep for the Nazis, who detest us with an envious hatred. Their politest epithet for us is "that damned bunch of aristocrats." And I've considered them and their regime, ever since 1933, an insult to all decent people, a catastrophe not only for Germany but for the whole of Europe. And by mentioning my family I'm trying to offer some background for my beliefs, my actions and even—yes, for my hesitations. I think of two in particular—when I began to hate what Germany had become with such hatred that I didn't think I could possibly live here any longer. The constant spying and the pressure put upon people like us made life a hell. Despite all my responsibilities, possessions and family I decided—when it seemed that nothing I could do would help destroy the tyranny—I decided to emigrate. To France, I thought, for I love France, or even further, to Brazil—but I hesitated on account of my old parents, whom I also loved and who were in despair at the thought of my leaving. And I hesitated again when, early last year, the leading men in the Plot chose me—in the event of its success—as Governor of Bavaria in the primarily Socialist regime that was to take over."

He paused. "But I'm not a politician," he continued, smiling, "and—as you may have guessed by now—not by nature a leader of men or a public figure. There again, it's not in the tradition. In other countries—in England, especially, as you know better than I—it's different; but then Germany is not like England. It's an odd thing, you know, but an American colonel here, he wouldn't believe me when I told him that my mother was alive before Germany became a united country!"

When he smiled again, I laughed and asked, "What did he say?"

"Oh—'Good God!' he said. 'I thought Germany was as old as the hills! It certainly looks it!' he said, glancing up at the Schloss! *Komisch, die Amerikaner,* like children—but children aren't good administrators. Things are going badly here. . . . But let me get back. I can see I'm wasting your time."

"Did you ever have any hope," I asked, "of getting rid of the Nazis once Hitler was in power?"

"Yes," he said, "I did—but only through the Reichswehr. That was why, long before the war, I volunteered as a Reserve officer in my old regiment, the 17th Lancers (*Reiter*) in Bamberg. There, I felt sure of finding anti-Nazis with whom I could fight and plan and organize to overthrow the regime.

But it was too late. They were there already—spying, investigating every volunteer. And I was pronounced 'unfit,' or rather, my character was what they called 'nationally unreliable!' This was a great blow. I didn't know to whom to turn, where to go or what to do. It was a lonely business. I felt isolated, cut off. I knew any number of men of my opinions. Ninety per cent of the 'damned aristocrats' in southern Germany were enemies of the regime. But none could suggest a sensible means of getting rid of the Nazis. My every movement was being watched, I knew. At that time my home was at Oberndorf, but things got so hot for me there I moved to Holzhausen on the Ammersee, where I built a small house. When war broke out I again volunteered for military service, hoping that now at last I'd be able to carry out my plan under cover of the army. This time I was accepted, as a training officer in a Driver's Division. But again I was to get a rude shock. I discovered that although some of the older officers were anti-Nazis, they refused—out of false patriotism—to take any active part against the regime. Completely misunderstanding the situation, they tried to console me with the idea of 'waiting till the war is over.' For not only were they convinced of victory, they were positive that the returning troops would overthrow the Government! Well, when I saw things were hopeless here, too, I tried to quit the army. If I couldn't work against the regime, I certainly didn't intend to work for it."

He stopped to light another cigarette, and in the short silence I remember repeating to myself that last sentence.

"Even this wasn't easy," he went on. "In fact, if it hadn't been for a kidney ailment and a sympathetic urologist in Munich who gave me a medical discharge, I often wonder how I'd have managed it.

"At a legal conference soon after I'd got out, I had a long talk with Dr. Franz Reisert, the Augsburg lawyer. I hadn't seen him for a long time. We have since become very intimate friends—and he's still, thank God [he crossed himself] alive. Our opinions, desires and fears completely coincided. We agreed that the Nazi regime could be overthrown only through organizing large groups of people. But owing to the Gestapo's system—I don't think anyone who hasn't lived under it could imagine what it's like—the complete dissolution of all professional organizations and unions, the obstacles, we realized, were almost insurmountable. We had one last hope—the two Christian Churches, the only organized bodies still in existence. We promptly got in touch with the Jesuits in Munich, and soon found three more ardent anti-Nazis in Fathers Rösch, König, and Delp. These men, we discovered, were already connected with the Kraisauer Kreis led by Graf von Moltke in Silesia.

"This group, as I understand you know, had managed with amazing secrecy to unite the active anti-Nazis among the other groups—the Protestant and Catholic Churches, those from the middle-classes under Goerdeler, and the more revolutionary group stemming from the old trade-unionist and socialist parties under Wilhelm Leuschner. Finally, they had put these men in touch with the activists in the Wehrmacht.

"In March, '43, Reisert and I attended a secret meeting in Father Delp's apartment in Munich. There we met two spokesmen for the Kraisauer Kreis—Dr. Mierendorf, the ex-Labor Union leader and Colonel Theodor Steltzer, a professional soldier. Steltzer told us that after Stalingrad, the OKW [the Wehrmacht's Western Command] was convinced that militarily the war was lost. They expected an invasion from the west and knew that Germany hadn't the strength to fight a war on two fronts. Under these circumstances, he said, opposition within the Wehrmacht would surely increase.

"We then discussed the new political program, should the Putsch succeed. We all agreed that the reconstruction of Germany in its present centralized form was out of the question, especially with the strong anti-Prussian, even anti-Reich hostility in Bavaria. Instead, the new Germany should be built on a federalist basis, with far-reaching independence for the different provinces. Prussia, of course, could not be allowed to continue with its present boundaries and population, and would have to be divided up. For the single districts, so-called Governors were to be elected. For Bavaria, as I've said, they chose myself.

"Later in '43 we called a meeting of Bavarians only, among them the former ministers Colonel Sperr, Gessler and the economist Hamm—all of whom we put in touch with the leading anti-Nazi circle in Berlin. Reisert and I managed to keep in contact with this circle through the Jesuit courier service. We were constantly hearing of new dates for the Putsch. The reasons for postponement were always described as 'tactical'—and with every change of date my skepticism grew.

"The news of the '20th of July' itself—after all the postponements and rumors—came to us as a complete surprise. My arrest, however, I took for granted. . . ."

I wanted to ask him what happened then, but I felt he wouldn't want to be asked and I didn't know how to word the question, or rather I respected too much his reticence which came, I was sure, not from a fear of reviving memories of what he had endured, but from the personal modesty that revealed itself in every word he'd uttered. Yet, now that I come to analyze my feelings, I know that to give the cause of my inhibition the name of respect is to tell only half a truth, and that the other half came from cowardice—from an old fear of having known and overheard too much at too early an age, of seeing as a child visions of men burying their own breed up to their chins on wild deserted beaches where they were forced to spend the last hours of their lives watching the long ocean-tide approaching, foot by foot . . . These visions haunted the mind long after the memories of country ambushes, of cars pocked with bullets, of being dragged along a road by a runaway horse, and of the operation in cold blood on a green gangrenous arm were half-forgotten and could be mentioned with a smile, because of the influence of spartan, God-fearing people who considered it "unmanly" and indecent not to put humor into the breath that dares to mention any kind of agony not suffered by an animal.

And so there was silence in the dark room for probably near a minute before I heard my voice, like a scared stranger's, breaking the silence as it said, for reasons I won't attempt to fathom, "Were you, sir, alone?"

The question seemed to evoke no surprise, neither a yes nor a no as answer, but with the same quiet smile, the smile of a man, I felt, of Faith and no illusions: "Oh, I'm accustomed to that!"

And then the whole face suddenly grew animated with a recollection. "But I wasn't alone for long. It was extraordinary. Not till I was thrown into the Berlin jail did I realize how wide the Plot had spread, how many and what different kinds of people all over the country had been working away in secret—in secret from their wives and families and nearest friends. It was extraordinary. I saw men there in the death-cells whom I hadn't seen and who probably hadn't seen one another for years. I saw friends with whom until recently I'd been corresponding—the usual careful, uninteresting war-time exchange of letters, you know—and whom I never for a moment would have suspected of living a double, much less a—a somewhat dangerous life! It was hard, all of them knowing they were going to be killed, and not knowing how, and not being able even to wave good-bye, for fear that the lifting of a finger might bring into that building another member of the family. That was the worst, the thought of all the innocent wives and relatives, whole families wiped out—and the little children carried off and given other names by people who—" suddenly he gritted his teeth and a look of passionate hatred brought a flush into the pale cheeks as he ground out: "who would inject them every day, every hour with the poison . . . !"

"Were you kept in Berlin?" I asked quickly, without thinking, for relief.

"No," he answered quietly, the flush of passion passed. "No, we were taken to Bayreuth in cattle trucks—ninety of us. The journey lasted over a week and only eighteen arrived. . . ."

He glanced up and saw in my eyes the question that couldn't be asked aloud.

"They'd been clubbed to death by the S.S. on the way," he said, as though it were common for the bravest to share the fate of bullocks; for a cattle-truck, not a slaughterhouse, to be the place of butchery.

"We were put to work in an underground sewer, with filth— or whatever you prefer to call it!—up to our waists, and fed on crusts and water. Our legs began to swell. I was surprised. I never knew that's what those conditions do. We soon learned —from seeing others go—that if the swelling rises above a certain height . . ."

He bent over suddenly and, as though from force of habit, began to pull up his trouser-leg; then he just as quickly stopped and laid the hand on my knee and exclaimed, *"Um Gottes Willen!* You shouldn't have allowed me to tell you all this . . . !"

"It's my fault," I said. "I did my best to ask you to!"

And glancing at my watch, I saw with amazement that more than three hours had passed since I'd asked him if I might see him for a "moment."

"You should have," he was saying as we walked towards the door. "It's a great relief to talk. Would there be any chance of your passing by again?"

"I would like to," I said. "Can you spare the time?"

He laughed out loud. "Time, my friend," he cried, "the only thing a prisoner never lacks is time!"

9

THE long day in the country—the drive with the pregnant girl and the visit to Kirchheim—had made me so absent-minded that on the journey back to Kempten I lost my way three times.

I arrived late in the evening to find the house full—Mervyn's dilapidated clothes spread all over "my" room, John strumming next door on the piano, the Professor and Frank and Dudley filling the kitchen with laughter, and at a writing-table in the sitting-room a stranger with a black mustache.

Mervyn was on the lawn, reading. "Who's that upstairs?" I asked him.

"The new Major," he whispered.

"Oh, of course," I said, "what's he like?" And I wondered if the stranger felt like the new master in a small school where all the boys are criticizing his appearance behind his back.

"Seems nice," Mervyn whispered. "Chicago. Classy, I guess. But not G.I."

"Have you met the chef, the parlor-maid?" I asked.

"Hedwig? My dear, d'you know I'd only been here two hours and she'd already washed my socks!"

"Thank God for Hedwig!" I exclaimed.

That night, over a delicious goulash served by Hedwig at the long table under the rubber tree, Mervyn observed that we were running out of wine.

"Is there a black market here?" he asked Hedwig, in German.

"*Ja, mei!*" she exclaimed, shaking her head.

"*Ja, mei!*" mocked Frank, whose knowledge and ear for German dialects was a constant source of envy to me.

Hedwig burst out laughing. "That's Kempten!" she said. "I picked it up here."

"Hedwig," muttered the Professor from a face bulging with ice-cream. "Hedwig's an evacuee."

"A refugee," corrected Hedwig. "I'm from Breslau."

"What *are* you talking about?" asked the Major with a bewildered, good-natured smile.

"Hedwig's sex life!" squealed Dudley.

At which the Major exploded and Hedwig ran blushing from the room.

"That reminds me," Mervyn said. "Kempten's apparently packed with evacuees. The *Bürgermeister* has given me the address of a man who evacuated hundreds of children from Essen. Someone's got to make a report on it for background material. Who hasn't had his day-off from interviewing?"

"I haven't," I said.

"Well, how about going to see this man tomorrow? And getting some wine?"

"Okay," I said, delighted at the idea of not having to sit cooped up in a room all day.

I got the address of the black market from Hans. "It's not easy to find," he said.

Hans was right. I found it with the assistance of a small boy. Passing the main station, which had been destroyed by a perfect piece of precision bombing, he conducted me up a grassy *cul-de-sac* to a lonely shuttered house. Here the boy pointed at a door and promptly ran away. The door was locked. I banged and shouted, but without response. I walked round to the back of the building and up some steps on to a truck-loading platform. Here the door was also locked. I was about to depart in frustrated anger when above my head a small window went up and out peered a yellow, swarthy, suspicious-looking face under a head of sleek black hair. Seeing my uniform, the face broke into an unpleasant, golden-toothed grin.

"The *Herr* wants something?"

"Yes," I said, refusing to divulge what until I got inside.

"Will the *Herr* please come round to the front?"

I stepped into what looked like an empty shop, but three dirty tumblers on the counter gave it the appearance of a bar.

"Will the *Herr* drink a little something?" asked the man, with the velvet, insinuating voice a brothel-keeper uses on a new customer. He was dressed in a dark suit, dirty shirt, and his fingernails were long and black.

Feeling like a drink but not like talking to the man, I said, "*Danke, nein*," and produced a chit which the Major had signed for the wine.

"*Tcha*," he said, gazing down at it and spreading out his hands, palms upwards, like a brothel-keeper who has been asked to produce the kind of girl he hasn't got. "*Tcha*, it's scarce—wine. *Wissen Sie, lieber Herr,* Kempten has no vineyards. . . ."

"What wines have you got?" I asked sharply.

"*Tcha*, the good wine's all gone. The French, you know, when they—"

"Will you please tell me," I said, louder, "what wines you've got?"

He glanced up, the full lips shutting over the gold, and turned and walked quickly away, disappearing into what I presumed was the store-room. In a minute he was back with a bottle whose label was written in Greek.

"Is this wine Greek?" I asked.

"*Jawohl, mein Herr,*" he said, smacking his lips. "*Aus Griechenland. Gut!*"

"I'd like to taste it," I said, and he uncorked the bottle and poured some of the thick red-brown liquid into a dirty glass.

I took one sip. "My God!" I said. "That's not wine!"

It tasted like syrup of turpentine.

"*Zu süss?*" he asked, grinning. "Too sweet for the *Herr?* Ach, how the ladies love it!"

"We are not ladies," I said severely, "and we want wine, not syrup swiped by Nazis from starving Greece!"

Suddenly a door opened behind me and an old man in his shirt sleeves trundled in, leaned over the bar and began whispering something to the man behind it. I walked quickly to the door he'd left ajar, passed through it and stood staring at the cases of bottles strewn all over the floor. I was bending down examining the label on a bottle of Rheinpfalz 1939 when I heard footsteps hurrying towards me and the man's velvet voice close to my ear: *"Tcha!* Such a shame! All ordered yesterday by the Military Government!"

"All?" I said, the long bottle in one hand and the other pulling out my wallet where I'd dropped the money Mervyn had collected from the team.

I watched the eyes following the movements of my hand, like the eyes of the brothel-keeper summing up the worth of the new customer. *"Einen moment, bitte,"* he muttered, *"aber ich glaube* . . ." And he vanished behind a tier of crates.

"Mein Herr!" he was saying while he noisily shifted some boxes about. "You are fortunate. With what pleasure I cannot tell you, I have unearthed a case of that superb vintage, the very wine you have in your hand."

He came towards me holding a bottle.

"My partner," he whispered, so near my face his garlic breath made me move away, "my partner—I tell you confidentially because I can see the *Herr,* like myself, is a connoisseur—he was keeping this consignment specially for an American officer, but I happen to know that the officer is in transit and I feel sure that once the *Herr* and his comrades taste a glass of this they will be excellent customers."

"Thanks," I said. "Thanks. I'll take two cases."

"It is thirty marks the case!" he said, opening his eyes so wide I thought they'd pop out of his head.

"That's okay," I said, "I'm not going to haggle over the price." And I thought: Three dollars the case—less than a bottle of rye.

The old man loaded the cases on a barrow and I followed him out and watched him lay them under newspapers in the back of the jeep. As I started the engine I looked up at the shuttered warehouse where the marketeer was bowing and flashing his golden teeth in the doorway.

"*Auf Wiedersehen, mein Herr!*" he was calling. "Till next time, much pleasure and many thanks!"

The man who had evacuated the children from Essen lived in Waltenhofen, a village in a valley five miles south of Kempten. Its *Bürgermeister*—a short, mild-looking man in shirt-sleeves—led me up a narrow path to some steps at the top of which he knocked on a door. It was opened by a woman of about forty with a beautiful, cream-like skin and enormous dark-brown, smiling eyes.

"Frau Rektor Hoffmann," she said. "*Grüss Gott!*"

"*Grüss Gott!*" I replied and stepped into a room spotlessly clean but reeking of that awful odor of sour stomachs, the odor of poverty which I'd last smelled as overpoweringly in the Champs Elysées.

At a table two children, with long plaits and the same skin and eyes as their mother, were sitting reading. When they saw me they gaped and the little one piped: "Look, *Mutti, Amerikaner!*"

"Quite right!" I said, and I split a piece of gum and gave them each a piece.

"Say 'Thank you'!" the mother said. The elder child gasped "*Ach, danke schön!*" and rolled her huge eyes, but the smaller one literally fell off her chair and tottered into the next room, shouting: "*Vati, Vati!* Look what I have—*Kaugummi!*"

Then she came running back with her hand in that of a tall, bald, powerfully-built man with a curiously blue-white, fleshy face, intelligent eyes and full, finely-shaped lips that were of a mauvish shade of red.

When I told him what I'd come for, he said, "Ha!" and shooed the children out of the room and asked if his wife might remain.

"We went through the evacuation experience together," he said. "I don't like her to be left out of accounts of it!"

"Of course," I said.

"Well," he began, "during two raids on Essen in the spring of '43, we lost everything we possessed. For me, the worst blow was the destruction of my library of two thousand valuable books. I am, incidentally, a geologist by—by nature!—and in that last fire a six-hundred page manuscript I'd just finished, on the history of Essen, went up in flames. Fortunately, my wife and three children had managed to get out into the country.

"Then in May, by which time most of Essen was a shambles, I was chosen to head the first transport of children to Bavaria. We left there by train on the 17th with 510 kids—"

"I think you should mention your health," his wife said, smiling. And to me, "My husband has bad heart trouble and had recently spent six months in a clinic at Bad Nauheim."

"*Ja, Ja,*" said the rector, with an impatient wave of his hand. "But that cannot interest the *Herr*—"

"As a matter of fact," I interrupted, "it does—though for a purely selfish reason. Now that you mention your heart ailment in connection with Nauheim, it suddenly occurs to me you may have met there the famous specialist—I was in Nauheim only a few weeks ago, but—"

"Gessner?" the rector exclaimed.

"That's right," I said. "I used to—"

"You know Professor Gessner?" the wife asked in astonishment.

"I was one of his patients," the rector said.

"I knew him," I said, "years ago in Frankfurt. One of his many sons married a friend of mine. Have you any news of the old man?"

"Not since nearly three years," the rector said. "I'm afraid he must have got into trouble. He was very outspoken, you know. A wonderful man. I only hope he didn't lose his job at the Clinic. *Na,* to return to our story. The journey with the five hundred children was not entirely uneventful. Between Darmstadt and Mannheim we were delayed for hours by an air-raid alarm—"

"Don't forget Rector Lieper," the wife said.

"*Ach, ja.* My colleague Dr. Lieper had traveled down ahead of us to the Allgäu, to get in touch with the official authorities in Kempten. When our train arrived in Ulm, Lieper was there to tell us that Kempten could put up only four instead of nine classes and that the rest would have to be billeted all over the country. Just how and where he didn't know. Since the children had been divided into classes according to their age, this news meant that all the brothers and sisters would have to be separated, that all clothes and ration cards packed in one trunk could be delivered at only one place. One result of this was that for weeks many children had no change of linen and no ration cards, and another that some parents were so angry they came and fetched their children back!"

"You've not told about our reception in Kempten," the wife said.

"I'm coming to that, dear," the rector said. "I will tell you first about how the children were welcomed. This, I'm glad to say, could have been much worse. But it was a sad reflection upon our countrymen—yet, I'm sorry to say, nothing new to me—to see how the poor behaved compared with the rich. There are quite a number of wealthy people here in Kempten, some at that time with six and ten and as many as a dozen empty rooms in their homes; but would you believe it that in all that suburban, park-like area where they live, only three—three out of over five hundred children—were taken in! It was the poor, the railway official, the bank clerk, the employee who gave, and willingly, our kids their temporary homes. 'That child is going to have a right good time with us!' they'd say, 'and be safe from those terrible bombs!' And most of them had already several children of their own, while the well-to-do had one child or no children at all—"

"Remember," the rector's wife broke in, "remember the bed-ridden woman who said, "I shall consider this child as my own, and I shall pray to God to be merciful to my older boy on the eastern front!"

"*Ja,*" said the rector, "and that woman, who couldn't walk, arranged excursions for that boy and other children—to Lindau and Oberstdorf and Füssen where they saw mountains and bathed in the lakes, which they'd never done before. . . ."

"We have a word in German," the wife said, smiling, "*Volksgemeinschaft*—Folk Community. We don't use that word any more. We've changed it to *Volksgemeinheit*—Folk Meanness!"

"How about yourselves," I asked, "and the other teachers?"

The rector and his wife exchanged glances over the table, then smiled a kind of hopeless smile as though this were a story they were already tired of telling and did not particularly want to revive.

"*Nun,*" the rector said, "that was not so good. I will tell you briefly about our own experiences; those of the other teachers were much the same. My family consists of five. The lodging chosen for us on our arrival was under the roof of an inn—a bug-infested attic with two camp beds and five people in the room already! When I asked the *Wirt*—a real bully of a Nazi—for some coffee or at least some water, he banged the door in my face. So we took our hungry and thirsty children outside, where they slept in the open beside a well. But the next night it was too cold and we had to bring them in. After the third night we noticed they had contracted a skin disease in that room, so we moved to another inn which was so expensive I ran out of funds before the end of the month. Then our begging period began. We walked out into the country and tramped from farm to farm, begging—begging for food for ourselves and for the other teachers who had been relying for funds almost entirely on me. Telegrams to Essen were useless; the banks there and in Cologne had been destroyed. When the *Wirt* threatened to throw us out of the inn if we didn't pay our debts, we started begging for room on the streets of Kempten. Everywhere we were refused, as I've already told you. Spinsters living alone—and I can give you their names [he did]—with eight and twelve rooms apiece would not offer us so much as an attic or a converted garage at the back of their houses. A retired music professor who owns a large hotel at Oberstdorf wouldn't give up his six-room apartment in Kempten, though he used it only a few days a year. . . .

"*Ja, ja,*" he sighed, after a pause. "*So is' es.* It's difficult for foreigners, probably even for you, to understand the feeling the Bavarian bears towards the Prussian. It might well be compared, I think, with that of the French towards the Germans. And the war has greatly increased the hostility. The only good we've seen come out of the war, or rather out of National Socialism, is that in the face of a common and ruthless enemy, the Protestant and Catholic Churches have sunk many of their differences and are today closer together than perhaps ever before."

"I have gathered that," I said, remembering the conversation at Kirchheim. "Tell me," I asked, "are most of the children you evacuated still here?"

"No, indeed they are not," the rector said. "I don't think we have more than a hundred in the area now. Most of them had returned before the end of the war. In fact, at least sixty went back within a week of their arrival—for two reasons: some because the mothers simply couldn't stand the separation, others because as city-dwellers they couldn't stand the country. Some returned later on account of acute homesickness, while others, we discovered, had chosen to come down here just for experience and the ride! Most of these children had already been evacuated to Thüringen and Württemberg. They were making a habit of it, grabbing at any opportunity to see a little more of the world. We used to call them the Sensationalists! Here, anyway, what they saw they didn't like. They found it too dull after the city—even though that city was in ruins! Then there was the difficulty of the different dialects. This caused constant brawls and ill-feeling between the natives and the newcomers. . . ."

"*Ja, mei!*" I said, and the rector and his wife laughed for the first time.

"Finally, on one day last August," he continued, "no fewer than eighty children were sent for by their parents. The reason was this: Kempten had been mentioned in an army report as having been raided by Allied planes. Although I wrote immediately to the Essen magistrate, who published my report in the papers, saying that not a single child from Essen had been hurt, seventy-odd mothers insisted on having their children returned at once!"

"How did you come to land up here in Waltenhofen," I asked, "and what are you doing now?"

"Now?" he smiled. "Now I look after—or rather, we have adopted—all the war-orphans, and I'm in the middle of a geological history of Kempten. Far more interesting than Essen. Kempten has amazingly rich and clear traces of the four Ice Ages. The moment I saw the formation of the land here and examined the strata of the boulders in the Roman *Campodunum*, I knew I was here for life—"

"Yes, dear," interrupted the rector's wife with a rare and most welcome flash of humor, "yes, dear, but I don't expect our visitor is planning to stay that long!"

I laughed, and the rector smiled indulgently, while she added, "Once I hear my husband mention the Ice Ages I always try to change the subject!"

"I will let you succeed this time!" the rector said, smiling still.

"You haven't told me," I said, getting up to leave, "how you managed to land up here in this house."

"That I shall be glad to tell," the rector said. "Primarily by chance—on one of our many wanderings from village to village, begging. But if it hadn't been for the generosity and perseverance of the *Bürgermeister*, the man who showed you up from the village, we might be wandering still. We owe our new home, this couple of rooms, to him—one of the two humane and decent men I've met in these parts. The other is the head of the Savings and Lending Bank, who saved us from actual starvation. This man, I should add, risked his own life to save that of an American flyer who was shot down here over the Menhölzerried *Moor* last July. He carried the wounded man more than a mile to the main road, loaded him on a car and took him to the hospital. *Ja*," he said, sighing and ushering his wife and myself out of the door, *"ja,* it's the few—the one or two—who make life worth living."

"And the Ice Ages, *nicht?"* his wife muttered, looking up at him, biting her lip, and slipping her arm through his as we walked down the lane.

From the lane in the evening sun the mountains looked as mauve-blue as the hills of Wicklow and Galway seen from the sea, and the women in white aprons and bonnets moved about like magpies pecking as they turned the hay in the fields below the village.

"Those women," the rector was saying, a hand guarding his eyes against the sun, "you might think they were Bavarians, but they're not, they're Poles—and they're the happiest, the most primitive people I've ever seen. No one has a word against them, for they work like slaves for almost nothing, and they love it. It's what they've been used to all their lives—cows and pigs and fields. They live all together in a barn, little more than a cowstall. . . ."

"But you should see them on Sundays," his wife said, as I got into the jeep and the two children, their plaits flying, came tearing down the hill. "They spend their few marks on things they've never seen before—cheap jewelry and ear-rings, fantastic hats with feathers usually worn by old ladies, even parasols they must have picked up in some junk store and which they use only when it rains!"

"Ja, ja!" sighed the rector, his arms hanging over his children's shoulders. *"Ja, ja!* Human nature! And their sons will become Bavarians and hate the Prussians and the Poles and—"

"—and emigrate to America," I broke in, "and become fat business men in double-breasted suits!"

"That's it!" laughed the rector and his wife. *"Auf Wiedersehen, mein Herr; auf Wiedersehen!"*

10

WHEN looking back on Kempten, my first vision is invariably of an ideal place for contemplation or vacation. It is in retrospect as though the weeks there—the mornings of sunlight, the serene evenings—had been passed in the comfortable house of wealthy friends who'd simply gone away, left you their home, garden, servants, and given you carte-blanche at all the local stores.

And is that, after all—despite geography and the moment in history—such a gross exaggeration? There was Hedwig to wash your linen, darn your socks, brush your clothes; the "treasure" upon whom even the Professor smiled because she put ice in his drinking glass without being told; the Hedwig who'd lost all she'd ever owned ("What's it matter? It wasn't much, and I've no use for possessions!"), who was a refugee from the dreaded *Russen,* who never looked downhearted and made some people feel homesick with stories of her wanderings in the States, and who was so much like an American ("Travel! Ach! That's what I like! Always on the move, that's what I like!") that everyone longed to stow her away in an outsize duffel bag and transport her across the Ocean. And Hans—the tall, stooping, modest, wounded veteran, the perfect handy man and cook combined—whose old mother had been thrown out of her home, all her belongings smashed or stolen by the conquerors, who occupied her house and insulted her son when he knocked on the battered back door and asked for a blanket; Hans, who smiled the philosophic smile and said: *"Ja,* in war it's all over the world the same; I've seen it!" and waved his paralyzed fingers and pedaled away on his or someone else's bicycle with the basket of flour, soap, and coffee on the handle-bars, to return with it overloaded to his chin with meat, vegetables, cheese, and occasionally cream and eggs which he whipped into feathery soufflés or Salzburger *Nockerln,* or just the cream alone, as thick and clotted as unstirred oil-paint, which Hedwig laid on the table in a huge glass bowl beside a bigger bowl of the raspberries and red currants she'd picked in the garden behind the house.

Nor was that all. That was just the house, the home from home, and which of us had ever known a better? There was also the country, always near and visible, the sun shining on the green fields and the mountains of periwinkle blue. And five minutes' walk away, along a lane deeply shaded by linden trees smelling of lemon and honey, one of those swimming-baths framed by mown grass, occasional young peach trees and all round it a trellis weighed down with bundles and bundles of crimson roses. Here the Major let off some frustrated steam with a handball when Frank and Dudley came back from work, and I cursed and swatted horse-flies on my naked body and finally stumped away because the sergeant in charge could not be persuaded to stop, even for five minutes, shattering the blessed country quiet with a juke-box going full-blast through an amplifier—with never more than half a dozen G.I.s to hear the inhuman din.

But what did that matter? There were the snow-covered summits and all the shimmering fields of Allgäu to gaze at or walk in, where the only sounds came from the bleary, fatalistic-eyed Tyrolean cows chewing the cud. There was the walk downtown, through the small park, where the beech trees and cedars turned the blazing heat of summer afternoons into cool and shaded evenings for the old men with long mustaches, who sat alone and silent, smoking long pipes on wooden benches. Here, too, rested aged women with buns of stained gray hair, lined parchment faces, and big bodies bulging from all the wrong places in long black dresses that were no longer black but aged by time and wear into the color of slate or a never-polished shoe. They sat, as a rule, on the ends of benches, knitting alone or maybe with a grandchild making sand-pies at their swollen feet, and you doubted that any of these old men or women could be or ever had been evil, because of the belief that no one of any age with a creaky conscience spends his afternoons on public benches under trees, alone and without speaking, hour after hour.

But the park was small and you were soon out of it on to the road of hospitals—large gray buildings for men with one leg or no legs, and beyond them one for the armless. They wore white singlets and sat or lay on the grass under copper-beeches in couples with their crutches, or in a line along the wall overlooking the road, like one-legged birds balancing on a telephone wire, gazing down with a perky interest on each passer-by, then turning the head quickly to make an apparently serious personal remark.

The shock at seeing them lasted only an instant, for you knew there were men in their condition sitting on grass and walls all over the world, in England and America. And still, for a fleeting second, you thought that the homes and families of the crippled American men had not been destroyed, the children and the aged neither maimed nor threatened with destruction; but that was not a new thought, rather one that had been present and never given expression, a small but constant ache of guilt, ever since the first bomb fell on Britain. The shock also passed off quickly because of something in the eyes, a look that did not suggest the bitterness and despair I'd seen on the downcast faces of the Wehrmacht soldiers on the *Autobahn;* but instead a steady gaze of almost peaceful resignation, as though their common and so visible affliction had relieved them forever of hard and hateful labor, of killing and maybe being killed, and had formed for them a kind of weaponless fraternity in which they felt secure, and to which all men in the future, even the evil ones, would be bound to offer a helping hand.

There were, after all, you found yourself thinking in the face of tragedy, greater tragedies. They were still able to see and hear, and when they'd been fitted out with limbs, they'd be able to hobble and finally to walk the few hundred yards down—not into the ruins of Europe—but into a town which war had made for the eye and ear almost as peaceful as on the day, three hundred years ago, when the local veterans of the Thirty Years' War had walked for the first time up the steps of the great, newly-built, green-domed Cathedral of St. Lorenz.

And there in Kempten's Old Town would be many more familiar landmarks to which the ancient veteran could lead the crippled survivor of Germany's Second Great Aggression. He would recognize the Rathaus-Brunnen (the fountain beside which Rector Hoffmann's children had slept their first night), the huge red baroque Schloss built for the prince-abbots and now a barracks, the same narrow streets, the placid river Iller, and the few horse-drawn carts (with oddly little in them). He might lift an eyebrow (though he'd be familiar enough with devastation by fire) at the charred remains of what he wouldn't know were two railroad stations; he would not be able to understand, any more than would his stumbling companion, the peculiar languages spoken by some of the "displaced" people; and he would be puzzled by some Germans who talked of "those terrible bombs" and "planes" and "no homes" and were constantly exclaiming: *"Ach, die Preussen können den Bayern alles abkaufen, nur die Dummheit nicht!*—Ach, the Prussians can buy anything from the Bavarians, except their stupidity!"—and by other Germans, local natives, many of whom frankly admitted they'd had nothing to worry about until *"Ja, mei,* those damned Prussians" came and plundered all the farms, crowded them out of their houses and in a year raised the population of the peaceful, law-abiding little capital from twenty to a hundred thousand souls. No, they'd had nothing to worry about, they admitted, until those "damned swine" swiped all their food and milk and homes, at which point they'd pull long faces and talk about "hunger" and "no bread" with popping, bitter eyes that looked far less famished than most of those who spoke of "bombs" and "planes" and "ruins."

Yet even the like of these stories the three-hundred-year-old veteran would have heard before, in different words. On the whole he would not have received many surprises in his home town, and but one monstrous disturbance, a single terrifying shock—shared, to a lesser degree, by his hobbling companion: the occasional roar and honk-honk of what people called a "truck" or a "jeep" as the bigger or smaller monster on four wheels appeared from nowhere and came charging down a street or round a corner.

But we didn't always travel by jeep from the Park Strasse. And that's one more reason why, when looking back on Kempten, my first vision is invariably of an ideal place for vacation. For instead of gulping down indigestible cushions at dawn, climbing into a jeep and driving blindly over awful roads into weeping devastation, you could rise in a civilized bedroom at seven-thirty, eat Hans's omelet at your leisure in the sunlight, then wander down through the park and the slumbering, peaceful-looking, untouched town to the house in the König Strasse, to a big, bright, empty room where . . . but *that* is where the vacation-idyll suddenly ends. For then I recall some of the things that were said, some of the stories I heard and some of the faces I saw in that other room—the big, bright, empty one whose windows looked out over the white street and the fountain and the great green-domed cathedral.

I have a vivid recollection of many faces which stared at me across the bare table in that bare room, but the one I remember best is that of a plain, blousy woman of about forty-five who wore a thin, yellow, red-spotted dress which had been washed or scrubbed until it was almost transparent, and on her head an old black hat of the cloche type which had been the fashion on Fifth Avenue in the 1920's.

She was an Austrian who had moved into Kempten from the Vorarlberg with her Austrian husband and children after the Anschluss. When, during the war, her husband and two sons had been drafted she had become a waitress at the Hotel

Post, the inn from which Rector Hoffmann had been evicted because he couldn't pay the rent.

I don't remember the color of her face when she first came into the room, but if it weren't crimson and the eyes not glazed and swollen like a drowned person's, they very soon were, for I can remember neither the face nor the eyes looking any other way.

"It is difficult," she began, in a voice normal and level, but with the lower lip, I remember, already beginning to quiver. "It is difficult for me to tell you how I'm getting along under the Occupation. You see—" and promptly, like a pricked balloon, all the life that was in the meager dress, under the ancient cloche hat, seemed to collapse. Only the arms—like a drowning person's arms as they quickly rise before disappearing for the last time—came up to hold the dropped head, while the words gurgled out as from a body saturated in water. "Oh, I'm sorry and ashamed, I really am! But, you see, all my men—all I still had to live for—my husband, my boys, my husband's brothers and all their boys—all my men, you see—are killed-or-missing. . . ." Then, "Killed-or-missing," she repeated several times, like a chant, like a chant that had stamped itself indelibly and forever on her brain from having seen it too often in the newspapers or in the dreaded official telegrams.

Well, what do you do and say, you damned Gallup-poller you, with your fatuous *Fragebogen,* its questions about prices and taxes, about wartime domestic problems, the military and political leaders already dead or jailed, about what plans she and her family have for the future, that charming rosy little Hell called the future? What do you do and say with all that Galluping nonsense on the table to be answered, and across the table the forlorn life with nothing to live for, and not the courage to take it because as long as the heart goes on beating life is dear, or because someone said long ago that this in the eyes of Almighty God is the Greatest Sin? What do you do and say, you who are no physician or priest or psychoanalyst, but a human worm with a full stomach and a wife and home and future and friends next door and a nervous system like a coil of taut and quivering copper wire? What do you do and say?

I once summoned up the courage to ask a tough, square-faced sergeant that, after he'd been knocking what he called "the bullshit out a crying Kraut." I asked not because I knew he was a "psychologist" by profession, but because I knew he was a different kind of a worm and I wanted to try and learn a lesson. "What did I say?" he said, as though what he said was all there was to be said. " 'Why!' I said: 'Madam,' I said, 'you better quit that blubbering quick. We gotta long way to go yet and they ain't gonna keep my dinner warm on accounta you!' That's what I said, and Jesus, was my dinner cold? No, siree!"

For a split second I envied that particular square-faced worm. But he didn't teach me any lesson.

So what did the worm with the coil of quivering copper wire inside him say? He said nothing for a while—just looked the other way and let the tears flow. He'd done that and seen and heard them flowing, God knows, often enough by now. It was nothing new, just one more out of all the millions. But one more doesn't help, doesn't make some worms any wiser.

Then, when silence fell and the wretched soiled handkerchief was a small sponge, I said, taking the chance which didn't always work, "You say all your men are killed or missing?"

"*Ja,*" she murmured, her eyes floating in the scarlet face. "Killed-or-missing, killed-or-missing. Every day now I go down to meet the prisoner cars, but every time I go I know none of them will be there."

Then I said it very quick: "Do-you-have-any-other-children?"

It worked!

The eyes overflowed afresh, but the lips parted in a smile, a pitiful ghost of a smile.

"*Ja,*" she said, "I've a daughter and—and a granddaughter—"

"Well," I said, "that—"

But she cut me short and suddenly the whole face changed. The lips snapped shut, the limp hand became a fist and it crashed down on the table as she growled out with eyes ablaze, "And do you know what those damned swine did to her, to my daughter? This is what they did! They threw her in jail and kept her there four months. And do you know why? Because she bought stolen *Schmalz* when her child, her three-year-old child was starving! She didn't know the *Schmalz* was stolen! She swore and I swear she didn't know it was stolen, and she didn't know! And the swine threw her into jail and the child into a damned Nazi *Kinderheim!—Herr Hauptmann!*"—the body was upright now and the swollen eyes dry and blazing—"*Herr Hauptmann,* I loathe the Nazis with a hatred I didn't know was in me. They screamed *Nie Wieder Krieg!*—No More War! And they swiped everything from us, starved us, and killed all our men, killed all our men!"

"You said you had nothing to live for," I said. "If what you say is true—"

"True!" she burst out, banging the table. "Is it possible the *Herr* doubts my word, that what I say are fabrications? I am an Austrian, and do you think I think it's a lie that the S.S. hanged Austrian soldiers in the Austrian streets three weeks before the Americans came in? Can I think such things are lies after what I've seen with my own eyes as a waitress here in that Gasthaus, where night after night we prayed and prayed for you to hurry, hurry—before in their last madness they not only blew up all the bridges (which they did), but also strung up all the innocent people here to lampposts! Ha, the innocent people! I don't think only of the decent Germans and Austrians. I can still hear the cries of the Hungarians and the Czechs and all the other foreigners who came to my window at night because they knew I was a waitress and dealt all day with some kind of food—I can still hear their cries in the night—*Hunger! Hunger! Hunger!* —never any other word because that was the only German word they knew or needed to know! True? The truth, *mein Gott*—"

"I believe you," I said, and I did; and because I did, I said, "But don't say you haven't got anything to live for. People like you will be needed. . . ."

That was a sincere but unfortunate remark, for she looked up, gave a ghost of a smile, then burst into a fresh flood of tears. "Me needed!" she sobbed. "Me needed!" as though the idea were a revelation.

And she clasped her red, chapped hands together and right there at the table in the bare room with the copper quivering inside the worm in front of her, she began silently to pray.

But they didn't all weep in that bare room. No, they certainly didn't all weep. There was one I didn't think ever had or could.

THE RED CROSS NURSE

She marched into the room.

Her manner and what she began by saying were so unusual that it never occurred to me to ask what the hell she was still wearing that gray Red Cross uniform for. Maybe she was entitled to. I really don't know. Anyway, it was good to think she'd never lean over my sickbed.

She was forty-five years old and unmarried. Before the war she'd been a music teacher and singer. That seemed so unlikely that you had to believe it. It was difficult to associate that bitter, genderless mask, the unflinching steel eyes, cruel lipless mouth with its frustrated, unhappy corner-creases—difficult to associate all that with music. And it was difficult to hear the emotionless, military voice clipping out the cold words and imagine that voice ever having burst into any song, except maybe the *Horst Wessel Lied* with a million others at the Stadium at Nürnberg. But whatever that woman was I'm pretty sure she wasn't a liar.

I altered the opening question a little, because when I asked it the way it was written I got nothing but a glum, insolent stare. So I asked her if she were satisfied with the way things were going under the Occupation. That did it.

"Satisfied?" she snapped, sitting up straight in her chair like a soldier on trial. "Satisfied? How could I be satisfied when Germany has lost the war? And the future as black as it is! I don't believe you Americans 'll stay here long. You won't be able to prevent the Russians from moving in, slowly, bit by bit. I hear they already have their eyes on Hamburg. You'll quit the country before long.

"What did I expect when the Americans came in? Not much. Or I might say I waited for you to annihilate the German people, as you were always saying you were going to do in your papers and leaflets. Where did I see these papers? In France and Holland where I spent most of the war. I don't know how they got there; I don't know the exact words, but that was more or less what they said. I'm also expecting you to draw up another Versailles Treaty, another League of Nations. The Versailles Treaty was the cause of this war."

"I didn't ask your opinion on that," I found myself saying, and I knew immediately I was getting sore and shouldn't have spoken. So I smiled sardonically in her face, and she pressed her lips together and if she'd been a rattlesnake she'd have struck. Keep that smile, I said to myself, it's the only good weapon you've got.

"How do I think I'd have got along during the next few years if Germany had won the war? Ha, mighty well, of course. It's fine for people who've won a war. *Bitte?* Wasn't fine for the English after the last war? Oh, well, the English didn't have a decent government! We had a good one here at last. It was doing wonderful things for the German people before this war broke out."

At this I let the smile break into a short guffaw, and asked, without thinking, a pointless question. *"Bitte?* No, I don't say it would have gone on for a thousand years. You don't have to be as literal as that. No one can see that far ahead. But it would have gone on for a long time.

"Chief reason why Germany lost the war? There were many reasons. Chief one was American superiority in the air, American production. America came into the war for purely selfish reasons."

This time I watched the smile make the fingers curl up like a nest of baby snakes in her lap.

"The military and political leadership? I felt very positive about both. Some leaders didn't do their duty—but only some. *Bitte?* Yes, I certainly think the idea of National Socialism a good one, very good. Communism? Ha, that's not the same thing at all. In the long run Communism is bound to fail because it tries to make all people the same, and all people are not the same. The Jews? Most Jews, as you know, fought against National Socialism, and in wartime that cannot be tolerated. *Bitte?* No, I don't say they should have been treated as they were, but the Race Question is important—especially here in Germany, where the great majority of people are of one blood. Those who are not of that blood cannot be expected to fight for those that are. The Jewish problem, however, is a great problem everywhere. You should know: you live in America. . . .

"I can't talk at first-hand about domestic problems, as I was abroad. But I do know that the problem of food was magnificently handled. And there was hardly any black market. You should have seen France! *Bitte?* No, the Germans couldn't control it there. Why? Because there were too many French and too few Germans!"

You couldn't see the baby snakes any more; they were doubled up into hard fists with the knuckles shining yellow through the taut skin.

"What did I think about? I kept thinking what the war was costing us, about the size of Germany, the size of Russia, and then France on the other side—after the Invasion, I mean. *Bitte?* No, I'm convinced we didn't declare war on Russia without very good reasons indeed. If we'd concentrated on trying to knock out England, then Russia would most certainly have stabbed us in the back.

"No, I don't think it would have been at all a good idea to have accepted Unconditional Surrender after July 20th. In fact, I thought we had a very good chance of winning after that date. How? With new weapons—not necessarily V-weapons as we knew them, but with some airplane which I always felt was in the making.

"Me take time off from work!" she exclaimed, as though stunned by the insult. *"Never!"*

I shrugged my shoulders as if I thought there were some sense in asking that of a German, even in peacetime. "Why not?" I smiled.

The eyes flared as she snapped, "Because the idea never entered my head!"

"Did I blame the Allies for the air-raids! Ha! Why, naturally! We never once raided America. England? England started them! England—"

"England started the air-raids?" I repeated, dropping the smile now and barely asking a question. "England started the bombing of open cities and villages? England, I suppose, started that before the Germans flattened Guernica in—"

"I don't know anything about Guernica and—"

"No, of course, you wouldn't."

"I know England started the air warfare against Germany by bombing Freiburg and Karlsruhe in 1940, in May, 1940, and—"

"And Germany, of course," I said, managing the smile again, "bombed Warsaw and Rotterdam in 1941—and of course Germany never declared war on England!"

"Of course not!" she declared, while I held my pencil still over the paper and stared—no doubt with my mouth agape—into the snake's steel eyes. "Of course not, the English declared war on us!"

"Well, well," I said. "That's very interesting. Just why did England declare war on Germany?"

"Why? Why? How would I know? *Aus Feindschaft gegen uns!*—From hatred of us, I suppose!"

I let the laugh out and said, "Did you ever listen to the Allied radio?"

The "Never!" was spat out like venom striking tin.

"Never?"

"Never, I said!"

"Oh, well," I said calmly, smiling. "Oh, well, that explains a lot!"

I was surprised some sound didn't come out of the straight thin line between the chin and nose, for the clenched fists went up to her temples and she looked as though she were about to spring or burst, or both.

I turned to the face-sheet, to fill in the personal details, and instead of inquiring what kind of education she'd had, I felt mean enough to fling a small dart.

"Did you," I asked, "ever go to a school?"

It fell flat in the middle of the table.

"Volksschule!" she snapped.

"Religion?"

"Gott-Gläubige!" *

*"Gott-*what?"

"Gott-Gläubige."

She was the first one I'd had, but I couldn't afford to ask the question I wanted to, which riled me and maybe helped me to load a heavier dart and ask her again one or two things I already knew.

"Were you a member of the Nazi Party?"

"Nein!"

"Nein?"

"I said *Nein!*" she barked. "I'm a Red Cross nurse!"

"Of course!" I acted. "I keep forgetting!"

It fell flat. But I had another, my last.

"And you said you were how old?"

"Forty-five!"

* Believing in God; Non-Confessional.

"And—and—not—married?"

"*Nein!*"

"And no children?"

"I-said-I-was-not-married!"

"I heard you," I said, smiling. "Maybe that, too, explains a lot!"

It swept across the table, and it stuck!

I can't say the snake wept, but its whole body coiled taut in just-controlled rage, and the steel eyes were screwed up and they were not dry in the hard, flushed, bitter mask.

THE S.S.

There can be little doubt that the fear the Germans expressed for the Russians in the summer of 1945 was caused far less by the years of Goebbels' anti-Bolshevist propaganda (which, after 1942, must have been superfluous) than by guilt for the behavior of the S.S. towards the Russian population and Russian prisoners. Not even the Gestapo could gag the mouths of hundreds of thousands of sickened German soldiers on furlough from the Eastern front. The stories they had to tell may have been told in whispers, but behind the whispering was not the fear of the Gestapo-man's ear, rather the thought of what would happen to Germans if and when Soviet troops entered Germany. Those who shuddered at stories of Russian raping and looting and murdering in Berlin should have heard what German veterans had to say of the atrocities committed by their own countrymen on Soviet soil. The same fear, to a lesser degree, haunted Germans who had fought in France.

In Kempten I interviewed a veteran who had spent four years on the two fronts as a medic. He was a Münchner, a one-time shoemaker, aged thirty-seven, who'd married a girl from the Allgäu.

"We were scared of Bavaria being occupied either by the

French or the Russians," he said, and you could still see the *Angst* in his eyes as he said it. "On the Russian front the S.S. took no prisoners. Naturally I feared reprisals for such horrors. We heard the Russians did the same, but I could never prove the truth of this. I was in France—near Gap, at Marseilles and Grenoble. There, things were different. A command came out: Anyone committing any form of atrocity against the French would be shot as an example. Well, commands don't come out for nothing—and I saw a lot of things happen in France which many Germans would not like to hear about."

Even so, this veteran had been "terrified that Germany might win the war—because I loathed being a soldier, and if Germany had won they'd have kept me in the army at least another four or five years. As a soldier I was treated even worse than if I'd been a civilian. I was very seriously wounded; my wife lost everything when she was bombed out of our home in Munich. My nerves were in a frightful condition from both the war and the raids. Yet, on furlough, when I tried to get help from the military to set up some kind of room for my wife to live in, they said, 'You're a soldier. Your home may be destroyed, but you're still a soldier—and soldiers don't need homes."

This man, incidentally, was one of the two or three who swore that Munich (where he was living at the time) had been bombed during the second week of the war—"on the 8th, 9th, or 10th of September, 1939," he said. "The planes were French and there were only three or four of them. We prayed they'd hit the Shit House—"

"The what?"

"The *Haus der Deutschen Kunst*," he said, smiling. "That's what we Münchners used to call that blot on the face of Munich."

Like many Bavarians, he blamed the Prussians for the war —"Prussian sword-rattling," as he called it. "We Bavarians," he said as he left, "we would prefer to be united with the French than with the Prussians. We and the French have quite a lot in common; we're civilized and we hate militarism."

An hour later, by an odd coincidence (since, as I've said, we were not supposed to interview ex-soldiers), in limped not only a Prussian but a veteran who had also fought on the Russian front.

He was fifty years old—a dark, swarthy, red-faced individual with a long nose—and one of the first things he said was: "In Russia, the S.S. swore that if Germany lost, we Wehrmacht soldiers would be deported to Russia as slave-laborers. Well, we knew what that would mean. . . . Down here in the Allgäu, the S.S. swore that Bavaria would be occupied by Moroccan troops. We thought we knew what that, too, would mean. . . .

"The soldiers didn't lose the war," he said bitterly. "It was the leadership, and particularly the S.S. They ruined our morale. I was in the Wehrmacht since '38. It was not long before I started trying to quit—promotion, everything was just one big racket [*Schiebung*]. But you couldn't get out. In 1941 I was badly wounded, near St. Petersburg [*sic*] and had to have my right leg amputated. (He pulled up his trousers and showed me a hideous bright pink shiny limb.) I spent six months in various field hospitals in Russia. When I was invalided home I tried once again to get a discharge. Instead, they sent me back to the Russian front with my wooden leg, at the age of forty-eight. On the way I passed through Elbing, my home town, and there were the healthy unwounded S.S. wandering round the streets. In Russia, whenever we in the Wehrmacht captured prisoners, the S.S. took them over from us and shot them. The S.S. had everything—all the food they wanted and the best, the warmest clothes. They got mad drunk and raped the Russian women and ruined our morale. While we watched this kind of thing going on, we heard from home that German women with one child and a husband at the front (that was me!) were being ordered to sleep with other men, and so increase the German population. That was the Führer's *Schweinerei* and it ruined our morale. So did the speeches in which Hitler, Goering, Himmler, and Gauleiters Koch and Giesler swore that every German village would be defended to the last man. We had seen what that meant. Ha! But what did they do? Here in Kempten, Bürgermeister Brändler—that drunk who used to go round boasting of the thousands of Bavarian women he'd had—at the last minute he ordered the S.S. to blow up all the bridges, not to stop the Americans getting in, but the population from getting out! Then brave Herr Brändler pulled off his uniform and tried to escape in priest's clothes. But they got him—the people of Kempten got him and bound him and stuck him on a wagon, drove him round the town and pelted him with stones! Then the Americans came in, the S.S. disappeared, the Nazi bigshots and the *Hilfspolizei,* they tore off their insignia, burned the records and put white flags out of their windows— the brave boys! And where are they now? Most of them are sitting right here, in the best apartments, helping the Americans to occupy and keep order. Brändler's adjutant is among them. I saw him the other day, wandering around. He lives in his own apartment, while we refugees—my wife, myself, and our child—live in an unheated attic. . . .

"You know what the people said to us when we arrived here in March and asked for a bed? You know what they said, after our two months' trip across all Germany, after escaping from the Russians in a speedboat to Swinemünde, after eight days and nights in a cattle truck and three nights in the open with the temperature at zero, after my wife had lost all her teeth from exposure and undernourishment and our child was, and still is, a nervous wreck from bombardment—you know what they said to us? They said, 'Get out, you swine from East Prussia, you can damn well bring your own beds!' "

He got up and limped towards the door. Then he turned round, and in a low, confidential voice he said, "You know, if only I could get some of my savings out of East Prussia, I really think I'd start a little farm here. I'm not a farmer, of course—I'm an electrical engineer—but that wouldn't matter because, you know, these people here are so damned lazy, they have so little idea about agriculture, I'm sure I could double their production in a year or two. But there!" said the man who had survived starvation, the Russians, and the war, whose wife and child were miraculously alive. "But there!" he said, spreading his hands. "How can I get my savings? How can I get the savings?"

THE CHEESE FACTORY

I don't remember whose idea it was, or why he should have been so intent on our visiting the cheese factory. Very likely it was the Major, poor devil, in desperate search of distraction. He could hardly have been in search of cheese, for the house had reeked of it since our arrival, and the only grudge I bore Hans was that he almost ruined my taste for Camembert by *cooking* it, in a good ripe state, in powdered egg! We ate cheese, indeed, in one form or another, at every meal, sometimes at the beginning, sometimes at the end, often at both. And I'd just spent one whole morning interviewing the managers of two cheese factories. God, they were bores! Their cheese was *ausgezeichnet, fabelhaft!* I must taste it, eat it, take some home, send a box to America! And they were wonderful managers: I must come and see for myself! Their factories had interrupted work only one day throughout the war, and that was the day the Americans came in and they all went out to celebrate! Their workers, those loyal and devoted souls, they had remained on after the Americans came in. What did I think of that? I didn't think much of that. But *lieber Herr,* it was *wunderbar!* They employed Letts and Poles and even Russians, all of whom wanted, nay, begged to stay on—"because they like us so!" Oh, no, the managers never had any trouble in their factories. . . .

Well, I had no doubt a Kempten cheese factory must be a wonderful place, a real democratic institution, but I had no desire to see one. I was fed up, literally, with cheese. And anyway I'd worked once, years ago, in an English cheese factory and I hadn't thought it so hot. I hadn't liked the smell of sour milk and all the other smells before a cheese becomes a cheese, and everything was too hygienic, too clean. No, give me a cow with its This-is-the-End-of-the-World look in its bleary eye, but not a shiny, sour-smelling creamery with all the men looking like tough male nurses.

But the Major didn't think that way. Nor, it seemed, did anyone else, except maybe Mervyn. They all thought, or pretended they thought it was a wonderful idea, and by the time we set out for the factory the team for once had developed a kind of team spirit, like college girls out for a Sunday excursion to the seaside, and it began to rain and I drove slowly behind Mervyn and sulked as I always did at school when the term ended and everyone scrambled into the train and lit cigarettes and unrolled the toilet-paper out of the window and began to howl:

> *"Pack up yer troubles*
> *In yer old kit-baaag!*
> *And smile—smile—smile!"*

On a hill outside Kempten we passed a sight that would have delighted the eye of Degas and Guys in their day, and that of the Polish artist, Felix Topolski, in ours. It so delighted us that for a moment Cheese was forgotten and we smiled and stared and went on smiling. It was a landau with the hood up. High up on the "box" sat a coachman in an old top-hat, his long whip out over the bony bay mare; and behind, leaning back under cover of the hood, Monsieur (impossible to call him *Herr, Herr Baron,* or even *Graf*) with leather motoring goggles under a *chapeau sportif;* and Madame, a bundle half-smothered in an *imperméable,* a wide-brimmed hat flattened down over her ears by a mud-colored motoring veil and tied beneath a vague promontory that must have been Madame's chin.

"The factory owners," I muttered, "taking their constitutional."

The idea had simply flashed in and out of my head, but—believe it or not!—I was right!

We'd been standing around—as people always do when no one takes the initiative—standing around the factory yard in the drizzling rain for several minutes, staring and being stared at by G.I.s who were occupying the large red-brick private house, when there came a jingle-jangle of a bell, the clip-clop of a horse, and into the yard drove Monsieur and Madame Fromage.

A man came out of the house opposite. Raising his right hand, he took the black-gloved fingers of Madame, who, lifting her veil an inch or two, placed a pointed black toe on the carriage step, lowered herself gingerly into the dung of the yard, and, clutching at her long skirt, quickly tripped away.

Monsieur, in his Burberry and green cardigan underneath, his spotted bow tie, and liverish yellow face, looked and behaved like the Spanish Duke who buys his breeches in Savile Row, and can ride his Arab stallion all the way from Madrid to Portugal on his own land. Lifting a silver-topped cane he uttered a curt command, whereupon a man in a white coat appeared, clicked his heels, turned about, and we filed behind him, all seven of us, through a door and into the building of milk-cans, churns, clean wet concrete floors, and dank, sour smells.

The door closed behind Monsieur, then as quickly swung open again to let in a short, youngish, ill-looking man with strands of black hair falling over a jaundiced brow. He seemed breathless, disheveled, and he was still arranging his tie as though he had just got out of bed.

"My son," said Monsieur Fromage, leaning slightly back, half-closing his black eyes as he gazed down at the younger man with a proud if somewhat supercilious air. "My son," he said. "He will conduct."

Oh, God, I thought, a regular Cook's Tour of Cheese!

"I must be excused for being so late," panted the son, shaking my hand. "I have not been well. I—"

"Pneumonia," muttered Papa, raising his silver-knobbed

cane and brandishing it like a sword at an enormous barrel. "Pneumonia."

"Excuse me," breathed the son, and ran off to the head of the line to "conduct" the tour.

"That," said Papa to me, aiming the cane at a small round hole in the barrel as though he were a torero and the barrel the head of a bull. "That is the only one of its kind in the country!"

"*So?*" I said. "What is it?" pretending I hadn't guessed the huge *Fass* to be a churn.

"Churn," he said, "churn. There may be none other like it in the world. It dispenses with labor and can turn milk to butter in a single process, straight from the animal."

"Good God!" I muttered, genuinely impressed. "In my time," I said, like an old retired milkman, "in my time, it took three days for the cream—"

"You a farmer?" he interrupted, the supercilious tone in his voice suddenly gone.

"No," I said, "I'm not. But I've worked on farms. I'm interested more in animals than machines."

"Animals! Ha!" he exclaimed, cupping my elbow in his palm. "Come and see my cattle."

"Thank you," I said to him, and to myself: Thank God!

The cow-stalls were in a field across the road, and they were any farmer's dream: a long brick building, with a line of a dozen cows separated from another dozen by white-tiled troughs, and at the side of each trough, like a huge cake of soap above a bathtub, a salt-lick for each animal. Strips of gluey fly-catching tape hung from the beams, and the cows— magnificent Tyrolean beasts, a little like Guernseys, with smooth silky coats the color of Siamese cats, velvet faces, flapping ears as soft and brown as a bulrush—the cows, they turned their heads to the clink of the chain round their dew-lapped necks, and with their great mournful eyes, a flick of the long tail and a momentary stillness of the jaws, they warned you of what, since the Beginning of Time, they had been waiting for, which was The End of the World.

I stared at them, inhaling the wonderful smell of milk and cow-breath, hay and fresh dung, and felt, as I so often do on a farm, that maybe I had, after all, mischosen my profession.

"They look strangely like Guernseys," I said at last, for something to say.

"Guernseys!" exclaimed Monsieur Fromage, the Lord of the Manor, the Gentleman Farmer, as he revealed two rows of discolored teeth in his first smile. "Like Guernseys, my friend! They should. In the old days the farm was never without a Guernsey bull."

So we talked shop for a while, exchanging opinions about Jersey, Guernsey, Hereford, Friesland, and Tyrolean cattle, about grazing, crops, sunflowers (as the best milk-producing fodder); about tubercular cows, foot-and-mouth disease, and artificial manures—until finally he waved his cane, cupped my elbow in his palm as I'd so often seen my parents do to horse-lovers in the stables at Bective, and conducted me out of the cow-stalls and into the fields.

I thought at first I'd *imagined* the neigh, the almost human, feminine, gentle whinny—but no, for when we'd climbed over a style and dropped into one of those short-cropped, daisy-dotted meadows that always remind me of mushrooms and September, there she was—a bright chestnut mare trotting fast but lame over the field, her ears cocked, eyes wide, snorting through her red, extended nostrils. Stopping abruptly short of us, she grunted, then stretched out the graceful head on its long, well-bred neck with the gesture of a giraffe through the railings of a zoo. I watched Monsieur bend down, snatch a tuft of grass and push it, on the flat of his palm, between the quickly nibbling velvet lips.

"*Nein,* no sugar, Dub!" he muttered. "No carrots! Just grass for your old age!"

"She's not quite sound, is she," I remarked, "on her off-fore?" And wondered if my German for that expression could be correct.

"Ha!" he snapped. "She wouldn't be here if she were!" Then he turned on me and a scowl made a wrinkled havoc of his jaundiced face. "Those swine took the lot!" he growled. "And left her, not because she's old—others were older—but because of that splint in her off-fore!"

"Has she been fired?" I asked, and wondered how he could possibly understand my German for that.

He did, though, for he looked at me, with all the wrinkles gone, and instead of them displayed again in an enthusiastic smile the uneven rows of black teeth.

"Can it be," he inquired, "that you are a horseman, too?"

"Well, no," I replied, "I'm not. But I used to be."

"In Virginia, perhaps?"

"No. Mostly in Ireland."

He threw up his arms (so that the mare took fright and stampeded away) and exclaimed, "Ireland! But that—" he waved his cane in the direction of the retreating animal—"that's where I bought her, where she was born and bred."

"Me, too," I said.

"So was!" he exclaimed, and somehow that hackneyed German phrase did not seem appropriate to the Latin-looking face.

"That's why I nicknamed her Dub," he said, "because I bought her in the Dublin Horse Show, from a breeder who used to live in Meath [he failed, of course, to pronounce the aspirate] not far from the city."

"Me, too," I said, but I did not show surprise, for I'd always believed what a wizened old Irish ex-jockey once told me. "When yez out in the Big World," he said, "and yer eye lights on Black Beauty—the short straight back, bold broad shoulder, the 'ristercratic head—stick up yer hand, me boyo, and keep it up, for ye can bet yer bottom dollar he'll be from th' Ould Counthry, and ten quid to two from the County Meath!" He spat. "Pull out yer pockut, then," he'd added, "the blood o' Black Beauty 'll soon fill it again!"

I tried to put that into German for Monsieur Fromage, but his surprise and excitement had transported him into a world habitable for and comprehensible to only lovers of horse-flesh; so instead of him listening to my little story I walked slowly across the field with him, listening to his longer stories of travels in search of the Best Blood, of pedigree mares and stallions from which, by crossing and recrossing their progeny, he might breed the Perfect Breed. Anyone overhearing this monologue might well imagine he'd been listening to a man who, with The Blue Book in one hand and the Almanac of Gotha in the other, was making a desperate effort to disentangle the complicated relations between the royal families of Old Europe. Or, were the eavesdropper of a tenderer age and Teutonic, he might more readily assume that, at the oft-repeated *Blut* and not-infrequent *Boden*, the aging German civilian was instructing the American "soldier" in a lesson which he, the blond *Pimpf*, had begun to learn on the day he had been picked from the cradle and layed across his mother's broad knee.

I found, I must confess, Monsieur's studbook theories extremely tedious—a horse, after all, is a horse, however long its nose! He, on the other hand, had found a foreigner who could speak and understand, however imperfectly, his "lingo," and I felt, by the time we sniffed the cheese again, that had it not been for the insignia on my uniform and that particular decade in history—I felt that Monsieur Fromage would have insisted on mounting me on his charger of the very bluest blood, girthed it with his most sumptuous Garadice saddle and led me off at a Balaclava gallop, if not to Portugal, at least from *Käse*-reeking Kempten, across the plains to the Prince of Kirchheim—had Monsieur but the faintest notion I knew him.

I entered the factory—to the sour smells, the milk-cans clanging on the concrete, the churns churning, the hairy-armed, white-coated men banging boxes about—I entered the sour house of uproar a little guiltily, to find what I'd been afraid I'd find: the team, that so recently gay group, on its "last legs."

Monsieur Fromage Jeune, the invalid, the sweat standing out in beads on his pasty face, was still "conducting" (in a churn-like voice inaudible above the din) to an audience in that state to which children fall when it's long past their bedtime. Dudley was prodding Frank's behind, while Frank was trying, in vain, to smother his "Ouch's" and giggles by biting hard on the scabbard of his bayonet. The Professor had wandered off in search, so it seemed, of smells even sourer than could be encountered standing up: all that could be seen of him were his hind-quarters, for the upper half of his stalwart frame—head, helmet, shoulders—was deep inside a barrel. John had simply surrendered: with his face in his hands and his eyes closed, he was more sensibly squatting, half-asleep, on a milkman's stool. Only the Major, poor devil, as is the fate and price of rank, stood steadfastly beside the "conductor," making a most courageous attempt to pretend to be listening (with barely a word of German) to the voice which droned on monotonously to the roar of machinery and churns. But even he, I observed, would look up now and again to wink, concealing the accompanying grin behind a hand. I couldn't discover, at first, for whom these winks and smothered smiles were meant, so I moved forward, the now somewhat deflated Monsieur Fromage still at my side, and there, down a dark corridor lined with shelves of ripening cheeses, I saw Mervyn, moving slowly, quietly, intently along, digging his forefinger into one after the other of the rows upon rows of Camembert. After each dig, he pulled the finger out, eyed it with interest, then popped it in his mouth.

I watched him for a minute, a handkerchief stuffed between my jaws, until finally he reached the end of the corridor, where he leaned his crossed arms against a shelf, placed his forehead on the soft circular cushion of a cheese, opened his mouth wide and let out a prolonged, exhausted sigh.

Then he glanced up and saw me. He came striding down the corridor.

"My God!" he almost hissed. "Where *have* you been?"

I jerked my head in the direction of Monsieur Fromage who, incredibly, gave the impression of being engrossed in the monologue of his perspiring son.

"But do you realize," Mervyn exclaimed, "do you realize we've been in this stinking hole two whole *hours!*"

Seeing my inability to speak, Mervyn turned from me to the Major, and because, for once, the Major could understand and Fromage Junior couldn't, said aloud, "Major, for God's sake, now that we're all here, let's get out of this smelly place!"

"Perfectly okay," the Major agreed, his eyes wide with relief, and nodding towards Fromage Junior, asked Mervyn: "Will you, for the love of God, give the victrola the works?"

So Fromage Jeune was given "the works" and, wiping his brow, switched off his droning as though he really were the leader of a Cook's tour or even a non-stop victrola. And with the command given, the Professor's helmeted head rose to the surface of the barrel; Dudley and Frank bit their lips and displayed, in place of grins, their politest party-leaving smiles; John, regaining consciousness with an audible yawn, stretched his legs and staggered from his stool; while Mervyn and the Major, approaching in leader-like fashion Monsieur Fromage, hummed and hawed until Mervyn, with a commendable attempt at a German ambassadorial bow, finally lied in a loud voice, "It's been awfully interesting, *Herr*—!"

But the Lord of the Manor saved him the embarrassment of mumbling-tumbling over the unknown name by raising his cane ceilingwards and in strident tones—to an audience, for once, of fourteen open ears—exclaiming, *"Meine Herr'n,* upstairs in our humble quarters a meal of cheese and wine awaits you—a meal of cheese and wine!"

For an instant there fell a hollow, horrifying silence, then a long drawn-out "Aaaah!"—an "Ah" of as forced a show of enthusiasm as can ever have been extracted from seven bored, bewildered men.

Mervyn caught my eye. *"Wine!"* he whispered.

"Cheese!" I choked.

So up we filed, Junior still conducting, Papa bringing up the rear, up a rough wooden staircase, and into a kind of loft.

"This," said Monsieur to me, brandishing his cane at two seemingly endless lines of clothes drooping from hangers on a couple of poles, "this until recently was our store-room, a delightful drafty place for cheese. Now, as you will observe, it is our home. Now it is our home."

Well, it was certainly a strange home. It was a great loft consisting mainly, so far as I could see, of clothes and women and children.

"And this," cried Monsieur, ignoring the clothes and pointing to a long trestle laden with plates of cheese and bottles, round which children ran and shouted, and young women, middle-aged women, old women sat and talked and knitted, "this," he cried, "this is the family—the family that survives!"

"All one family?" I gasped, staring at the sea of faces: the girls, the women, children, babies.

"In one way or another," Monsieur replied. "In the dormitory at the other end we sleep twenty-five." Then he left me stranded while everyone else sat down and he went off to the head of the table. "Just like horses," he called from there. "A mixed breed—like horses—from all over Europe!" he said, and seated himself in a high-backed chair.

Those were the last words I had with Monsieur before our farewell, for the table was of great length and I found myself far from him, between his son and the Major, faced by a whole sliced Camembert, some salt, celery, a couple of radishes, and a tall, labelless bottle of wine. I was staring at that bottle with—even for me—a rare thirst, when Junior's hand went round it and he asked: "You like wine?"

"Passionately," I breathed.

Then he did something which endeared me for the remainder of the day to that ill-looking man. He swopped my glass, which was little more than a large thimble, for his, which was a tumbler, and he filled it to the brim.

"It's only *Heurigen*—this year's wine," he said. "The swine swiped the rest."

"It's wine," I said. *"Prost!"* And swallowed the tumblerful in two gulps.

"Cheese without wine . . ." he said in German, pouring me out some more.

" *'Un repas sans vin . . . !"* I said.

"'... *est comme un jour sans soleil!*'" he finished in perfect French, and added, smiling, "You know, that's pretty near to poetry!"

"It is," I agreed, eating some cheese and polishing off the wine.

"During the war," he said, emptying the bottle into my glass, "I lived on poetry. I don't know what I'd have done without it."

I stared at him, at the pale, sweating face, the jaundiced eye of the man who had droned away all afternoon like the leader of a Cook's tour, and perhaps because he thought I hadn't quite believed his professed passion for literature, he asked: "Do you like poetry?"

I said I did.

"D'you know the most famous poem in Germany today?" he asked.

"The most famous poem?" I repeated. "No, I guess not."

"Don't you recognize these lines:

> *"Ein Ungeziefer ruht* *
> *In Staub und trocknem Schlamme*
> *Verborgen, wie die Flamme*
> *In leichter Asche tut* . . . ?"

"No," I said, "I'm afraid—"

> *Ein Regen, Windeshauch*
> *Erweckt das schlimme Leben,*
> *Und aus dem Nichts erheben*
> *Sich Seuchen, Glut und Rauch.*

"Who—?" I began, but before I could finish the question, he was off again, and had barely recited the second verse when a hush fell over the table: the women's knitting needles ceased their clicking, the children stopped their romping, even the babies only breathed; and in the church-like silence of the enormous room the Americans and the Germans listened to the most famous poem in the destroyed, defeated land.

*See end papers for literal translation.

*Aus dunkler Höhle fährt
Ein Schächer, um zu schweifen;
Nach Beuteln möcht' er greifen
Und findet bessern Wert:
Er findet einen Streit
Um nichts, ein irres Wissen,
Ein Banner, das zerrissen,
Ein Volk in Blödigkeit.*

*Er findet, wo er geht,
Die Leere dürft'ger Zeiten,
Da kann er schamlos schreiten,
Nun wird er ein Prophet;
Auf einen Kehricht stellt
Er seine Schelmenfüsse
Und zischelt seine Grüsse
In die verblüffte Welt.*

*Gehüllt in Niedertracht
Gleichwie in einer Wolke,
Ein Lügner vor dem Volke,
Ragt bald er gross an Macht
Mit seiner Helfer Zahl,
Die hoch, und niedrig stehend,
Gelegenheit erspähend,
Sich bieten seiner Wahl.*

*Sie teilen aus sein Wort,
Wie einst die Gottesboten
Getan mit den fünf Broten,
Das klecket fort und fort!
Erst log allein der Hund,
Nun lügen ihrer tausend;
Und wie ein Sturm erbrausend,
So wuchert jetzt sein Pfund.*

*Hoch schiesst empor die Saat,
Verwandelt sind die Lande,
Die Menge lebt in Schande
Und lacht der Schofeltat!
Jetzt hat sich auch erwahrt,
Was erstlich war erfunden:
Die Guten sind verschwunden,
Die Schlechten stehn geschart!*

*Wenn einstmals diese Not
Lang wie ein Eis gebrochen,
Dann wird davon gesprochen,
Wie von dem schwarzen Tod;
Und einen Strohmann baun
Die Kinder auf der Heide,
Zu brennen Lust aus Leide
Und Licht aus altem Graun.*

He, the factory owner's son, had recited by heart the whole extraordinary poem from start to finish, never once at a loss for line or word. When it ended and the reciter sat back and wiped his brow, there followed a silence all the more intense for the fact that now his voice was still and, for several seconds, the room was without sound.

Then Mervyn, the poet, leaned across the table and said in a strained, excited voice: "So Germany has a modern poet! Do tell us who he is!"

"You don't know?" asked Junior, smiling, glancing at me and across the table at Mervyn again.

We shook our heads.

"I thought you might know," Junior said, "because we often heard the poem quoted on the radio."

"But we didn't listen to the German radio," I said, "and certainly not to the German Underground."

"Ah," said Junior, smiling, "we heard it quoted not only by our underground, but by the Allies—that is, by the BBC, and the voice we heard was that of Mr. Winston Churchill—!"

"What's that he's saying about Churchill?" snapped the Major, poor devil, snatching at the one comprehensible word.

So I told the Major what it was all about, and he said: "Well, fer Christ sakes!" and Junior was telling seven astounded Americans that the poem he'd just recited was called *Die Öffentlichen Verleumder,* and that it had been written, not recently, but some sixty-odd years ago by the poet Gottfried Keller!

"Even the children know it," Junior said to me. *"Nicht wahr,* Noémi?" he asked of a beautiful blond child who'd suddenly presented herself at the table between Junior and me. *"Sag', Noémi, how does it begin?"*

"Ein Ungeziefer ruht," the child began,
In Staub und trocknem Schlamme . . ."

Then she blushed and laughed and ran away.

"That child," Junior said, "is the second happiest person on the farm today. The happiest is her mother. Though you might not think it, the child is half Jewish, and her father —who has worked with us nearly all his life—was taken away about eighteen months ago. He was one of those who refused to hide. Last month he was found at Theresienstadt, and freed. Last week he arrived back here, but he still cannot walk. . . . I rather doubt if he ever will. But Noémi doesn't care. She's so happy."

NÜRNBERG AREA

11

BEFORE we left Kempten, three things happened. First, the blond children of the Park Strasse (who preferred our garden, and I sometimes thought ourselves, to their homes and parents) were treated to a Farewell Party. The weather and the food were in their favor, for they were not condemned, oddly enough, to cheese. The hero of the occasion was Hans, who excelled himself and made, out of coffee, ice, and cream, a child's summer day's dream in the shape of a *Schloss,* with sugar garnishings for the windows and chocolate powder for the roof. Small wonder that the afternoon turned out to be, literally, a howling success!

The second thing that happened also concerned Hans. Though not twice a hero, he earned for himself—by the team's esteem, its appreciation of his culinary art, his character, the Major's sense of humor and co-operation—the enviable title of The Happiest Man in Germany. And the same act that gave him this name—news of which flashed, as though by secret radio, from southernmost Bavaria across all Germany to Hamburg and from there across half Austria to Linz (the Survey's geographical extremes)—also gave to the seven of us the title of The Team de Luxe.

The act was simple enough: Hans was dressed in a suit of U.S. army overalls; a helmet two sizes too large for him was dropped over his unbelieving eyes; the Major acquired from AMG a pass for "an indispensable addition" to the team (which its incredulous owner was advised to produce only under "the most provocative circumstances"); he was honored with a seat beside Frank in the back of the jeep, commanded never to take off his helmet, when passing patrols for inspection never to open his mouth and always "to look the other way."

Disguised thus as a G.I. the wounded Wehrmacht veteran, the ex-chef of the *cordon bleu* Munich restaurant set out—to the rousing, wildly envious cheers of wet-eyed Hedwig and the Park Strasse children—for Nürnberg, via Munich.

Most of Lower Franconia is flat, dull, characterless country, and the larger towns—Augsburg, Donauwörth and Weissenburg—were mountains of baroque smithereens.

Just outside Nürnberg the conquerors had omitted to demolish the yellow, egg-shaped signboards telling the traveler he is about to enter the *Stadt des Reichparteitags*. The swastikas on those signs were the only swastikas I saw displayed in Germany in public.

The moment we crashed over the awful road into Nürnberg I remembered—even though barely one street stood recognizable and intact—how much I had disliked it. It may be unfair to judge a city from a stay of a week in summer, but after a day, after a visit to a museum where a man, with ears like ping-pong bats, opened up for me the *Eiserne Jungfrau,* and with a devilish grimace pointed out the long rusty spikes of torture, I had wanted to get out. I hadn't liked the looks of the people in the streets, too many of whom were of the *Spiessbürger* type: too many of the men reminded me of the faces in the Frankfurt *Kneipen,* and the women of the witches and step-mothers in the Fairy Tales of the Brothers Grimm.

Against the pink, colossal Town Walls, the Towers, the wide dry moats round the Burg I'd borne a boyish, history-book grudge. When a German acquaintance took me down into the medieval city and we walked through the cobbled, cat-infested alleys, I'd had visions of shaven-headed, pock-faced perverts indulging in the most sordid crimes behind those crooked doors. And as we stood on a bridge above the canal-like Pegnitz, gazing at the flower-balconied wooden houses which seemed solidly stuck in the stagnant water, and he said: "Just like Venice, *nicht wahr?*" I thought, although I'd not seen the Italian city: No! No, this is not a gay or peaceful place. Can you imagine a Germanic gondolier punting up the Pegnitz, serenading a beefy blond *Fräulein* with a song? Can you imagine a German gondolier? And then I'd found that Nürnbergers for centuries had made machinery, toys, lead-pencils, dolls, ginger-bread, sausages, and beer—and that was just about what I thought they'd have made. I was sunk, of course, when we came to the house and statue of Albrecht Dürer; but I consoled myself with the reflection that the master was a cosmopolitan, a man not of provincial but international taste, and a traveler. And I felt, on entering Nürnberg again, that the Allies had laid waste not to the home of the sixteenth century genius but to the *Stadt des Reichsparteitags,* the sinister city Julius Streicher and his gang had chosen, most significantly, to desecrate.

Well, the job the Allied bombers had done had certainly not been half-hearted. The carnage at first glance was like that of Darmstadt, but worse, for Nürnberg is five times the size and, for the traveler, there was no relief for several miles. One of the first sights I saw above the rubble was a four-story modern building which had been split clean in half, as though by a knife, so that open to the public gaze stood four white-painted "privies," one under the other, all alike, and all intact down to the chains hanging from the ceilings. Strangely, despite its garbage-heap condition, the one wide thoroughfare—which half-encircles the city and keeps changing its name according to the round towers en route—was as packed with motor-driven traffic and pedestrians as Piccadilly or Times Square on an afternoon in spring. In the center of the Bahnhofsplatz—where purple-faced MP's waved their arms, shook their fists, and barked themselves voiceless against the overpowering roar of army engines—six men stood waist-deep in a crater, with bare backs, goggles, and drills which shook every bone in their bodies, but which, in that inferno, created a sound no louder than crickets in a field. Turning off the jeep's motor (you could tell it was turned on only by looking at the switch) in that motionless muddle of men and machinery, I looked up at the great black hulk, like a wounded battleship, that used to be Nürnberg's main railroad station, and saw, written across its blistered face on a long white enamel plaque: *"Victory! Victory! Or Bolshevism and Chaos!"*

As in Kempten, our billets were on the edge and above the town, but fortunately not high enough to offer a view of its roofless remains. Instead, the house—again one of those bourgeois villas built during the first years of the Hitlerian era and now camouflaged in a coat of ugly *feldgrau* paint—looked out over some rickety shacks and small plots of land covered with cabbages, potato-plants, and onions. Dudley and Frank were standing outside the house when we arrived, busily engaged with something in the back of their jeep.

"Come and look," Frank said. "We've brought Addy back from Munich!"

I glanced over their shoulders. In the jeep lay a bronze life-size bust of Hitler. Frank and Dudley had tied a white bandage round the forehead, pasted a cross of sticking-plaster over one cheek, a swastika on the fleshy nose, and now, over the blind, white-taped eyes they were giving the effigy of the Führer a squint with pupils of ink.

"What are you going to do with him?" I laughed.

"Stick him on the wall here," Dudley said, "and then watch from the windows the faces in the street."

I had a vision of Churchill's bandaged bull-dog face on a wall in defeated London, and wondered what the British would have done.

On the sidewalk outside the gate of "our" house, two small boys were playing in a heap of sand. One boy held in his hand an old tin can, while the other was building a kind of castle out of the sand. Suddenly the boy with the can let out a whine, like a siren. The other boy jumped away, picked up a second can, filled it with sand, and together, with the cans above their heads, they both started making noises like airplanes in flight. "I'm an *Amerikaner!*" shouted the one. "And I an *Engländer!*" piped the other. And together, with a wild flapping of arms and a bellowing "BOOM! BOOM! BOOM!" they dropped their sand-filled cans on the "castle," rolled themselves over on the remains and burst into shrieks of laughter.... From the doorway I watched them start the performance all over again. Then I went into the house.

In the hall a woman in a flowery pink dress stepped aside to let me pass, bowed, whispered *"Guten Tag,"* and bustled up a flight of stairs.

In a clean white room with an ominous-looking gash across the wall behind the beds, Mervyn was already unpacking.

"Seems a bomb just missed the house," he said, while I walked over to the long French window.

"Look out!" Mervyn shouted, just in time, for I was about to step out onto the balcony, where no balcony was. Instead, I looked down into a crater which had been converted into a garden of rocks and flowers. Beyond it lay a lawn with a few young cherry trees and a vegetable garden: bushes of gooseberries, red currants, raspberries, and a strawberry bed over which a young girl, with a basket, was bending. Then an elderly man in a long cream-colored coat came out from somewhere under the house and began watering the grass from a long rubber hose.

I walked out of the bedroom through sliding doors into a study, with writing-desk and radio, all shiny, square and "modern," and from there into the dining-room where the long table and chairs and shiny sideboard looked as though they'd just arrived from a Grand Rapids store which sold all the same furniture to all the other proper and prosperous middle-class people in this semi-suburban street. From the dining-room I could see the inevitable piano, the glass bookcase, the low round table and the "modern" striped upholstered chairs in one of which sat the Major, stripped to the waist.

"Hya, Jim," he called, looking up from the *Stars & Stripes* and handing me my mail. "How yer doin'?"

"Fine, thanks, Major," I said. "You certainly have an eye for good billets."

"Isn't this something, though!" he beamed, gazing round the sunlit room. "Twice the size of Kempten! Showers in the bathrooms! And best of all, a sunbathing deck up near the roof! See what a tan I got already?"

"You certainly have," I said, eyeing his pink chest. "Say, who was the woman I passed in the hall?"

"Dame in the pink dress? Frau Model, Muddle, or Middle, I guess! The owner."

"Is she living in the house?"

"In the basement. Well, what the hell, why shouldn't she?"

"Why not, indeed!" I said, and wondered if the Major had also been visited by a Nazi with an evil grin.

"Her old man's down there, too," he said, "and the daughter, Hertha, quite a cute kid."

"Is there a Herr Model, Muddle, or Middle?"

"No," laughed the Major. "Seems he's been missing since '43."

So that was the house on the Luisen Strasse, with more rooms upstairs (rooms the Germans use only at Christmas time, New Year's, for wedding and funeral receptions). Each of them contained a brand-new-looking Grand Rapids drawing-room suite, complete with antimacassars on the sofa-back and arms, embroidered lace mats on the glistening tables. And that was the household, with one further addition—a fat, shy little kitchen-maid called Trude, with a face like a pleasant pig. I found her in the kitchen (as modern as any in America) with Hans in his apron and high chef's hat.

"Grüss Gott!" beamed the Happiest Man in Germany, putting down the potato he was peeling and offering me his paralyzed hand.

"How was it, Hans," I asked, "being an American?"

"Prima!" he cried. *"Prima!"* which sent Trude into giggles over the sink.

Then the owner (whose name turned out to be Miedel) came in, smiled and bowed while we introduced ourselves.

"Ach!" she exclaimed, in a semi-flirtatious, too familiar

manner. "Another German name! *So* many Germans in America!"

"*Na ja,*" I said sternly, trying her out, "what can the Germans do, with so little *Lebensraum?*"

She shot me one quick quizzical glance which assured me she was no fool; then she threw up her head, clapped her hands, uttered a little squeal and exclaimed, "Ach, it's so wonderful to laugh again!" Then she put a hand to her head as though suddenly remembering something. "O!" she said, "I forgot, there is a letter for you. There was a *Herr* here this morning—" And she bustled out of the room.

"An American?" I asked, in the corridor.

"*Nein, ein Deutscher.* At least, he was in civilian clothes." And she handed me an envelope from a table in the hall.

"Dear Mr. Stern!" the type-written letter began in English.

Seldom I have had so joyful a surprise as was the news of your being in Germany and news from our dear friends we all know. Probably I am absent from Bamberg next week, but at all events I must have a talk with you because I want to tell many things of importance about our way of living in Germany and about what I have lived to see as a lawyer during the preceding years in the intellectual and social life of Germany.

There is still another question to ask you: Could you help us to obtain any news of my son in case he is a prisoner in Russia?

Yours truly,

Gustav Schulz

Gustav Schulz? I had, of course, first glanced at the signature, which meant nothing to me. Nor had I ever known anyone who lived in Bamberg. I learned who Gustav Schulz was when I settled down in the bedroom and opened my mail. Among the letters was one from a German refugee I'd known in Paris and met again in London in May. He wrote:

Three days ago I received a message from an American officer "somewhere in Germany," giving me news of the Schulzes, and that they are now living in Bamberg. It seems

Schulz is representing two concerns there (of course he would not be bothered to represent just one!) so I replied immediately, giving the American officer your name, army outfit, etc., to give to Schulz in case you are anywhere near Bamberg. I suppose you will remember the couple of meals we all had together in Paris. I certainly haven't forgotten them! Anyway, it might interest you to talk to him. . . .

I remembered now who Schulz was. He was a large, permanently smiling German, with a gash across one cheek; and in the awful fall of 1938 he had sat behind a *caneton aux oranges* in one of the most expensive restaurants in Paris and argued, with an optimistic, almost convincing boyish charm, how now that Hitler had got what he wanted he wouldn't ask for more. . . . Yes, I thought, as Frau Miedel started ringing a little bell in the dining-room, maybe it would be quite interesting to talk to Gustav Schulz. And I wondered how he had managed to travel from Bamberg to Nürnberg and back.

What Hans and Frau Miedel produced between them from the kitchen in Nürnberg made the meals at Kempten seem comparatively simple fare. We started off that night with a big bowl of *Kalte Schale*—a cold fruit soup—followed by *Rindfleisch* with dumplings the size and color of dirty tennis balls, and ended, in speechless stupor, with thick hunks, cut by Frau Miedel, of a chocolate cake. When I left half of my cake on the plate, Frau Miedel looked at me and asked, quite seriously and in an offended tone, "*Na,* Herr Stern, no hunger?"

For answer, I clasped my stomach with both hands, staggered to my feet and collapsed in a chair beside the bookcase. There, when fit enough to read, I found a shelf devoted to picture postcards and automobile maps of Germany and Switzerland. The Miedels, evidently, had done some traveling. Judging by the books, they also seemed to have a taste for opera and music. But it was difficult to tell, for they, like so many Germans, were "collectors." They belonged to those millions one used to see with mugs of beer at long tables under chestnut trees and in all the postoffices of Germany and Austria, red-faced and rucksacked, scribbling *Herzliche Grüsse!* on the backs of picture postcards of villages, mountains, or waterfalls. They collected everything—not only postcards, but theater and concert programs, Christmas cards, mementoes of a visit to the Leipzig Fair, an Oberammergau Passion Play, and the catalogues of art exhibitions among which I discovered the entire war series of the annual "salon" at the Munich Kunsthalle. Looking at the illustrations was like—so far as art was concerned—going back to the middle of the nineteenth century. For subject-matter, war took a back-seat; instead, the glossy pages confronted you with Big Girls, Big Goats, Big Cows, Big Boys—the last usually sculpted naked, with big biceps and ferocious faces. Then, of course, there was the Farmer's Family in front of the Evening Fire: the Führer frowning over the mantel; Poppa with a beard, Momma smothered in children and looking glum, all their faces golden in the light of the embers, all listening to The Voice on the radio and the whole sentimental German horror entitled HOME!

The combination of the Museum and the meal must have been too much for me to stomach, for I woke up in the night with the *Rindfleisch* and the chocolate cake rending that part of my anatomy asunder.

"Are you sure you won't be able to do any interviewing today?" Mervyn asked on his return from breakfast.

"Positive," I groaned. "I can't stand up."

"That's awful," he said. "John's down with the same trouble."

"Well, for God's sake," I said, "tell Miedel our innards are not made of rubber. Tell her, too, if it's her intent to fatten us up for the Christmas slaughter, that we won't, thank God, be here."

Then there was a knock on the door and Frau Miedel put her nose in.

"Ach, the poor Herr Stern!" she exclaimed. "He's caught a chill on the road, *nit?*"

"I've done nothing of the kind," I said. "I've eaten too much of your heavy food!"

"*Aber* Herr Stern is not serious," she said, frowning, and I knew I had insulted her, and didn't care. "You are so thin; you must put on weight at Miedel's."

"I won't," I said, drawing up my knees and screwing up my face. "I'm by nature a scraggy bird."

"*Na, so was!*" exclaimed Frau Miedel. "I will go and get a hot-water bottle."

"Thank you," I said, "that's just what I need."

She bustled out, then in again with the bottle in a towel; then she bustled round the room, folding Mervyn's filthy clothes. "*Mein Gott!*" she exclaimed, picking up his socks. "Have the *Herrschaften* no one to do their laundry?"

I didn't answer: I didn't want to talk, least of all to Frau Miedel.

"Herr Stern," she was saying, "what you want is some good hot coffee."

"No, I don't," I said. "I really don't want anything." And I rolled over and pretended to go to sleep.

She bustled out of the room with an armful of dirty clothes; but a moment later she was back again, with a thermometer.

"You have, perhaps, fever?" she said. "I can understand anyone catching cold in those open jips!"

She came up to the bed, too close for my taste, but for the sake of peace I took the thermometer, and while I held it under my arm she stood over me and said she wondered what the wives of Herrn Haynes and Stern would say if they knew their husbands had gotten ill in *her* house.

I was about to mumble that I'd had stomach-aches in many houses, including my own, when there was a loud knock on the door and in walked a giant of a man in blue breeches and high black military boots. Then I saw the gash on his face, knew who he was, and made no effort to stifle the groan.

"Ha-*ha!*" boomed Gustav Schulz with overpowering gusto. "Found you at last, Herr Stern!" And he reached out to me a huge hand.

"How d'you do?" I said. "I've got the stomach-ache."

"*Na!*" he said, pulling up a chair, sitting down and slapping his great thigh. "*Na, das wird bald vorbei geh'n!*—That'll soon go! Fancy finding *you* here!"

"And you, too!" I said. "I thought you lived in Berlin?"

"*Ach wo!*" he said. "Berlin's a mess. We moved out in the spring. But I've been to and fro since. Been very busy, right up to the end."

"You still are, I understand?"

"*Tcha,*" he grimaced, "nothing much doing in Bamberg. Dull place. Not that there's anything doing anywhere in Germany. I'm thinking seriously of going to Switzerland. In fact, I shall go to the border next week—"

"Go to Switzerland?" I interrupted, forgetting my stomach. "How will you get there?"

"*Ach, mein lieber Freund,*" he beamed, "I have an automobile, a motor-bike and side-car. . . ."

"And gas?"

"*Aber freilich!* Certainly. I have a couple of little concerns in Bamberg, you see."

"Oh, of course," I said, seeing nothing but a large, healthy-looking man with a round face and a gash across one cheek.

"Next thing, *lieber* Herr Stern," he said, patting his knees with both hands. "What about my boy?"

I said nothing.

"You see, it's like this," he went on, unabashed, "he is probably in the Russian zone. It would be very difficult for me—in my position, you understand. . . ." He smiled a very charming smile.

"And out of the question for me, in mine," I cut in.

"Well, anyway," he went on, laying on the bed a sheet of paper, "here are the particulars of the boy. If you would be so kind as to use your influence. . . ."

"I have no influence," I said, and added: "I wish to God I had!"—which, of course, was lost on Herr Dr. Gustav Schulz.

"Well," he said, drawing his massive bulk from the chair, "it's a great joy to see you after all this time. Kindest regards to our friends from Paris when you get back to London. Remember Paris? Ha! I was back there again in '42 and '43. As beautiful as ever, but somehow not quite the same."

"I was there in May," I said; "it certainly was not the same."

"*Na ja,*" said Schulz: "France will recover. I put great hopes in the French. Wonderful people. Although, on the whole, I prefer England. There were no damned Nazis there, and in London I have some good friends. I shall look forward to phoning them when I reach Basel. After that, Herr Stern, I hope to have the pleasure of seeing you in Bamberg. We have much to talk about. My wife remembers you well, and your charming wife. *Auf baldiges Wiedersehen,*" he said, smiling, his great hand clutching mine, "*und recht gute Besserung!*"

"Thank you," I said, and thought how Hans had a rival for his title of The Happiest Man in Germany.

In the afternoon the stomach-pains wore off, and by the time Frank and Dudley came bursting in from work, I was feeling a little weak but otherwise almost normal.

"Hi, you old crock, you!" Dudley said, seating himself where Schulz had sat. "Gee, I'd a good one today, Jim! He was eighty-six and looked a hundred. Know what he said?" Dudley burst into squeals of laughter at the memory. He enjoyed more than any of us discussing, by the hour, his respondents and what they'd said. "He said today was the first time he'd been out of bed in two years! He said he'd been out of bed only once during the war, and—" Dudley couldn't contain himself and off he went again into peals of laughter— "he said that was when he'd been blown out of bed by a bomb! His wife, he said, always insisted on going out to the shelter when the alerts came. But he always told her to stay right where she was, in bed, he said. 'And what happened?' he said. 'I never saw her again. She simply disappeared with everyone else in the shelter. Women, they have no common sense,' he said. Then he leaned right over the table till his nose nearly touched mine (he was as blind as a bat), and he said: '*Junger Mann,* bed's a great place, *nit?* Ach, how glad I'll be to get back there tonight.' The old boy took about five minutes to reach the door, he was so weak he could hardly walk!"

While we roared with laughter Dudley hobbled across the room towards the door.

"Did he say *'nit'* all the time?" Frank asked.

"The whole damned time!" Dudley said.

"So did mine," Frank said.

"Nitwits!" Dudley said, and from then on all Nürnbergers were known as nitwits, which was just what many of them were.

"What was yours like?" I asked Frank.

"A prostitute," he said. "The morning one."

"No, really? Professional?"

"Sure. Special report Mervyn wanted."

"Oh, do let's hear what she said."

"Well," said Frank, looking at his typed report. "It's not so hot. Really want to hear it?"

"Sure, some of it, anyway."

"Well, she was about thirty. On the beefy side, but not bad-looking. Before the war she'd been 'working at her trade,' as she called it, in France, Belgium, Holland, Switzerland. 'I never liked to work *under the Nazis*,' she said—"

"That's good!" I laughed.

" '—because they made life miserable for us. But I'm a German, so when the war broke out I had to return. I chose Nürnberg because it's a good city.' "

"*Good* city?" Dudley repeated.

"Sure," Frank said, continuing to read: 'It was a great commercial center; there were always any number of business men. Things were bad at the beginning of the war because the Nazis were against us. However, as the war went on, many of the police were drafted into the army or got jobs abroad, and gradually there were only the old officials left. These old gentlemen didn't bother us any more. In fact, during the last three years, so long as we reported to the doctor regularly every week and went to the hospital when we were sick, we hadn't much trouble."

"What did she say about the army men?" I asked.

"Army? Let's see. Oh, yes. 'We didn't like the soldiers too much,' she said, 'because most of them were diseased. Nearly all the Luftwaffe men had syphilis, and those who came from France usually had the most infectious kind. We examined every man who came in, and if he was diseased we didn't do business with him.'"

"Did she say anything about the Party people?"

"Oh, sure," Frank said. "The great time for the whores in Nürnberg was during the *Reichsparteitag*. 'Big business,' she said. 'Nazis gathered from all over Germany. S.S. men were posted outside all the houses to see that no Party member in uniform got in. That was *streng verboten*. Of course the Party people got around that by simply borrowing civilian clothes. They usually stayed in town a couple of weeks and many came several times. Of course, the rank and file of the Party couldn't come because they were too busy reporting, marching, drilling, parading. But plenty of big-shots came and even in uniform. Like everything else in the Party, exception was made for the big shots. If they were caught in a house by the *Sittenpolizei*—the police controllers—they were never written up. Many times the police would apologize for breaking in. I remember one time an elderly man came in. He wanted something to drink, so I sent out for a couple of bottles of champagne and some wine. Like most old men, he wanted to be whipped by a naked woman. We were drinking and talking when the bell rang and I went to the door. It was Fischer of the *Sittenpolizei*. He saw the bottles and the whip and asked me, "Don't you know it's against the law to serve drinks in here?" I said the gentleman had brought the drinks with him and he agreed that he had, saying he just couldn't come and start right in—that he needed a little stimulant first. Then the old man produced his papers and Fischer went off. But the next day I was called before the Court and they told me that if I were caught again whipping a man or drinking in the place with a man, I'd go to the concentration camp. Then two days later they passed a law that drinks could be served in houses. That's the way it always went. From one day to another they'd make different rules; they never wanted to let us alone.' "

"Any idea what she took in in a day," I asked, "or rather a night?"

"Oh," said Frank, "she was quite interesting on that. Let's see. Here it is. 'We often had more than enough money,' she said, 'but it wasn't much good, for we couldn't buy any food with it; the rations were too little to live on, and in our trade you can't work if you're hungry. So we usually asked customers for something to eat. Some men would bring enough for a meal or two. Farmers would bring a pound of butter—which was worth more to me than 30 or 40 marks. We also got quite a lot from the French and other foreign workers who worked in dairies, bakeries, and meat-packing plants. They stole a lot and shared their loot with us. We also got food from the street-walkers. Many of them went around with S.S. men who worked in the canteen. These men swiped food and gave it to their girls who in turn sold it to us.' "

"What happened to the gals during the raids?" Dudley asked.

"You mean what did their customers do?" Frank said, smiling. "That's easy. 'When the alarms went,' she said, 'off they'd go to the bunker or cellar, and after the All Clear they'd come right back again! . . . Civilian trade stopped almost entirely towards the end,' she said, 'when the attacks got really heavy. Not so the soldiers, though! They went right on coming,' she said."

"Frank!" mocked Dudley. "I'm surprised at you!"

"What's the poor harpy doing now?" I asked.

"Still at it," Frank said. "Mostly kraut POWs. 'But we also get some American soldiers,' she said, 'both white and colored. So far, AMG hasn't bothered us at all. All we have to do is register and go to the doctor every week.' "

"Did she make any personal remarks about her customers?" I asked Frank. "I mean, did she compare types or nationalities?"

"Don't think so," Frank said, thinking. "Except she did say

something about the German soldier—wait, now—I don't think I put it in—yes, I did. 'About the most pitiful type of customer we ever have,' she said, 'is the soldier who has returned from the front and found his house and family gone—destroyed by the bombings. They come to us for comfort, dozens of them, very bitter about the whole war. Lots of them never went back to their regiments. Just deserted. Even today we get German POWs who haven't seen Nürnberg for two years. The look in their eyes after they have seen the city for the first time is a terrible thing to see.' "

"That's a mighty good report, Frank," I said. "She sounds like a decent soul."

"She was," said Frank. "I liked her very much."

I could well understand the soldier looking the way the prostitute described him on his return to Nürnberg, even if the poor wretch hadn't lost everything in the world. Though the city had been raided less than half as often * as Munich, it gave the impression not so much of having been bombed as devastated by a terrific fire. And this, in fact, was what had happened. Nürnberg would not have looked the way it did, had not so large a part of it been a medieval city, where the four-hundred-year-old houses were built of a little brick and a lot of wood which, touched off by a few phosphorus bombs, went up in flames like paper. Even so, the extent of the damage would probably not have been so great had not the zero-cold weather on the night of January 2, 1945, been accompanied by a howling wind. That was the wind which helped wipe out the Old Town of Nürnberg.

The descriptions we heard of it took place in what had once been a school for Arts and Crafts, a red building intact except for its plumbing, lighting, its windows of cardboard, and a few cracked panes of glass. All round it lay a sea of smashed glass and brick, and in the narrow street outside a

* Raids: 47. Planes: 7,190. Tons of explosives: 17,115. Killed: 6,120. Seriously injured: 12,000—approximately, since the records were destroyed during the last great raid on April 5, 1945.

high and foul-smelling garbage-heap. The house would have been perfectly adequate as a place for interviewing had not the AMG elected, on the day after our arrival, to turn all the rooms not occupied by ourselves into a *Wohnungsamt*—offices where the homeless came to seek official aid for some form of shelter. The result was permanent pandemonium; not only were the corridors jammed all day with impatient, howling, squabbling, often weeping women and children, with men screaming vain orders for silence; but many of them, having waited several hours in a queue which stretched down the stairs and into the street, would finally break out of it and, dragging behind them a couple of children, come bursting into our rooms, demanding of us a roof or at least a hearing. Even when we put up large PRIVATE and KEEP OUT signs on our lockless doors, the destitute would often ignore them in their desperation.

So the days at Nürnberg were not like those at Kempten; nor did the people to whom we talked in the schoolhouse have much in common with those who'd confronted us in the König Strasse. They were city-dwellers, of a much lower class, the *Spiesser* type, and their health and clothes were in a poorer condition. None, naturally, were evacuees, or refugees from the Russians, and many of them were sullen. The sullen ones —often wives of S.A. or S.S. men—were Nazis, though not one I talked to ever came out and said so, as had the Red Cross nurse in Kempten. Instead, when asked why Germany had lost the war, they'd shoot you a quick, guilty, hostile look, like bad-tempered children who have lied but are determined not to confess, then lower their eyes and finally mutter: "I don't know," or, "Germany had too many enemies!" or, "*Auf so was kann ich nit antworten!*—That I can't answer!" or, "*Ich bin wirklich zu wenig im Bilde*—I'm really not informed about such things!" and add, "My husband, he never discussed politics at home," or, "My husband, if only he were here, he could tell you all about that kind of thing!"

Another point where the natives of Nürnberg, the center of German anti-Semitism, differed significantly from the inhabitants of other cities was in the numbers who expressed deep-seated feelings of guilt over the treatment of Jews. Often they gave this fact as their reason for Germany's defeat. "The deportation of the Jews was a terrible crime," said a girl, at the end of an interview during which she had shown no signs of intelligence and very little of life. "The Jews," she added, "were the best doctors in Germany, the best dentists, and the best merchants." Another girl, of seventeen, said she considered Nürnberg had been bombed "more heavily than any other city" because it was "Streicher's home and where the Jews were treated so abominably." And there was the woman who hadn't slept out of her clothes in two years, whose husband had gone off his head from the bombings and whose one son, she said, had been forced into the S.S. in 1944 and never been heard of since. "I was sure," she said, when asked if, after the first raid on Nürnberg, she thought more raids would come: "I was sure more would come, because they wanted to punish us for what happened to the Jews. We lost the war because of our persecution of the Jews."

Possibly the only interest of these remarks is that they were neither solicited nor extracted as a result of "probing," but came impromptu from people of, even for Nazi Germany, below average intellect. What I remember most vividly about the Nürnberg respondents is that they were mostly middle-aged charwomen, of an ugliness almost as tragic as their ignorance (two were barely literate), and of a standard of intelligence so low that no better name could have been found for them than nitwits.

There were, of course, exceptions. Among them was a woman who'd have been exceptional anywhere outside Hollywood or an asylum. She "saw things." What, after the first bombing of Nürnberg, did she think future raids would be like? *"Tcha,"* she said, "now I'll tell you something." Whereupon she went into a kind of trance, stared through me from eyes that were not quite sane. "I'll tell you something. I knew the Time of Destruction was at hand. The planets, the stars— they were all set for it. Back in 1929 I read a book. You should read it, *The Horoscope of the Twentieth Century* by someone called Grimm. *Bitte?* No, I'm not exactly a clairvoyant, but I see things. . . ." She rose from her chair and began to walk round the room, staring at the ceiling. "Listen, my father was a barber, but he could also foretell the future. Of course I've inherited some of his gifts, even though I'm just a working woman. . . ."

Then she sat down and insisted on opening a large handbag, from which she produced a pile of faded photographs of her family dating back to the nineteenth century. When told to put them all back in her bag she became very sore.

"The *Herr* is not interested in Time," she said. "This is the Time of Destruction. The Destruction must come from the air, I said, because that is where Man has risen. And once up there, I said, he would drop explosive things on the cities and blow them all sky-high. *Tcha*, that's what happens when the Time of the New Scientific Technique arrives. . . ."

"*Bitte?* Did I continue to fear the raids? *Nein!* I got used to them. This is the Age of Iron, I said. It maketh us like iron. Three times through Fire, my dear man, I went. My eyes were burned. Now I am like iron.

"*Bitte?* Nürnberg bombed more heavily than other cities? If you really wish to know that, my dear sir, I suggest you take a journey!

"The chief cause of the war? Ha, God's word. It came from God's hands. There must have been a call from Heaven. BOOOOOM! There comes the Devil—Satan, the Evil One, Lucifer, the Black Rider—bringing Death and Destruction!"

She rose to her feet, stood at attention.

"I follow Knowledge, not Politics!" she cried. "Now," she roared, "my—Mission—is—over!" And picking up her bag, she bounced out of the room.

Another exception was a man who had spent three years of the war in Poland. Before embarking on his experiences there, he took some cracks at AMG, then expressed his opinion that the only popular foreigners in Bavaria were American Negroes. "The children adore them," he said. "And I have reason to like them myself. One day last week I saw a Negro smoking a cigarette by the roadside, so I asked him if he'd exchange a cigarette for something else. He looked at me a moment and noticed that I was wearing dark glasses. Then, in perfect German, he said, "My glasses don't fit; let me try yours!" So we exchanged glasses, and found that we were both more satisfied with each other's glasses than with our own. The Negro then handed me a couple of cigarettes."

His reasons for Germany's defeat he listed in this order: "Terror from the air. Sabotage by the generals and aristocrats, beginning with the murder of Schleicher. The behavior of the homosexuals within the Party, of whom Streicher was the worst. The massacre of the Jews in Poland. I was there and saw it. The massacres were carried out by the S.S. and the Ukrainian police."

From then until the end of the interview, nothing could distract his thoughts from the Jewish massacres he had witnessed. He gave them as the answer to almost every question, no matter how irrelevant. "The Jewish massacres in Poland," he kept repeating. "No nation capable of such atrocities could possibly win a war. This *Kulturschande* is the end of Germany. Germans can never again be called decent. I shall never forget. I am haunted always by what I saw at Lemberg. My greatest difficulty since, has been to convince people of what I saw with my own eyes. Even my wife won't believe me. . . ."

12

THE evenings of July were beautiful and long. But what could you do? Where could you go?

You were too restless to read. Having typed, from notes scribbled in frantic haste, some five thousand words and talked German for several hours every day, you didn't feel like writing or talking any more. And your mind was a vacuum, because—from constantly moving about—you were cut off from the world. We'd not heard a radio in Germany. Mail caught up with us by accident, arriving in batches two to four weeks old. In Nürnberg, for the first time, *Stars & Stripes,* a "pony" edition of *Time* and the *New Yorker* made an occasional appearance. Even their lack of advertisement was regretted. The novelty of communal living, of listening all day to "schimpfing" Germans had worn away. Boredom had set in—not so much from the monotony of the work as from the sense of the "conspicuous waste" and pointlessness of that work. And we ourselves had grown to know one another a trifle too well. Harmless remarks, repeated once too often, began to rankle and sound like insults. When Dudley and Frank and the Professor turned on their baiting disk at breakfast, the civilians would sigh and our eyes say, "Oh God, there they go again!" What used to irritate me even more was that in the late evenings, with a barrel of beastly beer, they would gather together with Frau Miedel, Hertha, Hans, Trude, and howl with laughter, often until the early hours, in the garden right behind my head! It was all horribly like school.

The Major, poor devil, whiled away his days by typing long

letters to his girl in London, and sunbathing on the top balcony. Then he and Dudley and the Professor extracted from me (to the misfortune of all concerned) the confession that years ago I used to play bridge—en famille and on long ocean voyages. But by now my bridge was so abominable, the Major's so expert, that he had to be unusually desperate for distraction before I was called upon to make up the four. Instead, he and Frank and Dudley and the Professor put on baseball gloves and went out into the street and threw a ball at one another until they were all purple in the face. Then they came in and watched, through the Venetian-blinds of the sitting-room window, the passers-by as they stopped to stare at the bandaged head of the Führer on the wall. It might have been interesting—if you *had* to have a Gallup poll—to employ someone to take careful count of the native reactions to this bit of questionable taste on the part of the conquerors towards the conquered. From my own observation I would have divided the pop-eyed starers into two groups: the young and the middle-aged. The young took one look and burst into roars of laughter. Then they clustered round the bust, investigating every detail, and finally went away giggling and with a lighter step. Their elders stood stock-still in the middle of the street or sidewalk and glared, their eyes screwed up in fury and their fingers twitching with frustration at not being able to reach out and remove what they may have considered the crowning insult to the defeated Reich. Then they'd trudge on, muttering to themselves.

Occasionally Mervyn, who met more people privately, would invite a German to dinner. Once I came home to the sound of Beethoven being played—even my tone-deaf ear could tell—expertly on the piano. I stood in the passage, listening. And as I listened I looked up and saw Hertha, the Miedel daughter, standing outside the sitting-room door, her head on one side and her eyes closed, lost to the world. I tiptoed away into the kitchen and told Frau Miedel that she should persuade her daughter to go into the sitting-room if no one but the pianist were there.

"Mein Gott!" exclaimed Frau Miedel. "She has no business listening outside the door!" It was all I could do to prevent her from sending the girl away. "She loves music so, that child!" she said.

"Can she play the piano herself?" I asked.

"Oh, *ja,* she plays all day when we are alone."

"Wouldn't she play for us one evening?"

"Mein Gott! For nothing in the world, Herr Stern! She's much too shy!"

"Who's the pianist anyway?" I asked. "Isn't he playing rather well?"

Frau Miedel laughed. "He is, and he should," she said. "That's Herr Ledenfels—one of the best pianists we have. Ach," she sighed, clasping her hands before her face and raising her eyes like a sentimental Madonna, "ach, I could listen to him all day!"

It turned out that Mervyn had met the pianist and asked him in to dinner. He was an oldish, meek, emaciated man and he promised to play for us after the meal. In the dining-room he told us he'd been invited by AMG to give a recital in what remained of the Opera House.

"By the way," he said, smiling a wan smile, "do you know what the last opera was they played here before the end? *Götterdämmerung!*" he said, and added: "And the last play in a Nürnberg theater was *Much Ado About Nothing!*"

Then, in his hunger, the pianist ate six of those dumplings the size of tennis balls. Twenty minutes later he almost collapsed from what seemed like a heart attack, and had to be taken home.

Another man who came to dinner I couldn't believe was German. Youngish, dark, handsome, he looked French or Italian. But he wore a suit—not new, but in good repair—which I knew immediately had been made in England. And when he opened his mouth and spoke English I could hardly believe that that was not where he came from, too. He didn't, but he'd lived there several years. He was a Berlin art historian, and when he heard I was interested in painting he asked if I knew the Director of London's National Gallery.

"Kenneth Clark?" I asked. *"Sir* Kenneth, I should say."

"Quaite," he said.

"Just thirty years ago," I said, "he used to sit behind me at a desk and throw paper pellets at me when we were supposed to be writing our Sunday letters home. I remember being wildly envious of him because he had a typewriter, the only one in the school. He also had an enormous head, like a brown busby!"

"That's him!" said the art historian, whose name was Möricke, "he was a great friend of maine."

"I've not seen him since," I said. "He went up in the world, while I went to America!"

So we talked of painting and mutual friends, and remarked how odd it was we'd never met between the wars in London, Paris, or Florence, instead of today in the ruins of "this damned place," as Möricke called Nürnberg. He couldn't stand Nürnberg, he said, but the Kaiser Friedrich Museum in Berlin had sent him there in 1943 to take charge of the crating and evacuation of the treasures—among them the priceless Holbeins, Burgkmairs, Cranachs, Dürers, and the Riemenschneider sculpture—from the Germanisches Museum. These, Möricke said, had all been stored in the great rock caves under the Burg, probably as impregnable a fortress as any in all Europe. But now, to his horror, he discovered that many of the masterpieces were showing the effects of damp, and he could get neither the permission, the labor, nor the transport to have them moved. After dinner Mervyn and I took him back in a jeep to his "home" just outside the Altstadt. When we reached the door of a high but more than half-demolished building, Möricke warned us he not only had nothing to offer us but that we might find the ascent to his apartment a little too giddy an undertaking. "If aither of you are given to vertigo—" he said, and left the sentence unfinished.

He lived on the fifth floor. For four flights the staircase had no banisters and on that side no walls, so that while you climbed there was nothing between you and destruction; and if you looked down you saw, between the stairboards, more stairboards below and under them the rubble heaped over the foundations of the house. At the fourth floor you walked out onto a small ledge, open to the world, and from there mounted a rickety ladder into a kind of crow's nest which had four gashed and charred walls and a piece of corrugated iron for roof. On the one divan sat a pale, haggard woman, all bones, whose age it was impossible to tell.

"May waife," said Möricke. "We've been bombed out so often we dessayded—so long as the floor and the four walls hold up—to stay. In any case, we've nowhere else to go, except into the open air or into the caves with the pictures! And may waife isn't well enough for that."

I looked at the man in the expensive London suit, the art historian with the "refained" accent, at the colored reproductions of two Vermeers tacked to the shattered walls, at a piece of Greek vase amidst a clutter of carpentering tools and old newspaper on a trestle table, at the skeleton-thin woman, and finally, between my feet, at a hole in the floor through which I could see, a hundred feet below, the tiny heads of human beings crawling over the debris. Then I thought of the Director of the National Gallery, one of the most Important Men and Hosts of London, who—at a time when Zeppelins were exploding in flames over England—had pelted me with paper pellets while I tried to think of something to say in my boring, dutiful Sunday letter home. It's a queer world, I thought once again, as we made, with the aid of some matches in the dark, that steeplejack descent into the ashes of the one-time imperial city.

When no guest came to dinner and I was not hauled in to play bridge, I sometimes went for walks with John. One end of the Luisen Strasse led to open fields, to what had recently been an S.S. barracks (now occupied by G.I.s), and two woods— the one an overgrown park with young trees rising out of long grass, the other a forest of firs which spread north from the city as far as the eye could see. The smaller wood I christened "Conception Copse," for there, between six o'clock and curfew, lay a prone G.I. and girl, whispering in the grass under every tree. On the lane outside, a single soldier would stand guard, on the lookout for the prowling officer or M.P. The fir trees on the other side of the road whispered, too, but in different languages, for this was the playground of the D.P.s. Most of central Europe was represented here. Dressed in American uniforms, you could distinguish them in the distance from G.I.s only by their less furtive look and the fact that they, with no fraternization ban, walked or swaggered along arm-in-arm with their girls, who might be German, Hungarian, Czech, Italian, Lett, or Pole. As the result of an order divesting us of our U.S. insignia (an order prompted by American officers who resented American civilians occasionally being taken for officers), we ourselves, both on the open road and among the fir trees, were often taken for D.P.s. I was twice asked—once by a Filipino patrol and once by a Hungarian Displaced Person—whether I knew any English!

If you walked down the Luisen Strasse in the opposite direction, you came to a street of Nürnberg's grander houses, all undamaged and all occupied by the higher-ranking American officers. Crossing this street and continuing for about a mile, you arrived at Mögeldorf, a suburban village of no interest except for one house which we called "Our Favorite Ruin." Standing alone and conspicuous above the main street, it had presumably been hit by artillery fire. Most of the lower floor and all the outer walls had been shot away, but the pumpkin of its tower still hung crazily out in space; and though the tiles of the roof had gone, some of the rafters, a staircase leading to a non-existent attic, and a magnificent bathroom on the ground floor, were still intact. From the street you could see the tub and over it the shining green and white tiled wall. You got the impression that if you leaned against the ruin and shoved, all the precarious timbers would collapse like a castle of cards and go crashing down the hill.

When we wanted gas and preferred not to run the dismal gauntlet of Nürnberg's ruins for the fifth or sixth time in a day, we used to pass through Mögeldorf—and thus circumnavigate the town—to the motor-pool, which was located on a concrete parade ground outside the Stadium. This vast area looked as though it contained all the gas and gas-cans in the world. It's a pity, I used to think, that the anthropologists of racism, led by Goebbels and Rosenberg, could not be marched down to this motor-pool, for it was operated—and more efficiently than any other military organization with which we had dealings—by a gang of powerful-looking Negroes, all stripped to the waist, their torsos gleaming like molten copper in the evening sun.

Of all the sights I saw in Germany the most disappointing and the most ridiculous was the famous Nürnberg Stadium. It didn't even look big. Or perhaps because its area was so large, the tiers of seats all round it looked absurdly small, much less impressive than the empty grandstands at Ascot, Auteuil, or Saratoga. The whitewashed steps of the grandest "stand" at the Stadium, from the center of which the Führer, surrounded by his ferocious-looking yes-men, used to fume, were covered ludicrously with bricks (for camouflage), and the white walls (always photographed from below in order to create the impression of size) looked as sugary as the crust of a monumental wedding cake.

Most of the long, golden evenings in Nürnberg I spent alone. I'd set out in a jeep from the Luisen Strasse to the Old Town, drawn there partly by a morbid fascination, partly because of the feeling that if you live for weeks surrounded by destruction (knowing you're not, thank God, going to stay there much longer), you may as well familiarize yourself with some of the worst conditions under which the native people exist. I was aware, too, that one constantly recurring question still remained unanswered: If only some 20,000 Nürnbergers had been killed and seriously injured by air-raids, and half of the 400,000 inhabitants had dispersed into the surrounding country, where were the remaining 200,000—or even 150,000—now living?

If the ancient bridges over the Pegnitz had been destroyed,

it would have been almost impossible, even on foot, to move about in the Old Town. But for some inexplicable reason they still stood. So did the green, pencil-pointed steeples of the Lorenz Kirche—two of the astonishing number of German Gothic towers to survive where nothing else had. And in Nürnberg's Altstadt nothing else had. Which is not strictly true. For, as usual—and again no one knows why—a few statues remained. Surrounded by deep holes full of twisted, broken drain-pipes, Albrecht Dürer stood high up, erect, like a lonely saint in his stone robes. He could not be reached by jeep. You had to climb the tiny foot-trodden paths over bricks and boulders, past a crater, at the bottom of which lay some stinking, stagnant water. And there, every evening, under the master's outstretched hand, gathered a group of gangsters whose ages ranged from four to eight. They were clothed in rags—or rather, from head to foot they were perfectly camouflaged in filth, so that until they moved you couldn't tell they were there. At sight of you, they scattered in different directions, soundless on their cracked, dusty feet, like rabbits over an old warren. They simply disappeared, behind and under the debris, into holes. If you remained long enough in the same place, they'd emerge again, slowly, like rabbits, sniff the air and stare. And then you'd see that they carried stones or sticks or bars of iron, that their teeth were black and broken, or that they had no teeth, that one had a single arm, another a crutch, and that the only clean spots on their bodies were the whites of their eyes. But when you looked at their eyes a second time you saw that they were not ordinary human eyes, nor like the soft, scared eyes of rabbits, but wild, reckless, fearless, heartless—like the eyes of a famished, diseased leopard-cub, whose one enemy is man.

Stumbling down the hill from Dürer and the young generation of Nürnbergers, you passed the corner of a wrecked alley, where you stopped suddenly and stared again; for here, in the center of what was once Julius Streicher's city, still nailed to its shattered wall, was the blue plaque bearing the alley's ancient name: *Judengasse*—Street of the Jews.

A few hundred yards further north, picking your way over a smashed bronze breast and arms, over rusty bedsteads, bottomless kettles and a cracked, overturned bath-tub, you heard the sound of voices—which was strange, for people did not speak above a whisper in the Old Town. Glancing up, you saw a setting straight off the Elizabethan stage: men and women seated in chairs in a room on the third floor of an old house which had lost its façade. The face of the house—its front wall, windows, and all—had simply fallen away; so that as long as warm weather lasted the house's many occupants could sit comfortably in their sitting-room, gossiping in their chairs, surrounded by all their own familiar objects, and pretend they did not know that if they took three steps forward they would fall into chaos.

On every visit to the Old Town I returned to this spot. It was the only place in Nürnberg where you felt a few people were sitting where they'd always sat. Unlikely as it may sound, this "house," with its interior open to the elements and the human eye, had window-boxes (on the floors, like footlights on a stage) filled with pink and purple petunias, and on a round table in the living-room, in front of an upright piano, stood a china vase of marguerites and corn-flowers. I grew so fascinated by this family's public private-life that I used to stand, hidden by the rubble, and watch them live. With the evening sun turning the whole gaping apartment gold, a heavy big-boned woman would waddle across the crowded room, open a door into the kitchen and light what looked like a kerosene stove. I couldn't believe—from where I stood, a witness to all—that she would return to the door and close it (from habit of a lifetime? To be alone? To shut off the smell of cooking?) but she did. And when she'd placed a pan on the burner, and something in the pan, she slowly, painfully, lowered her bulk onto a wooden chair and, as people are more apt to do when alone, promptly let her chin fall onto her expansive chest. While the family talked and argued and gesticulated in the living-room, a door in the background would open, a blond girl, her hair aflame from the sun, would stand on the threshold, all the heads would turn, and you almost felt like referring to your program to see who the heroine was, in real life.

One evening I scrambled up behind the house, to have a look at what these people saw from where they sat, from where I imagined they'd been sitting all the evenings of their lives. And it was this view, rather than the panorama of moonlit horror from the hotel balcony in Stuttgart, which has remained most vividly in my memory. I climbed beyond the level of the house, higher and higher, until I reached the battered Burg, which dominated the city. What you saw from here you could not compare to anything you'd ever seen, not even to a dream, for dreams are too detailed, and here the sight was too vast, too overwhelming for the eye to rest on details. I have since seen moving pictures of the remains of Hiroshima. Nürnberg from the Burg bore no resemblance to them, for the Japanese city appeared almost flat, and the German one was nowhere in as clean a state. Nor was it like Stuttgart, for Stuttgart still possessed habitable-looking buildings, some roofs and houses with at least their outer walls intact. From the Burg, to the limit of vision in every direction, and that was a long way with long sight, you saw—with the exception of the Gothic towers—an endless unbroken brickscape of jagged walls. Months later, back in America, I came across a photograph of the ruins of Ypres, after the First World War. It was a dead city, without a growing tree, a human being, a sign of life. Nürnberg looked like that photograph, magnified many times.

But the Altstadt was not a dead city. It was *total beschädigt* —totally destroyed, as the Germans called it, but it was inhabited, and not only by gangsters in embryo. By daylight you could not tell, or even believe that anyone lived there, because you could not detect any livable space. Nor did you believe that the few people you saw stepping over the debris dwelt in this foul arena. Many of them were not badly dressed, and they looked surprisingly clean. Carrying bunches of wilting wild flowers in one hand, and on their backs a rucksack or a bundle of kindling wood, you presumed they were making a short-cut through the ruins to some more habitable region elsewhere. But you couldn't tell for sure. You could tell human beings lived day and night in the Altstadt only by entering it after sundown, after curfew—an hour when there fell over the desolate scene a weird, sinister silence, like sudden death.

In the mauve dusk I used to leave the jeep in the hands of an M.P. in the König Strasse, walk slowly through what used to be the Market Place, past the Schöner Brunnen (which had survived in concrete), and—at a spot where pedestrians had trodden lanes through the mountains of garbage like the lanes the African native makes through the veldt—I'd stand still, and listen, and hear not a sound.

Twice I stood on this spot, hearing nothing and seeing nothing move. But not content, incredulous of that silence, I came again, this time penetrating a little further into the gloom of the lanes; and suddenly, standing still, holding my breath, I heard, so near it seemed as though it were under my feet, a sound as of many muffled voices murmuring. Since the lane, I reasoned, must lead somewhere, I tiptoed forward. I had covered maybe a couple of yards when the silence was shattered by a cry, the cry of a woman shouting: "*Kartoffeln!*—Potatoes!" And on the instant, all about me, the grave-like rubble leapt to life. In the gloom, dark figures appeared from nowhere, scurried like frantic rats over the hills, some rushing headlong into a hole I hadn't noticed, and from which, as I was about to pass it, there came, like something solid, the appalling stench of sickness. I stood a few yards from the hole and saw that it was a kind of cave covered over by some canvas and sheets of corrugated iron, that within there flickered the light of one candle, round which I could see the blurred glowing outline of five or six faces, and beyond them, in the background, a dark mass which I took for coats or blankets covering many living, prostrate people.

I walked quickly on, thinking of the witches of Endor,

and all of a sudden there came over me the feeling that I was being followed. I walked faster, stumbling over rocks and refuse, and then I knew that I was lost. I stopped, stood still, and all round me I could hear a sound as of many muffled voices murmuring. At first, in the darkness, I could see nothing but the rubble and smashed walls, all indigo against the ink-blue sky and stars. Then, right beside me, something moved. I heard a sound like a spoon or fork hitting a plate, and I could just see the form of a woman, in a seated position, outside what looked like a small hut.

"Could you tell me where I am?" I asked, and my voice seemed as loud, as sinister as a fog-horn at sea. "Could you tell me how I can get to the König Strasse?"

"*Ja,*" a female voice said, "that's complicated."

And she got up and in the dark began giving me the most complicated instructions. When she'd finished, I asked her if this was where she lived.

"*Ja,*" she said, "would the *Herr* like to see? But, unfortunately, I have no light, no matches. . . ."

I struck a match, and followed her over the few yards of rubble to where she had been sitting. Here she bent down and, picking up a sheet of old newspaper, rolled it tight and lengthwise and put it over the dying flame. In the sudden flare of light I saw that she was a woman of about forty, ashen pale but quite good-looking, with a long scar across her forehead.

"Here is my home," she said. "I made it all myself."

You could just manage to enter her home without getting down on your hands and knees. It was like a large, dilapidated dog-kennel, made of planks about four feet high, with a sheet of corrguated iron for roof, and another sheet, covered with two overcoats, on the floor.

"That's where I sleep," she said. "And there's my table."

The table was a board, charred black, nailed onto four rickety pieces of wood, and on the table I saw a hammer, some nails, two plates, a cup, and a broken knife and fork.

"Are you all alone here?" I asked her.

"Oh, *ja*," she said. "I wouldn't live where those other people live for anything. It's disgustingly dirty down there. And there's no air. It's horrible."

I talked to her for about twenty minutes. Then I left her my matches and went away. Back in my room I wrote to my wife, describing briefly that evening and this particular woman. This was her war-history.

She'd been bombed out of seven different places; her husband had been killed in a raid; her mother had been killed in a raid; her sister had been killed in a raid; she herself had had four major operations during the war; her only daughter, aged 21, after the sixth bombing-out, had been evacuated to Kiel in February of this year and not heard of since. Her one son, aged 16, had "gone wild" and kept disappearing. She never knew where he was, and hadn't seen him for a month. For six weeks she had slept in a bunker with 200 others. But she preferred her own company, so she'd made herself a shack in the ruins of the Altstadt. She had one great fear. The ground on which she had built the shack didn't belong to her. "You see," she said, "I don't *own* my ruin. I don't own anything except two coats and the clothes I stand up in. I'm afraid the people who own this bit of land may come back and turn me out."

Early next morning, a Sunday, I returned to the Altstadt. I stood on the spot where the lanes converged, but I didn't hear any murmuring. I found the hole of the cave-like place where I'd seen the faces in the candlelight, but now, by day, I couldn't see inside. I just held my breath at the overpowering stench. I spent half an hour looking for the shack where the woman lived alone, but I couldn't find it. On returning to the König Strasse to pick up the jeep, I passed through the deserted desolation of the Haupt-Markt, and out of the silence I suddenly heard the sound of voices singing a psalm. They sounded as sad, as timeless as the sea, as silver-voiced as a trained choir of boys—more beautiful than any singing I'd ever heard before. While listening, I noticed at my feet a small green weed growing out of the ancient, battered cobbles, and all of a sudden I felt convinced that man would sing as long as weeds could grow, that however destructive, he was as indestructible as the Oceans or the Earth.

Back in the Luisen Strasse, I told John what I'd heard, and he said, "Yes, I believe there's a German Protestant pastor who conducts a Sunday morning service down there—in the crypt of the Frauen Kirche. I wanted to go, but it's too late now. So I'm going to Fürth instead, to a G.I. service. I've not attended a service since I left the States. Why don't you come along?"

I laughed impulsively at the idea. Then I thought: Why not? So I said: "Okay. I don't think I've 'been to church,' as we used to call it, for about fifteen years!"

"In that case," said John, "it should be quite an experience."

Fürth is a suburb of Nürnberg, with today two claims to fame: the five miles of local line from the city, built in 1835, was the first railroad in Germany; and its second, far more important claim, is that it suffered very little damage in the Second World War.

The ugly red-brick church was surrounded by jeeps and trucks and hundreds of blond German children. Then, the moment we stepped over the threshold into the gloom of the hot, G.I.-jammed interior, Something Awful Happened. . . .

Many years ago, as children in Ireland, we used to be dressed up in our Best, and when the bells began to ring every Sunday morning we'd set out, *en famille,* with prayer-books in our hands and a sixpence (for the plate) in our pockets, down the mile of avenue, to church. Church—a gaunt, gray, prison-like building outside—was like a morgue inside, smelling of dust. The moment I crossed the threshold I knew Something Awful was going to Happen. It began in earnest soon after we'd reached our pew, which was up front, past the rows of empty pews, under the pulpit. It began with a feeling of nausea as the wrinkled-skinned skull in soiled robes started droning in his corner under the dirty windows, where there always fluttered a dying peacock butterfly and a few dying flies. It started in the stomach and went up into your mouth, which was parched, and into your ears, which began to ring. It got really bad, so bad you presumed this was Death, when, holding on to the prayer-book rest, you had to stand up and pretend to sing the *Te Deum*. The crying question was: Should you just roll over and vomit right here or try to make a dash for the door between the pews? But at this critical moment between Here and the Unknown, my mother's hand would grip my elbow and I'd go with her, unsteadily, past the half-dozen villagers, past the old harmonium-pumper on his stool, and out into the glorious life-restoring light of day. And there, on a wall beside the moss-covered tomb of a famous Master of Fox Hounds, I'd sit out the Service with that sense of blissful well-being which only those to whom Something Awful has Happened can properly appreciate.

To feel faint among your family when you were young was not much fun, but to feel that way at the age of forty in Fürth was humiliating. To be surrounded by hundreds of strange men in uniform; to stand, holding on to the prayer-book rest, between two tall G.I.s who cannot figure out why you don't wish to share with them the Words; to have lost your one friend in the crowd coming in, and to see in that hot, gloomy interior no sign of getting out—that was Awful with a vengeance!

Under the spell, you strain every nerve to concentrate on one particular object; but your eyes don't focus properly; everything is blurred and your sense of balance is precarious; so you close your eyes and concentrate entirely through your ears.

The hundreds of male voices singing sounded like a great slow wailing in a cave.

> *I would be true, for there are those who trust me;*
> *I would be pure, for there are those who care;*
> *I would be strong, for there is much to suffer;*
> *I would be brave, for there is much to dare....*

I would be friend of all, the foe, the friendless;
I would be giving, and forget the gift;
I would be humble, for I know my weakness;
I would look up and laugh and lift. . . .
                                                            Amen.

The Words were a great help, for you'd never heard them; but somehow the singing was like all such singing you'd heard before.

When it ended and the world all round sat down, you looked at your watch and wondered, and were still wondering, when a single American voice forced your chin out of your cold perspiring hand and your eyes towards the pulpit where, instead of a skull in robes, you saw a figure like those on the cover of *The Business Weekly*, its curves framed tight in immaculate khaki.

"We may well be pleased with ourselves today. Two Sundays ago 380 of you attended service; last Sunday 300; and this Sunday there are not enough hymn-books to go round, because 500 of you have turned up. . . . I want you to tell that to the folks at home in your Sunday letter. . . . I want you to tell the folks that, because rumors are being spread by irresponsible tongues. . . . The folks are thinking of us out here, far from home, as disintegrating under the influence of wine . . . women . . . and worry. . . . I want you today to banish any such fears the folks at home may have. . . . I want you to tell them that this morning you shared the Book of Common Prayer with a Christian comrade, because there were not enough for all of you. . . .

"And now—while on the subject of sharing, I want . . . I want to tell you about the man—an ordinary man—he might be you or me . . . who, by sharing, came nearer to God. A simple man he was, an American, like you or me, who worked hard and made his fortune and was not happy. Why? Why was he not happy? Because his fortune brought him no nearer to God. . . . But there lived in the now rich man's town another man—a simple man, an American, like you or me—who worked hard but did not become rich. Why? He did not become rich because . . . because the rich man had procured all the business in the town. And when the rich man saw that his competitor was poor, he set to work to strive all the harder, to make even more money, an even bigger fortune. . . . Why? Not that he himself might become even richer, but that he might share his riches with his competitor, who was worse off than he. And that was what the rich man did. He shared his wealth with his competitor . . . and he came nearer to God."

I don't know what I'd have done without the Irresponsible Tongues and the Rich Man. Even if my head were not held high as I tottered out into the life-restoring sun, at least I could say, after too many years, that I'd endured the ordeal and put Something Awful, at last, to shame.

Next day, another awful thing happened—but of a different nature.

It's not a pretty story, but no record of Germany in 1945 would be complete without a glimpse into at least one of the many seamy little recesses of Occupational life. Nor is it an easy story to tell. It's not so simple to be honest when you've made a fool of yourself. The fact that you were not the only one doesn't help, doesn't lessen the sense of shame. The other one, the other villain, was the Major, poor devil.

Quite a time before our Sabbath visit to Fürth, it was becoming increasingly clear that the Major was growing restless. It began to show, by degrees, in small ways. At night, after what should have been a blissful day on the balcony, he would provoke a discussion, usually of a political nature, which led invariably to a battle of words over Russia, against whose government the Major, son of a wealthy Chicago banker, would brook no criticism. Stalin casting an eye on lands or territory the Soviet Army had not itself conquered in battle! What an outrageous suggestion! Prove it! Conducted in a friendly enough fashion, these arguments always proved pointless. Nothing could convince the Major that in the world of Power Politics all is not black and white; and the more pointless the discussions became, the more heated the Major grew, the louder he shouted, the longer they lasted.

"The morale of the Team is sinking!" he would say. "You're all a bunch of reactionaries! You talk like a Hearst editorial!"

In his increasing hunger for distraction, the Major began thinking up ideas on his own. One morning at breakfast, with a mischievous light in his eyes, he dealt out to each of us a slip of paper on which he asked us to write what we would like to eat for dinner that night.

"You know more or less what there is," he said, trying not to smile. "But I want each of you to state your favorite dish."

In a fractious, facetious mood, instead of mentioning any known food, I made a drawing of a Bavarian church with its pumpkin tower. It was just a piece of whimsy that happened to pop into my head; with the wildest stretch of imagination it could have suggested, I suppose, that my one desire was to swallow a church.

At lunch that day the Major seemed as pleased with himself and the world as a child with a secret he is about to divulge to his unsuspecting parents. By dinner-time he was beaming with anticipation, and when the door opened and Frau Miedel came into the room we understood why. She was carrying before her an immense platter on which there stood, surrounded by a green carpet of parsley, an astonishingly accurate model of a Bavarian church. As she deposited this colorful structure in the center of the table, we discovered that the tower was made of a length of hard red sausage (the first we'd seen in Germany), on top of which perched a shining, peeled onion. The body of the building was composed of layers of yellow cheese, with slabs of a darker cheese for windows and doors, while the roof was tiled with the outside shavings of radishes. Hans, as usual, was called in and congratulated on his feat, and the Major blushed with pleasure at the success of his idea. No political discussions were provoked that night, and the Major no doubt would have started conceiving another idea of a similar kind if something altogether unexpected hadn't occurred, next day, to divert his attention to a matter far less frivolous.

The trouble began with Hans bursting into the sitting-room while we were waiting for lunch. His face was flushed and he seemed unusually agitated. Mervyn, who had been strumming on the piano, stopped playing, looked round, asked Hans what was the matter.

"Ach, etwas Furchtbares!" breathed Hans. "Something awful's happened! Food has been stolen from the garage!"

"What's he say?" demanded the Major, sitting bolt upright in his chair.

"Oh," said Mervyn, who hated scenes, "just some food missing." And back he went to his strumming.

But the Major had leapt to his feet. "Food missing!" he cried. "Where? How? What? Preposterous!"

And away he went, followed by Frank and Dudley, to the scene of the crime.

A thorough investigation revealed that the thief or thieves must have possessed an intimate knowledge of the place, and that they had not been clumsy. Carefully selecting several heavy cans of beef, some pounds of fresh fruit, a can of gas, they had gone to considerable pains to conceal traces of their work.

That night it was quite a different Major who sat at table. He was silent and he glowered. One felt that he considered his authority, his position of responsibility to have been assailed—in a word, that it was he who had been caught napping, and that he would not rest (or rather, sunbathe) until the food and the culprits had been cornered.

When everyone in the house had been questioned, it appeared that the crime could only have been committed during two hours of the previous afternoon, a time when Hans had omitted to padlock the garage door, and when the one person present in the house had been the Major! Where, then, had the Major been? Why, he'd been up on the balcony, as usual, sunbathing! This balcony, however, overlooked the garage.

"How could anyone come in off the road by that gate," demanded the Major, "walk into the garden under my nose, open the garage doors, and go off with that amount of loot without my hearing the bastards?"

To this question there seemed to be no answer. Perhaps the Major had been asleep? Preposterous! The Major had never slept a wink on the balcony. So the native members of the household were questioned again. Had they ever seen a stranger in the garage? Had Hans? No. Frau Miedel? *Mein Gott, nein!* Trude? *Nay, nay.* Hertha? What was it the *Herr Major* wanted to know? A stranger in the garage? Hertha hesitated. Surely the excessively shy, pretty young Hertha, so rarely heard to breathe a word, was not going to shatter this silence with a bombshell! Bombshell or not, hers was the only evidence anyone had to offer.

"*Ja,*" she whispered. "I saw children."

The Major found the news sensational. "Children!" he pounced. "Ask her *what* children!"

Hertha dropped her dark brown eyes, blushed with embarrassment. "I don't know who they were," she whispered. "But not—not nice children. They were—rough-looking."

"What did she do when she saw them?"

"I told them to go away."

"And?"

"They went, but they came back again!"

The Major did not join in the titters which greeted this remark. He dismissed the Germans and looked glum. He continued silent and morose all that evening, and I had a feeling he was planning some secret coup on his own.

The following Monday, the day after the visit to Fürth, my afternoon interview had been brief, so that I returned to the house early and alone. I had just sat down over a dog-eared *New Yorker* in the sitting-room, when in burst the Major—not, for once, naked to the waist, but in full battle dress.

"Jim," he whispered, gripping my arm in great excitement, "I guess we've got 'em!"

"Got who?"

He almost pulled me out of the chair. "Take a look out of that window," he breathed. "But keep back—don't let yourself be seen."

Taking a look out of the window, I saw a couple of children standing between the privet hedge and the gate leading into our garden.

"Recognize them?" he asked. "Are those the kids I've seen you talking to outside here?"

"No," I said. "Can't say I've seen them before."

"Keep close watch on 'em," he said, "while I go up onto the balcony and scan the horizon from there."

The two children were boys whom I judged to be about five and seven years old. I didn't know them. As I watched, it did strike me that their behavior might be considered suspicious. The attention of the elder one was quite clearly directed towards our garden, while the other seemed to be on the lookout for someone down the street. Then they moved off and were lost to view behind the hedge. They'd been gone only a few seconds when I heard the Major come rushing down the stairs. As he dashed into the room he was fixing his revolver holster to his belt.

"Come on, Jim!" he cried. "They've quit. Gotta catch 'em. Quick. Stick your cap on, man. Jump into the jeep. Drive down the road till I tell you to stop. . . ." (The Major, poor devil, being an officer, was not allowed to drive a jeep.)

We were already out of the house.

"Major," I said, as we came out onto the road, "what on earth are you going to do?"

"Don't ask questions, man. Do what I tell you."

I put the jeep into gear, turned it and, looking straight ahead, sent it roaring down the road.

"Stop!" yelled the Major after a couple of hundred yards.

The Major leapt out. "Now follow me!" he ordered.

I wished—then no less than today—that I had been a spectator of, rather than a participator in the following scenes. From now on I was borne along by the impossible social position of the civilian vis-à-vis the army officer. Gradually losing my identity, I found myself acting as though under that kind of spell imposed upon the layman by the lunatic.

The instant the Major's feet touched tarmac he started charging across the road towards a large, dirty, vacant plot of ground. On a mound in the middle of this open space, I saw half a dozen children silhouetted against the sky. At this moment I watched the Major whip his revolver from its holster and brandish it high in the air. Simultaneously he doubled his speed and let out a kind of war-cry. The children, as though playing their part in a mock-trial of war, promptly collapsed and disappeared from view. Reaching the mound, I found them gathered together in a deep crater full of ash and garbage. They stood there, their arms stretched above their heads, staring blankly down the barrel of the Major's gun.

All six children were boys, healthy-looking and dressed in shirts, shorts, and shoes. The two eldest were adolescents—one very handsome, the other with a sullen, peculiarly evil face. The middle couple were around ten years old, while the youngest were those we had seen outside the house, mere tiddlers of perhaps five and six.

"Now then," breathed the major, still panting from his recent gallop, "ask them what the hell they think they're doing here."

It is not easy to sound aggressive when you don't feel it; and since I had less reason to feel as the Major felt and would not have agreed that the best, most dignified way of rounding up children suspected of thieving is to hunt them to ground in a garbage dump, my duty as interpreter of the Major's intentions was neither simple nor pleasant to perform. When asked coldly what they were doing in the garbage, it was not difficult to anticipate their answer.

"*Nichts,*" muttered the bigger boys.

"*Nichts,*" squeaked the smaller.

What did they mean by "*Nichts*"? the Major wanted to know. They must have been doing something.

"Playing," said the elder boys.

"Just playing," piped the tiddlers.

Meanwhile the Major and I, unknown to one another, had been watching the boy whom I shall call Evil, casting his eyes surreptitiously at something on the ground. The Major made the first move. He walked over to where Evil was standing and after a few seconds' search picked up a full beer bottle.

"Take a look at this," said the Major.

Taking the bottle, which had a rubber valve stop, I prised it open and put it to my nose.

"This is gasoline," I said.

"Gas!" exclaimed the Major, agog with triumph.

I turned the bottle to the light, poured out a little of the liquid on my hand. "I'm pretty sure it's pink," * I said.

"Ask him where the hell he got it!" demanded the Major.

"I found it," said Evil.

"Where?"

"Here—buried in the ashes."

"A damned lie," snapped the Major. "Tell him he's a liar."

"Major," I said, "do you really think that would get us anywhere?"

But the Major insisted. So I informed Evil that he was a liar, which I considered probably true. But Evil, as might have been expected, didn't even deign to repeat his statement: he simply shrugged his shoulders and said nothing.

"Ask him what the hell he was going to do with it!"

"Take it to my mother for her spirit lamp," Evil said.

The Major, still heartened by his one discovery, seemed undaunted by the apparent deadlock. Thrusting his foot into the heaps of ash, turning over chunks of decomposed garbage, he began touring the immediate area in search of further booty. Returning, empty-handed, he wanted to know where each of the children lived.

* U.S. military gasoline was colored pink, to distinguish it from any other. The Germans had already devised an ingenious method of extracting it from the jeeps' tanks. A German beer bottle just fitted into the hole by which the tank is filled. Provided the tank was not less than half full, these bottles could be dropped in, allowed to fill while in the tank, then withdrawn.

"Near the North East Station," they repeated one after the other. This station was about a mile up the road, and it appeared that they lived in couples in the same block of houses.

Why did they come here?

They were out for a walk.

Had they ever been here before?

Nein.

"Ask each of them," demanded the Major.

"But, Major," I protested, "so long as they are together they're all bound to say the same thing!"

"Never mind."

Nein, none of them had ever been here before.

"We'll take them back to the house," the Major said. "Tell them to follow me. You drive the jeep back."

The Major walked off, carrying his revolver and followed by six children, while I returned to the jeep, carrying the bottle of gas.

The children were assembled in the garden, facing the door of the garage.

"Now then," said the Major, "ask them if they've ever been here before."

I was about to repeat what I'd just said about them being "bound to say the same thing," but my small powers of self-assertion were dwindling fast, and I refrained.

Nein, none of them had ever been here before.

What had those two standing by the gate been doing there?

"Just looking in," muttered the taller tiddler.

"Ja," repeated the smaller, "just looking in."

"A damned lie," snorted the Major. "Tell them they'll be carted straight off to jail if they don't confess."

I looked at the Major. But I said nothing. To the children I said, "It would be better for you to tell the truth."

"But we are!" they chorused. "We haven't done anything wrong."

At this point in the humiliating proceedings, I felt at one moment an almost uncontrollable desire to run from the scene, at the next to burst into shrieks of hysterical laughter.

"Jim," I heard the Major saying, "go and fetch Hertha and ask her if she can identify any of the damned brats as those she saw in the garage."

This, at least, was action; it at least relieved me of continuing to face the children's dumb, bewildered stares.

I found Hertha with Hans in the kitchen, and when I told her what was expected of her, I gathered from her embarrassed smile that she did not exactly relish the prospect. But she followed me meekly out of the house. There, standing on the terrace above the group of kids, like an inexperienced school-mistress about to deliver her first lesson, she glanced at the row of expressionless faces. Then, slowly, gravely, in a negative motion, she began wagging her head from side to side.

There are situations in the tragicomedy of life that defy relief. One might select such moments as the test of human balance. The nervous—hovering with tightly closed eyes on the edge of the abyss—either surrenders himself to hysteria, or, seeing red like the proverbial bull, lowers his head and goes berserk. The utmost the more stable constitution can manage is to hold himself taut in a state of perspiring paralysis. It is always within the bounds of possibility that in this condition temporary salvation can appear by a miraculous flash of the grotesque, of the inscrutable, issuing from a world bordering on that of the dreamer, the drug-addict, or the drunkard.

How the suggestion I made entered my mind, to be expressed unsmilingly in speech, I am powerless to tell. When put into practice, it was an idea for which I imagine only a surrealist or a lover of the perverse would have given me credit.

"Major," I heard a voice, which was mine, saying, "how about getting Hans out to nod his head up and down, instead of wagging it sideways?"

Was my condition contagious? Had the Major, poor devil, also drunk of the cup of Queerdom? How else could he, instead of suggesting I go and stick my head under a cold tap, have instantly and with a straight face accepted my idea, have reckoned it, indeed, reasonable? (Did he think he might convince the "damned brats" not only that we considered them liars, but that we had a reliable witness to prove that they were thieves?)

Reasonable was hardly the word Hans could have been expected to accept as a fit description of my flight of fancy. Frying onions in the kitchen and totally unaware of the strange events, he did precisely the opposite of what I, now sobered by his white chef's cap and the kitchen calm, was asking him to do outside. In silent, stupefied disbelief, he slowly, gravely wagged his head from side to side!

"Oh, Hans!" I sighed weakly. "This is one long Tragedy of Errors, and you are asked to play so small a role! A man, after all, does not commit perjury by a nod of his head!"

Hans, God bless his soul! had a sense of humor. A smile slowly began to dispel the gravity of his face, and wiping his hands on his apron, adjusting his cap, he followed me out onto the terrace. He stood there a moment, gazing down on the children, glancing from face to face; and he had just begun to nod, to play his part to perfection, when suddenly at the end of the garden the gate clicked open, and the massive, bull-necked figure of the Professor, in gloves and helmet, bayonet dangling from his belt, came marching up the path —followed by Frank, Dudley and John.

Seldom have I heaved a deeper sigh of relief.

The ensuing consultation quickly developed into an argument, and from an argument into moments of silence broken by burst of hot-tempered words. I tried to explain the situation to the Professor, but I could see he was already too incensed to listen.

"I'll be damned if I'll have anything to do with the whole f——— business!" he growled, digging his huge boot into the ground.

As though he had overheard this remark, the Major shouted, "We'll now drive these brats back and search their homes!"

For a moment I thought a mutiny was about to break.

"I've never been taught how to search a house!" barked the Professor.

"Nor 've I!" piped Dudley, whose squeal for once failed to provoke a giggle.

"Then it's about time you damn well learned!" shouted the Major. I noticed that his face had turned a deep red, and I suddenly felt sorry for him.

"Come on!" he ordered. "The enlisted men get their rifles and revolvers. Two kids to a jeep. John, you take the lead with me."

I got into the Professor's jeep, with the handsome youth and one of the tiddlers in back.

"That guy's plain nuts," growled the Professor, as we shot up the road behind the Major. "He's sure got me pissed off."

"I'm not far from that condition myself," I told him. "Look here," I added, "I don't know what you intend to do in these kids' homes, but I'm through. If we're supposed to search a house, I'll do some face-saving by opening and shutting closet doors, but that's all. You'll have to do the talking for once. I've already had to say more than enough."

I was under the impression that the Professor had so much to say just then, that he'd have exploded at the wheel if he'd so much as uttered a word. As we pulled up behind the Major's jeep, outside a row of gray, unbombed modern tenement houses, his bull-dog jaw was set and there was an ominous glint in his eyes behind the horn-rimmed spectacles.

The Professor spoke the most peculiar German—a German pronounced exactly as it's spelt, with no trace of German accent, without inhibition and very loud. As he let himself out of the jeep he turned on the handsome youth.

"*Heraus!*—Get out!" he roared. "*Wo ist dein Heim?*—where's your home?"

Neither Handsome, nor the tiddler, as they jumped down from the back seat, showed any sign of alarm. Perhaps that was the most surprising, as well as the most disconcerting feature in all this appalling performance: at no time had any of the boys, not even the smallest child, revealed any emotion. They just stared at us blankly, as though at some not quite sane strangers putting on a mad but harmless act.

In the street each jeep-load dispersed in different directions. Handsome, followed by the five-year-old, led us under an archway into a courtyard. A few G.I.s were standing about, apparently billeted here. Outside a tenement entrance a short, round-shouldered, rat-faced man, who had been sitting on the ground, stumbled to his feet. The youth stopped in front of him, glanced at us, then muttered that this was his father. I gazed at the yellow, wizened, inferior-looking weasel of a man and wondered how it was possible for him to have sired the blond, blue-eyed, exceptionally good-looking boy. When the Professor barked at the father that we had come to search his apartment, the latter began to tremble, to stutter, to point accusingly at his son, then look questioningly at us.

Father and son led us up a narrow staircase into two tiny rooms which, while looking clean enough, reeked of stale sweat and sick stomachs. While Handsome stood near the window, the father's eyes shifted menacingly from his son to the tiddler who sat huddled in a corner. Then the Professor broke into a vociferous tirade which I shall not attempt to reproduce. His voice filled the room. In his excruciating American-German he informed the father that his boy and other members of a gang had been found in a garbage-pit in possession of American gasoline, that gasoline and food had been looted from our garage. In the midst of this raucous, declamatory speech the father, with a burst of incomprehensible curses, suddenly lunged towards Handsome and struck him twice across the face with the back of his hand. The son, making no effort to defend himself, flinched under the blows, but stood his ground without uttering a word. When the father continued to attack him with a volley of accusations, the boy simply shook his head.

"I didn't do anything," he finally muttered through his teeth.

This seemed to infuriate the parent all the more, and as

he again prepared to lay into the unfortunate youth, we stepped between them. The man's arms dropped to his sides, and he glanced up at us with his jaundiced eyes full of a cringing fear.

The Professor then ordered him to open all his closets. This so-called search was a farcical performance that might have taken place on an amateur stage. At the end of it we had found, between us, a bottle of questionable vinegar, some stale bread, and a few potatoes. When I considered the rumors that had undoubtedly been circulating about the meals which twice a day were laid on our table, I did not wonder that the more courageous local people were ready to risk their "freedom" to relieve us of some of our edible reserves. Nor did I wonder, when the Professor had administered to the cowering father a final warning as to the behavior of his son, and we were out in the street again—I didn't wonder, glancing up at the tenement windows, that on most of the faces looking down on us as we drove away, silent and empty-handed, there was a smug, sardonic smile.

ERLANGEN AND BAMBERG

13

THE last week at Nürnberg we commuted to Erlangen, the university town some seventeen miles north, on the main road to Bamberg.

We didn't take that road, but clattered early every morning through the city's periphery of ruins, past the meaningless mass of American military roadsigns heaped one over the other on telegraph poles, past the sleepy Negro traffic-directors and over a crater-ridden lane which bumped you out of the suburbs into a pine forest and out of that again onto an *Autobahn,* where you could race into Erlangen in ten minutes at sixty miles an hour.

Erlangen is a dull town, lying in dull, flat country. The low eighteenth century houses still "lend the place," as Baedeker says, "a comfortable bourgeois air." On the main square, in front of the Schloss, stood a statue of Margrave Friedrich of Kulmbach-Bayreuth, founder of the University. Looking a little like Oliver Cromwell, he was being used by the Americans as a telegraph pole, with coils of wire twisted round his ruffled neck. At his feet stood the town's proclamation board, tacked to which I saw the first notice, in large black type, of American films for the German public. One was a movie of the Wild West, the other was called OIL.

For interviewing in Erlangen we had, for the first and last time, a whole house to ourselves—a onetime schoolhouse which the Nazis had turned into a museum for the purpose of discrediting Freemasonry. I heard later that it was the only one of its kind in the country. Round the walls of the upstairs rooms stood glass-covered showcases full of Masonic symbols, gavels, and deformed military Iron Crosses with typed labels attached that informed the visitor they had been desecrated by Masons. On the walls hung framed charts, convention cards, and colored reproductions of Masonic pictures belonging to members of lodges in California, Pennsylvania and other American States. Some of these membership scrolls were written in Hebrew.

Like Kempten, Erlangen had been very little damaged by air-raids and was consequently packed with evacuees from Nürnberg, the Saar, the Ruhr, with refugees from Berlin, Dresden, Breslau, and other cities in the East—all of whom "schimpfed" as usual about the way they had been made to suffer at the hands of the natives.

The natives had suffered mostly from the fear of being raided, from hearing every night the thunder of the planes passing overhead on their way to Nürnberg, and then, a few minutes later, feeling the foundations of their homes rock as the big city quaked under the deluge of bombs. Even when the earth ceased to shudder they never knew whether the Allied pilots had not been ordered to attack Erlangen on their way home; but they did know that if they were attacked they stood little chance of survival, for of all the towns we visited I think Erlangen's defenses and shelters were the most inadequate. This, of course, worked both ways. There were those, like the nineteen-year-old girl I interviewed, who said: "Nay, we had only our cellars, and they were useless. I thought if we were going to be bombed, at least we'd have had decent shelters. . . . Of course," she added, "the Party people had them, up in the hills."

Erlangen seemed overrun with girls from all over Germany. On some days the onetime anti-Masonic museum sounded like a school for young females. I had one girl, from Pomerania, who simply refused to speak. She just stared at me out of eyes that registered absolutely nothing. Finally, in desperation, I swopped her with the Professor for a deaf, toothless old moron of a man who answered almost every question with a grin full of gums, a nod and a "Yaw! Yaw!

That's the way it was!" When I peeped through the Professor's door an hour later, I heard him giving "my" girl one of his lectures on democracy. Another girl, a native of Erlangen and very handsome, told me she was a member of "the small German intelligentsia"—which may have been true, but her ignorance of anything outside Germany didn't say much for this "small" and apparently exclusive group. The girl I remembered best was an eighteen-year-old blonde who'd been forced into the Luftwaffe late in the war. She'd worked on an airfield at Bayreuth where, she said, the Germans used six-motor Italian Savoia planes. Once, when two hundred of them were assembled on the field, the Allies had raided Bayreuth and destroyed almost all of them. In 1944 she'd been forced into the *Feuerschutzstaffel* and with five other girls and three men had driven into Nürnberg on a Fire Brigade engine, to fight fires.

"We always drove first to the Deutscher Hof," she said, "where Hitler and the big-shots used to stay. In February of this year I was on the third floor of the Deutscher Hof in the middle of a raid, when the hotel caught fire. I had on an asbestos suit which saved my body, but flames from phosphorus bombs burnt my arms, my legs and my head under my helmet. The pain from the burns was terrible."

She was violently bitter against the Luftwaffe. "They gave us girls," she said, "almost nothing to eat. I really think if it hadn't been for our parents, we'd have starved to death. We used to sing all night to try and prevent ourselves thinking about our empty stomachs. We were too hungry to sleep. We weren't allowed to speak to any Luftwaffe men, in case we heard too much."

Even Germany's defeat she put down to the Luftwaffe—or rather to "old Meyer,* that *Lump!* There'd always been too much talk about the Luftwaffe," she said. "The men in it

* The Germans' nickname for, and one of their oldest jokes about, Hermann Goering who, at the end of a pre-war speech, boasted that if ever a foreign plane should drop a bomb on a German city: "Then my name is Meyer!"

were half mad with bitterness and despair. If any of them was heard or reported to have said the war was lost, he was promptly taken out and shot. I was in the Luftwaffe, so I know. I tell you, I was really ashamed of being a German."

At noon we didn't return to Nürnberg, but took our Hans- and Miedel-made sandwiches out of town into the pine forest, and lay there in the silence under the trees and talked or dozed until it was time to return for the afternoon interview. When that was over we used to wander back, slowly and reluctantly, to the ruins. One afternoon I drove off in the opposite direction, to Bamberg, partly to take a look at that city and partly to call on Gustav Schulz, and see for myself under what conditions that garrulous opportunist was living.

If there ever again comes a time when students and lovers of architecture wish to see with their own eyes the great monuments of Europe's past, I believe that Bamberg is the only city left in Germany today where they can be found. The most superb examples of all styles, from the 12th to the 19th centuries, are here, and all are intact. In spite of this, you get the impression that the city suffered several quite severe raids. All along the arms of the river Regnitz, single buildings lay in ruins; all but two of the city's dozen bridges were blown up, and in such a way that the ancient houses near them were also destroyed. This damage was done, however, not by Allied planes or artillery, but once again by the S.S. during the last days of the war.

Gustav Schulz lived behind the Romanesque-Gothic-Baroque church of St. Jakob, in one of the most beautiful sections of Bavaria's most beautiful city. His apartment in the lovely eighteenth-century house had a view from its front windows over the green fertile valley of the Regnitz, and from the rear over lush and shady private gardens that reminded me of the cool patios of Seville.

"Such a pleasure to see you, Herr Stern!" he said, turning on me that super-charming smile as he led me through the cool spacious rooms. "Pleasant here, isn't it?"

"It certainly is," I agreed. "You're lucky to have chosen Bamberg to live in!"

"*Tcha,*" he sighed, hunching his huge shoulders. "Bamberg! It's no place for an active man, you know."

"No? What's wrong with it?"

"Ach, there's nothing doing here," he snorted. "And the people! So dull! So provincial! They're all asleep. Terrible! Just now a man came to ask my advice—used to be one of the editors of *Die Dame* in Berlin. D'you know, it was a relief—to talk even to him!"

Then a door opened and a woman in a spotless white dress came in. She looked as though she were just off to a garden party.

"You remember my wife?" asked Schulz.

"Of course," I lied, and thought how sad and ill Frau Dr. Schulz looked compared with her big, boisterous husband.

"*Na, mein lieber Herr Stern,*" said that man, smacking his hands and drawing his bulk out of the comfortable armchair. "What shall it be? How about some fresh fried eggs, some—?"

"Eggs?" I gasped.

"Ha!" beamed Schulz. "Why not? And some coffee—black or *Crême, comme à Paris?* Or wine—a little iced hock?"

"I'll take the wine, thanks," I said. "We haven't much, and what we have is bad."

"Ah, my poor fellow," sighed Schulz, striding from the room, "I always say there's nothing worse than bad wine."

"What a world!" sighed his wife when he was out of earshot.

"Yes, indeed!" I muttered, and guessed she meant—consciously or unconsciously—the world of Gustav Schulz rather than the world in general.

"Has your husband already been to the Swiss border?" I asked.

"No," she replied, and she couldn't have shown less interest. "I believe he plans to leave tomorrow."

"Here we are!" he cried, returning with a bottle and a couple of glasses.

When his wife got up and left the room and he had filled the glasses, Schulz took two small framed photographs from an antique writing-table and showed them to me, one by one.

"My boy!" he beamed, as though he alone had conceived the tall, handsome young man in white flannels. "Still missing," he said and handed me the other, of an intelligent-looking blond girl: "And my daughter."

"Is she here, too?" I asked, for something to say.

"*Ach, nein,*" he said, and chuckled, and turned on the smile like that of a mischievous boy. "She and I—we had a little—a little tiff—and off she went! You know, of course, how it is with temperamental young girls!"

"Oh, of course," I muttered.

"*Ja,*" said Schulz, stretching his long arms and legs and lying back in his chair. "It's a pity you were not here the other day—the 20th of July. I was thinking of coming over and picking you up in my car, but then they held the service so early. We had a memorial Mass here in the cathedral for Graf von Stauffenberg and all those other poor men. His widow was present. It was very moving. I defended one of the Generals, you know. I've copies of a long correspondence with the widow. It should be of great interest to the American military government."

"I'm sure," I muttered, and then Frau Schulz reappeared with two fried eggs, some potatoes cooked in what tasted like butter, and some coffee.

"Aren't you having some?" I asked her.

"Thank you, no," she said. "I'm not hungry."

"We dine later," said Herr Dr. Gustav Schulz.

"Oh, I see," I said, and finishing my good meal I rose to go.

"Well, *lieber Herr Stern,*" said Schulz at the door. "My kindest regards to everyone in London. I may be over there one of these days. Who knows?"

Who, indeed! I thought, as I got into the jeep and drove, in the sublime summer evening, out of Bamberg, through Erlangen, on to the *Autobahn,* and into the forest of pines.

ERLANGEN AND BAMBERG

All the way I had been thinking of the Schulzes of the world, wondering what it was in their make-up that allowed them to get away, even in Nazi Germany, in the Europe of 1945, with so much, when I happened to notice, in the silent forest lane, a U.S. military sign that was not, to me, a meaningless letter or anagram, nor even a pseudonym such as "Garbage" or "Ashcan," denoting God knew what unit of American occupation. It was just a simple sign—large black letters on a white background, with an arrow pointing left —saying exactly what it meant: U.S. MILITARY CEMETERY.

I debated a moment, then turned the jeep left and scrunched down a cinder-covered lane. Suddenly the forest opened up to form a small circular space over which a floor of wooden planks had been laid. In the center of this deserted spot stood another sign: VISITORS' VEHICLES. Parking the jeep, I got out and walked toward an opening in the trees through which I could already see line upon line of neat white crosses. Reaching the fringe of the cemetery, I stood still and found myself admiring the good sense and taste of the man who had chosen such a spot to bury the dead. In a large, protected circle cut out of the pines, hundreds upon hundreds of crosses—all identical except for an occasional, surprising Star of David—gleamed white against a background of beautifully mown, very green grass. It was the first clean, orderly, peaceful place I had encountered in the neighborhood of Nürnberg. I stood for several minutes in the intense evening silence and thought: If I should die tomorrow, this is where my bones, if not my dog-tag, would lie forever. . . .

The scene was so peaceful, so still, so lonely that I had begun to imagine it inhabited only by the dead, when suddenly, moving forward a few paces, I saw, just beyond the periphery of graves and set against the background of forest, a small house of stained wood. Approaching it, I noticed that its wall facing the cemetery had carved on it, criss-crosswise, a series of sporting symbols—a tennis racquet, a club, what looked like a lacrosse net, and under these a ball, cut out of the wood.

While examining this example of "Aryan" art, from which I gathered, correctly, that what was now an American military cemetery had recently been a German *Sportsplatz*, I had the sensation that I was not alone. Looking up quickly, I saw above me a small window, from behind which there gazed down at me—sleepily, uninquiringly—a coffee-colored face. I heard the sound of slow footsteps from within, and a moment later a door opened and out came a lean, pleasant-looking Negro corporal.

"I was just having a look round," I said, by way of explaining my presence.

"That's okay," said the corporal. He then lit a cigarette, pulled up a stool, sat down and leaned back against the doorpost. Behind him I noticed a pile of narrow wooden planks and a large can of paint.

"You lookin' for anyone special?" he asked, his glance turning on the sea of graves behind me.

"No," I said. "I was just passing by and saw the sign."

And then, more for the sake of conversation than from genuine interest, I asked him from what battle area these casualties had been taken.

"Battle?" he said, frowning. "Why, the war's been over two months and more. . . ."

"But surely," I began, but he cut me short.

"What with the dozen this morning, that couple at noon"—he put the cigarette between his lips and began doing some mental calculation on his fingers—"that makes one thousand and twenty-six. Out o' that number, I guess there's no more'n a couple o' hundred battle casualties out there."

"But what about the others?" I asked. "How come they—?"

"Oh, there's all kinds," he said, pulling on his cigarette. "Mostly on the road. We average about thirteen a day. Jeeps, trucks, weapons-carriers. Specially bad in wet weather. 'Careless drivin',' they call it. Guys get boozed up, you know. A long time and a long way from home, they do all kinds o' crazy things. There's what they call 'accidental deaths,' and others not so accidental. There's soocides—just had a couple this noon. . . ."

"A couple?"

"Well, that's the way I understand it," said the corporal. "These two were buddies, see. Ever since they left home, about three years back, they were always together. That's the way it gets some guys. . . . One of 'em was married and had just heard he'd got enough points to go home. He was all set to leave for one of them French ports end of this week —today it would have been. Then he gets a letter from his wife. A short letter. Just to congratulate you, she says, on bein' the proud father of a beautiful baby boy. . . ."

The corporal hesitated, looked at me a moment, then continued in a toneless voice. "Well, this guy, after he reads the letter, he gets his gun and goes and looks for his buddy. I guess no one knows, never will know, just what was said, but anyway the bodies were found in a wood back of their billets, and the guy that wasn't married, he was holdin' the gun. . . ."

The silence that followed seemed endless. I gazed down at the grass between my feet, while my eyes watched a faceless girl writing a letter. . . . "A beautiful baby boy," I found myself muttering.

"Yep," I heard the corporal saying in his matter-of-fact way, "yep, that's the way it gets some women."

I turned and faced the graves. The sun, now sinking fast, came streaming through the forest onto the acres of crosses, painting their whiteness a delicate shade of pink. The trees, darkening in the evening light, seemed to be drawing closer, as though intent on forming a solid, intimate circle of protection against the oncoming night and all the nights to come.

"It's a peaceful place you've got here," I said, turning once more to the corporal.

His lips parted, and for the first time a smile spread slowly over his face. All of a sudden he beamed. "Glad you like it," he said. "Come again."

FRANKFURT

14

WELL, our work was over. We had eaten our last Gargantuan German meal, taken our last interview. Only in our sleep should we ever again ask anyone how he was getting along under the Occupation, how many hours' work he had voluntarily avoided during the war.

An embarrassed farewell had been taken of Frau Miedel, Hertha, Hans. All three had feared our coming; they were mighty sorry to see us go. "What shall we do without you?" sighed Frau Miedel, and her eyes asked: Shall we get kicked out of our basement? What shall we get to eat?

Standing beside the mother and daughter, a small bag at his feet, Hans waved his shattered hand. How he was going to get back to Kempten no one knew, and no one seemed to care. All we cared about was that our circle was completed. Tonight we'd sleep where I'd slept the first night, a few miles from where I'd slept the first night I ever spent in Germany—at Bad Nauheim.

In Nauheim everything was different—more as I'd expected it to be when we arrived in May. The entire Survey was reuniting—or rather uniting for the first time. Enlisted men, officers and civilians had converged on the Spa in jeeps from all parts of Germany and Austria outside the Russian zones.

At the entrance to the Park Hotel two MPs—each with his weight on one leg, like bored horses at the gate of a field—were standing guard, surrounded by groups of gaping children. One pale, constantly laughing boy kept pirouetting on his one leg and crutch with the agility of a ballet-dancer. He drew from every observant eye special regard, for after the shock of the hanging stump, you noticed that half of one of his ears, three fingers of one small hand and all the fingers of the other were missing. A Belgian orphan cut to pieces in a raid on Aachen, he had become a great favorite among the German children and G.I.s, enjoying the attention caused by his crippled condition as much as the scraps of gum and candy his wounds elicited from the pockets of the conquerors.

Inside the hotel, life was like that of an ant-hill. In one hour I ran into Frank Knox (off for a sulphur bath), into the little man with the mustache whom I'd first seen skipping from telephone to telephone in the Pentagon; in the lobby I met Hindler breezing through with a brief-case ("Cood Cod, clad to see you! Cood-bye!") and the German-American with the apoplectic face who told me he'd just run into an acquaintance of mine in Frankfurt. "Still vorking in ze *Metallgesellschaft!*" he spluttered.

Everyone was running into Everyone; men who had never exchanged more than a word greeted one another like lifelong friends. At one moment it was like Old Boys Day at an English public school, and at the next—because we knew we all had to be "off the Continent" within seventy-two hours— it was so much like the Last Sunday of Term that I half-expected to be ordered into the ugly Gothic church, there to join in the rousing chorus of:

>   *"Lord, dismiss us
>   With Thy blessing;
>   Thanks for mercies
>   Past received. . . ."*

Then, after the first hour—after the disappointment of finding four occupied beds in Room No. 88 and of having to share a dark hole of a room with a captain I'd never seen— the rumors began. Two topics—both, of course, scandalous— were humming through the hotel. The first concerned a number of officers and civilians who'd been caught returning from the Russian zone in trucks piled high with priceless gems. The treasure ranged anywhere from sacks full of Nazi-looted pearls and diamonds to the Russian crown jewels gladly handed over to the Americans in exchange for ten thousand cartons of Camels and a few cases of *Courvoisier*. The culprits—some of them big-shots—were at large, awaiting no one knew what fate; and Everyone stared at them as at a fresh consignment of lions straight from Darkest Africa.

The second scandal proved, for me, of more interest, and more disturbing. In our absence, it seemed, the few officers and wretched coders (who for weeks had sat behind mountains of our interviews and documents) had grown so bored with the monotony of life in the dead Spa that in their spare time they'd filled up all the remaining jeeps with gasoline and gone off to spend days and weekends as far away from Nauheim as the gas would take them. The consumption of this life-giving liquid had reached such staggering proportions that, by the time we returned, the motor-pool was rumored to be running dry and on the Hotel Notice Board an order had appeared forbidding anyone to leave town in a jeep without special permission. With Frankfurt a dozen miles away and only seventy-two hours left to us on the Continent, this news came as a grave disappointment.

If I can't get to Frankfurt, I thought, I'll try Homburg—look for the doctor and Maria and that family whom I'd not seen in eighteen years. But even Homburg was too far to reach on foot; and anyway, in Germany in the summer of 1945, an American didn't set off alone on a ten-mile cross-country hike, least of all when in three days a plane was going to fly him in as many hours to London.

In my dilemma I sought out the few officers I knew. I consulted Frank, who was shooting snapshots of friends outside the hotel door. "Ah'm darned if Ah know what you can do," he said. "Ah guess we're stuck here."

Everyone said the same. Some bored, enterprising civilians decided to tramp to Friedberg, for no other reason than that it happened to be another small town, and nearby. But I had no interest in Friedberg. Then I ran into the Major, poor devil, who was champing at the bit of frustration because his girl in London had written him a letter whose tone sounded sinister.

"For Christ sakes!" he said. "If I don't get to London tomorrow or the next day I'll burst! What the hell's the good of sitting here, anyway! Can't even go to H.Q. in Frankfurt for a decent meal!"

I mentioned my personal predicament, and I watched a light come into the Major's big brown eyes—the same light I'd seen in Nürnberg when he'd conceived the idea of asking us to choose "our favorite dish" for dinner.

"Say, Jim!" he asked. "Have you any friends in Frankfurt itself?"

"I had," I said, "years ago. That's why I want to go there."

The Major banged one hand on the other. "Boy!" he cried. "Maybe I've got an idea. Meet me in the bar in a couple of hours."

When the Major had disappeared I wandered off through the park on my own, wondering who, of all the people I had known in Frankfurt, might still be alive and living there in its ruins. I came out of the park and was thinking of walking through the town and into the country, when I happened to notice an impressive, beige-colored building with steps leading up to its columned façade. I might not have given it a second glance, had there not been nailed, just under its roof, in huge block letters, one of those German words which, even with a fair knowledge of the language, you have to read twice in order to disentangle all the other words which have been telescoped to make up the one: HERZFORSCHUNGSINSTITUT—Institute for Heart Research.

The moment I'd read the first syllable I thought of Rector Hoffmann, near Kempten, and immediately of our mutual friend, Professor Gessner, the heart specialist who during the war had treated the rector. The Professor, so the rector had told me, was alive in 1942. "A wonderful man," I remembered him saying. "He was very outspoken, you know. I only hope he didn't lose his job at the Clinic."

Two well-dressed girls were standing outside the Institute, their heads bent over some sheets of paper.

"Could you tell me," I asked, "if Professor Gessner still works here?"

"*Herr Professor Gessner?*" repeated one of the girls, looking up. "*Ach nein.* He doesn't. And the Institute is closed."

"But I believe he lives here," said the other girl. "In a pension. I know the street, but not the number, I'm afraid."

"The street might do," I said, and when she told me its name I went off in search of it, and found it. Trees shaded its sidewalks on both sides, and its houses stood back from the road, with small patches of lawn, rosebeds and bushes of white hydrangea between. Twice I walked up and down the street without seeing any sign of a pension; and the only people I saw were an old couple on the balcony of a stucco house which badly needed a coat of paint. I had returned to this house and was leaning over the wooden fence, about to ask the old man or woman for the whereabouts of the Professor's pension, when I noticed that the old man had a beard, and when I noticed the beard I didn't say anything, but looked again, and then I realized that I was looking at the Professor and his wife, who were seventeen years older than when I had last seen them. Then I noticed something else: that the Frau Professor—the big, masculine, peasant-like woman who used to sit like a matriarch at the head of the table in front of her brood of children and grandchildren—I noticed that she was staring straight at me, without moving. Even when she opened her mouth and muttered something to the Professor, the eyes still stared at me and only her lips moved. Then it occurred to me that maybe she wasn't seeing me or the street or the sun, but only darkness. So I lifted the latch of the wooden gate and walked into the garden and stood under the balcony.

"*Herr Professor,*" I said.

The old man's head went up from his reading and he looked at the door giving onto the balcony as though expecting to see someone standing there; and when he saw no one he shook his head as though distrustful of his hearing, and went back to his book.

"Herr Professor," I said.

This time he leaned over the balcony and, taking off his spectacles, gazed down on the American uniform and the upturned face.

"Bitte?"

I'd never been one of the Professor's patients, nor known him well, so I re-introduced myself to him via Kurt, one of his many sons, and Gisela, Kurt's wife, whom I had known very well indeed, both before and after that marriage, which was her second. To place another rung in the broken ladder of years, to show the Professor how many of them had passed since our last meeting, I spoke the name of the strange Dr. Wolfgang Dunkelmann, Gisela's first husband, her second husband's mentor, who worshiped and physically resembled Goethe and had been dead a dozen years, whose life had been spent studying the art of the insane, interpreting dreams, living with and marrying beautiful women, and who, on being informed by Gisela that she was about to leave him for Kurt, glanced up from his desk and said: *"Meine Liebe,* I congratulate you! This is the first time I've been surprised by a human being!"—then went on with his work.

"Dunkelmann!" exclaimed the Professor, at the sound of that name. And raising his eyes from mine, he turned them on his wife, who was still staring in my direction seemingly into darkness.

"Ein Amerikaner," the Professor said, "who knew Dunkelmann and Gisela!"

The old lady didn't speak, didn't move, just went on staring.

"That must have been a long time ago," the Professor said. "Gisela, if you would like to see her, is still in Frankfurt, at the Funk Strasse, number 18, top floor. Kurt has been missing since March."

"I'm sorry to hear that, Professor," I heard myself say, and as I said it the balcony door opened and out came a sturdy blond boy with bright blue eyes and a flirtatious smile. I knew who he must be before the Professor said: "This is Ferdinand, Gisela's eldest son."

"You're the image of your mother," I said to Ferdinand, and the boy hunched his shoulders, cocked his head on one side and smiled just as Gisela always had as the fourth and youngest of Dr. Wolfgang Dunkelmann's wives.

"Have you any brothers and sisters, Ferdinand?" I asked.

"Five!" he said, smiling.

"Five!"

"His father had a dozen!" the Professor said, in a voice that sounded both proud and sad.

"Last time I saw your mother," I told Ferdinand, "she had a one month-old baby—"

"That was Constantia," Ferdinand said.

"She's already six-foot tall," added the old man.

"Good God!" I exclaimed. "She can't be more than thirteen!"

"Nearly fourteen," said Ferdinand, and I remembered that all the Gessners I'd ever seen instinctively lowered their heads on entering and leaving a room. I thought of Kurt, Ferdinand's gaunt gigantic father, with his mane of hay-colored hair, high wide brow, sunken eyes, every bony feature larger than life, the black velvet jacket he wore and from his long neck the heavy silver chain, like that of a *sommelier,* dangling to his waist. The memory left me chilled. I had not forgotten the look that had greeted my impulsive guffaw and question, nor the hostile glare he shot at me and then at Gisela, still Frau Dr. Wolfgang Dunkelmann, when her throaty Garbo giggle had joined mine and she muttered behind her hand: "Stefan George!"—which in retrospect explains more than it did then, for that was one of Germany's most exclusive Intellectual Worlds in which the works of Nietzsche, Spengler, Klages, George, the words Superman, Nordic Man, *Geist, Kultur, Seele, Volkstum* and *Tod;* the slogans Mysticism, Nationalism, Racism, Totemism were discussed in semi-bated breath; the music of Bach, Brahms and Beethoven with as much humor as famished cats over a fishbone; and psychology, pathology, anthropology, genealogy, graphology, morphology, musicology and mythology behind doors guarded jealously (I suspected later) against all but the "Aryan" elite.

It was perhaps the only world in which I—young, ignorant and a foreigner, yet nevertheless and necessarily at that age a bit of a chameleon—could not find, figuratively and often physically, a comfortable seat. There was over it all an air of superiority, an arrogant, humorless, intellectual, cabal-like clannishness—a *Bund*ishness through which I always sensed a sinister streak, but just what or why I did not know until years later, when I'd read more, thought more and come by degrees to the conclusion that many of these men, highly intelligent, responsible specialists in their various fields, were *pro* all the isms mentioned above, *anti* everything and everyone not of German *Blut,* German *Boden,* and therefore highly dangerous.

One whom I never suspected, and know today never to have been anything but an archenemy of this *Bund,* this brand of Germandom, was the old Professor under whose balcony I was standing. And another of whom I still was not suspicious, despite her marriage (if only because of her animal-like laziness, and her ability to giggle at the clan, at the mysticism, and all the other isms, even at her husband and the ridiculous wine-steward's chain), was the Professor's daughter-in-law.

So "I hope," I told the old man, "to be able to call on Gisela during the next couple of days."

"She will be pleased to see you, I'm sure," he said, and I said good-bye to him, to young Ferdinand, and to the old lady whose eyes still followed me as I walked away through the quiet green and golden evening, to the boisterous American military badinage in the hotel bar.

The Major pounced on me immediately, and—with the look I'd seen as Frau Miedel had brought into the dining-room Hans's edible effigy of the Bavarian church—he slapped me on the shoulder.

"I fixed it, boy!" he beamed in my ear. "For tomorrow! Jeep, gas, and all!"

"Major," I said, "you're a marvel—a bloody marvel, as the English say!"

"I'll buy you a lunch at H.Q.!" he said, and I beamed him back a smile of delight that was not entirely sincere.

"That would be wonderful, Major," I said. "But—well, would you mind if we drove over to Homburg first? I used to live there, years ago. . . ."

"That's perfectly okay, Jim," the Major said, "lots of time." And I told him briefly about the doctor and Maria, about the Professor I'd just met, about Gisela whom I hoped to find in Frankfurt, whereupon (not having listened to a word) he said: "That's perfectly okay, Jim. How about getting off around nine o'clock?"

"Perfectly okay, Major," I said, and went to the bar to celebrate, before going to bed.

Though I woke in the dark to the clatter of crockery and the reek of cushions cooking in the kitchen below the dingy room, the morning outside was magnificent. Birds sang in the acacia tree and in the umbrellas of chestnuts covering the row of idle jeeps.

"Let's make it snappy," the Major said. "The less we're seen the better."

We shot out of town, onto the *Autobahn* and off it at a turning from which I could see the spires of the church at Homburg. Yet nothing else was familiar as we drew near. I didn't know the road. My memory must have gone, or the road have been a new one. A new one? Well, less than twenty years of age.

Then we turned a corner, to emerge all of a sudden onto the Haupt Strasse—the long straight street with the two rows of tramlines; and the moment I saw the shining rails I could hear the heavy trundle of the trolley-cars, the gong-gong of the bell as the grim conductor in spectacles, black uniform and shiny peaked cap pulled the cord and commanded in his harsh strident German voice: *Einsteigen!*

Einsteigen! All aboard! And off we went, I sitting on one of those ribbed, upright, single wooden seats, opposite—opposite —who on earth was that dolled-up woman with the hooked nose, the large fake pink carnation on the brim of her blue straw hat and the over-rouged lips with their frightening, secret, sensual smile?

My God, what two decades can do to one's memory! Now I knew who she was, but only now—which was hard to believe! She of all people getting left out of the picture of the doctor and Maria and the other girl (what *was* her name?) who was often overcome with fits of weeping in the evenings after Maria and I had returned from a walk or from playing bad tennis on the good courts! She—Hawknose (*that* was my private name for the Old Girl of fifty)—she the doctor's wife, she the Frau Doktor! Imagine her getting left out of the picture! And this was the spot; from this very corner here she used to take the tram into Frankfurt once a week, and every time she went her face and behavior used to change. She had one bright-gold front tooth and a chin that stuck out and up towards the hooked nose, so that when she came down to breakfast on those mornings, all dolled-up under the blue hat and fake carnation, with brooches on her breast and dangling ear-rings and bracelets, and grinned as at no other time and yapped in her tense, tinny voice: *"Na, Kinder! Was wollen die Herrschaften aus der grossen Stadt?*—What does everyone want from the big city?"—when she said that with her secret, anticipatory smile and licked her rouged lips, I remembered thinking she looked like an evil Mr. Punch dressed up as a woman.

"I?" I could hear Maria whine in her peevish virgin voice, "I don't want anything from town, *Mutti,* I just want to go along with you!"

"Na, du!" pounced Hawknose over the slices of hard *Wurst* and the brass-potted aspidistra or *Palme.* *"You*—you are too young, child—" But, having let that escape, the lips would snap together over the golden tooth, and Hawknose would blush and shoot a look at me, who'd be already scarlet in

the face before she'd leer: *"Du, Maria,* you can give *dem Chimmy* German lessons—you can, *na ja*—Maria can do all kinds of things—*gel, Chimmy?"*

With that and the golden-toothed smile on me, I'd feel the sweat breaking out all over my body and I'd try in vain not to glance at the doctor as he quickly took the big flat watch from the pocket of his green knitted vest, and rising from the table, said: *"Na, los, Kinder!* It's already late!"

Whereupon Hawknose would begin to hum a tune and run up to the corner to catch her tram.

That evening every week there'd be a row. She'd come back, the smile gone and a dark, ominous look on her face. Arriving just in time for supper, she'd stand on the threshold of the dining-room, jab her sharp knuckles into her hips and with her elbows sticking out she'd rap out in her rasping tinny voice: *"Na, so was!"*

"Was denn?" Maria'd mutter, with the fear that came into her eyes only on these evenings.

"Was denn?" mocked the mother. "Child, have you really no eyes in your head? *Ach, ja,* I know who you keep your eyes for! [Oh, stop! I'd almost say aloud, the heat rising in my face.] The poor palm, the cactuses, covered in dust, and all day long not a drop of water!"

Maria would flush and lower her head. She had forgotten. So had I, and thinking why we'd forgotten I'd blush again.

"Sofort! That's easy!" I'd say, taking out my handkerchief and lifting the water-jug from the table. "Won't take a minute!"

"Chimmy!" the doctor'd shout from his end of the table. *"Lieber Chimmy!* One does not dust plants at table!"

"Und warum nicht? Why not?" snapped his wife, and suddenly my whole body'd freeze as I felt Hawknose behind me passing her bony fingers slowly over my hair.

"And why not?" she'd croon, the tinny voice soft as velvet now. *"Der Chimmy, der gute Chimmy* is probably right!"

Horrified, I'd finally shake my head free of her hand.

"*Na, nu!*" she'd grunt, in a suddenly low, insinuating tone. "The old one's hands are not—not soft enough, *gel?*"

"*Mutti!*" shouted the doctor, his head high, his eyes suddenly flaring.

"*Und?*"

It was like a grunt from an animal, and suddenly like an animal, like a wildcat creeping on its belly towards its prey, she'd move soundlessly round the table, the chin out, head low, the red fingernails twitching on her hips, towards the father of her children—the quiet, modest, patient man who kept the home going by sitting hours every day at bedsides, caring for the ill. She'd stand glowering over him, the hooked nose close above the bald crown of the head, and in the silence I'd try to prepare myself for the dreaded moment when the painted claws would at last shoot out and up from the hips. . . . But they never did, not in my time, for just when you couldn't stand it any longer the father'd look up and with a smile that would always make me want to take his hand, he'd smack his knee with that hand and say: "*Ach, Mutti!* What a fool I am! Know what I've done now?"

"*Was denn?*"

"I," he'd say, pointing a finger at his bald forehead, "I've gone and left the car in the Haupt Strasse—tomorrow I'll be fined!" Or: "I also forgot to dust and water the plants!" Or: "Once more I've gone and lost my spectacles! Fool, idiot that I am, *Mutti!*"

She never got used to it, somehow was never prepared for it when it came. It worked every time, and for the naive young man, the twenty-year-old youth, it was always wonderful. For after her little triumph, expressed in tin: "Ha! *Das du ein Idiot bist hab' ich leider immer gewusst!* Unfortunately, I've always known you're an idiot!"—after that, she'd sit down and like a voracious eagle eat—eat everything in sight, and with the crook nose turning like a bird's beak from face to face, she'd start telling stories of what she'd seen and heard in the *grosse Stadt*, and everything would be the same again. Next morning the hat, the rouge, the brooches and bracelets would be gone; she'd be the slightly sophisticated, unusually vital, vulgar German doctor's bourgeois wife, and everything would be the same again.

But the naive young man with his English public school education, his months at a Paris *Ecole Secondaire* and a military college, who'd sailed away to Africa and become a farmer, gotten ill and become a bank clerk in London, and was now "learning German" to become a banker—he didn't know what it was all about, just didn't or maybe couldn't be bothered to figure it out at all. Until one day, a couple of years later, someone wrote and told him, when he was in America or maybe on an island in the Pacific, that Hawknose had been found in some house in Frankfurt with her throat gashed open and a plain razor in her hand. . . .

And then, but only then, did he put the smile, the morning song and the evening row together, remember the doctor and Maria and feel for a day or two—in San Francisco, Honolulu or Hilo—very sorry; then promptly forget about them and Hawknose until, past forty years old, he saw the tramlines again and the corner where she used to stand, while driving with an American major in a jeep down the Taunus Strasse, where he and the suicide's family used to live.

"My God, Major!" I said, pulling up outside the familiar house, "the old man's name's still on the door!"

"Well, wha' d'yer know!" the Major exclaimed, and pulling open the dashboard pocket in front of him, he took out a detective story and began to read.

"Look here, Major," I said, "I'll make it as snappy as I can. Maybe I'll be back in a minute, but . . . Say, would it interest you to have a look round that hotel opposite? Old King Edward used—"

"That's perfectly okay, Jim," the Major said. "You go ahead, stay as long as you like. I'm perfectly okay. What's that you said about some hotel?"

"Oh, just that it's where all the Old European monarchs used to stay in the early 1900's."

"Well, for Christ sakes!" the Major said, and settled down to read his paper-bound book.

Inside the gate I saw a wooden chair, painted white. I stood for a moment, staring at it, and then not at it, but at a photograph I'd taken (with an old camera an Irish aunt had given me and which I lost years later in a field near Fontainebleau), a photograph of a young woman with a wide mouth and a spotty white face, and beside her an Alsatian dog whose name was—I had it!—*Bari*. The girl was sitting, giggling in the chair and the dog had its tongue hanging out, as much from embarrassment, I like to think, as from the heat of that faraway summer's sun. The girl was the family's *Dienstmädchen,* but I couldn't remember her name. She must be over fifty now, I thought, but the chair looked the same age and was in the same spot as on the day I took the photograph.

I was about to write that I rang the bell. I didn't. With my head down I walked, or my legs took me, straight in at the door and up two of those twelve stairs. Then I stopped, for on about the sixth stair I saw two black shoes and a pair of dark trouser-bottoms. I looked up quickly, into the face of a boy of maybe seventeen.

"Oh, excuse me," I muttered impulsively, putting out my hand to the banister which fell into my grasp without my looking. "I forgot—" And my legs were about to turn and take me down to the bell, when at last my reflexes reminded me of the year.

So I said: *"Bitte schön,* is the Herr Doktor at home? I mean, does he—still live here?"

Neither the scared look in the boy's eyes nor his evasive answer brought any relief.

"Einen Moment, bitte," he said, and swinging round, he leapt up the six stairs and disappeared.

Who the hell is he? I wondered. Then I smelled the musty smell of the carpet and at the head of the stairs I suddenly saw the naive young man sitting with Maria. *"Nicht doch!* Don't! *Mutti's* coming!" she was saying; to which the young man replied: "Well, let's go on upstairs—!" But *"Um Gottes Willen!"* Maria exclaimed, and she got up quickly and bounded up the next flight of stairs into her room and locked the door. The young man followed slowly after her, but at the top of the stairs turned into his room, flung himself on the divan and picked up a Tauchnitz edition of *The Importance of Being Earnest*. . . .

The dining-room door was open and I stood on the threshold staring at the brass-potted aspidistra or *Palme*. Tiptoeing in, I looked at it more closely, at the plant's dusty leaves, and my hand went to a spot over the heart where I used to keep my handkerchief, but when the fingers found a brass button there the arm dropped to my side and I sat down in the chair by the window. I looked at the chair where Maria used to sit, at that of Hawknose at the end of the table, at the tassel-shaded lamps in two corners of the room. I looked at the heavy sideboard with the brass candlesticks, at the deep drawer from which I occasionally used to sneak a gulp of the doctor's hock, and only then did I look at the door into the sitting-room, to find that it was open and that where the old sofa used to be, there now stood an operating table, a couple of plain white chairs, a couch covered with a white cloth, and beyond that a door marked *Privat*.

Well, a doctor must still live here, I said to myself, and as I said it the door marked *Privat* swung open and an oldish, slightly stooping man in a long white coat with a Red Cross on his arm came walking through the room with his head down. I could see as he approached that he was wearing spectacles, but he carried his head so low I couldn't see his face.

When he was almost upon me his legs drew up suddenly, the feet in white canvas sneakers side-by-side. Then he raised his head, dropped it in a slight bow, raised it again, looked me straight in the eye and with lips that trembled a little, said: *"Bitte schön?"*

Only when the words were uttered and I heard the voice, was I absolutely positive, and a single thought flashed through my mind: Good Lord, he must be well over seventy . . . !

He stood there, the lips trembling, even the head ever so slightly shaking, like an old soldier or a Dreyfus standing court-martial for a crime he hadn't committed twenty years ago or ever; he stood there as though summoning his last strength to withhold the tear from falling, the cry from escaping at the sound of the atrocious sentence; he stood, a stooped, bald-headed, frail old man—without a flicker of recognition, only the look of fearful premonition, in the yellowish, rheumy, aging eyes.

That was how he stood, for what seemed an hour, before I could bring myself to say, in a voice that sounded not at all as I had meant it to, but that came out barely above a whisper: *"Herr Doktor?"*

"Bitte schön?" he repeated, like a man who can stand the strain of suspense only a little, a very little longer.

"Herr Doktor!" I said quick and loud now. *"Herr Doktor!"* And then in English, to help crash the gulf of years: *"Herr Doktor,* don't-you-remember-me? Don't-you-remember-Jimmy-Stern? Don't-you-remember-the-*verrückte-Engländer*-who-used-to-live-with-you-here-in-your-home! Don't-you-remember-me-and-Mar—?"

At last, slowly at first, the trembling mouth opened, the old eyes grew wide behind the glasses. Then rheum turned them bleary, the trembling lower lip sagged—and all of a sudden the arms were flung up above his head.

"Der Chimmy!" he half-groaned, half-shouted. *"Der Chimmy!"*

And down came the arms, with all the small weight of the frail body, on my shoulders.

"Weisst du?" he half-sobbed, half-laughed. "D'you know—d'you know, *Chimmy* . . . ?"

"Was denn?" I muttered, holding him, like the son the acquitted father. *"Was denn?"*

"Ich dachte—I thought—I was convinced that you—that the Americans, I mean—had come at last—to-put-me-out-of-my-home!"

I forced a laugh, as though the probability were an impossibility. "They won't do that," I said, with a vision of the Kempten Park Strasse, Frau Miedel's and the undamaged street in Nürnberg.

"They've turned out everyone else in the Taunus Strasse," he said, standing back from me now.

"Well, isn't that proof enough!" I said. "You're a doctor."

"*Tcha*," he breathed, slowly shaking his head, "still a doctor!"

Then he looked at me, and the smile—the one that used to melt his wife when she came towards him like an animal—spread over his face, and I could almost see the past moving slowly into his head, creeping down into the sad, disillusioned eyes. Then the smile faded like a small sun sinking, and he looked as men do who've made a quick, unpleasant decision.

"Maria's dead!" he blurted out.

I dropped my eyes and while he said something about "three months ago" and of an illness whose name I couldn't catch, I caught sight of the left hand hanging out of the white limp sleeve and shaking there as though the fingers were not even those of a dead hand, but a cluster of brown leaves held to a branch by one living nerve and trembling in maybe their last hour of life in the summer's barely perceptible breath of wind. Then, as though my gaze were challenging them to make the effort, the fingers curled a little as he said: "Johanna (*that* was her name!) was in Stuttgart some months ago. But I've not heard since. She isn't married. . . ."

At that, unwillingly, I looked up and thought: She must be thirty-five (the sixteen-year-old who had the fits of weeping); and I could see that that was what her father was thinking and that the thought hurt the man whose wife had committed suicide, one of whose daughters was dead and the other, no longer a girl and unmarried, not positively alive.

Then he smiled and reached out his arm, slipped it through mine, and walked me slowly round the table. "*Tcha*," he said, "it's a strange world, *lieber Freund*. Who'd have thought, in those days—! *Na,* one mustn't think. D'you remember," he said, turning quickly and standing before me, "d'you remember your tobacco pouch?"

"Tobacco pouch?" I repeated. "My tobacco pouch? I never had such a thing! I never—"

He threw back his head, clasped his hands together, and laughed out loud.

"You don't remember? It had the first zipper we ever saw! *Ach, lieber Chimmy,* you mean an old man's memory—?"

"My God!" I exclaimed. "You mean I had that here! You mean I smoked a pipe . . . ?"

"*Oh Gott, oh Gott!* And what a pipe! What a stink!" Bursting into giggles, the old man held his nose.

"You mean I smoked that filthy Springbok here?"

"Springbok! That was it! You had yellow cotton bags of it, and after you'd filled your pouch or the pipe the children used to pull the zipper backwards and forwards until you said they'd break it. Remember?"

"Yes, yes," I said. "I do now. My associations with that pouch have always been so African."

"*Ach ja.* Your stories of Africa. I must say, I never believed them . . . !"

We both laughed out loud and sat down at the dinner table, with the brass-potted *Palme* between us, and the old man covered his face with his hands (so that I saw a large ring I didn't recognize) and went on silently giggling. "And the tobacco was so dry," he muttered through his fingers, "it used to fall out of the pipe and burn the carpet—*oh Gott, oh Gott!*—and you said how much you liked being here because no one in England allowed you to smoke your Springbok in their houses! *Ach, lieber Chimmy,* the stink of that stuff!"

"And every evening," I said, smiling, "you went into your room and read two pages of *The Outline of History!*"

"*Ja, der Vells—der H. G. Vells!*"

"Did you ever finish it, *Herr Doktor?*"

"I never did," he sighed, and wagged his head and glanced

away as though in shame or because the memory revived a pain. "I had my troubles," he murmured.

He looked up over my head suddenly, with his mouth open, as if the banging of a door outside and footsteps approaching were bringing him from calm contemplation of the past to the unreality of the present with too great a shock. Then he got up, and I looked round and saw a big, red-faced, middle-aged woman in shirt and white slacks coming through the door.

I didn't hear what the doctor said, but as I shook hands with the robust, vital- yet vulgar-looking woman I caught a glimpse of embarrassment flash across his face. With a fleeting vision of the blue straw hat and pink fake carnation, I guessed immediately the role this woman played in the old man's life, and I thought how unfortunate it is that when seeking instinctively in women the opposites of themselves, men—particularly the modest, the masochistic—so often fall for the extremes; and how, as though the experience of being bitten by one for years were not enough to make them forever shy, they almost invariably, after divorce or death offers them their freedom, repeat the error once again.

The moment the doctor's second misfortune had heard the reason of my visit, she created such a rumpus with her voice alone that you felt the quiet room since her entrance had filled with people. She first went out into the hall and shouted a name, whereupon the young man I'd seen on the stairs (her son by a former marriage), came in and shook hands and sat down with some embarrassment. Then she sent him out again and started haranguing the doctor for having entertained an old friend for an hour on nothing but air and reminiscence.

"Not even a glass of wine!" she howled.

At which, under my fascinated gaze, the old man looked up and with the smile that had always made me want to take his hand, he smacked his knee and, looking at me, exclaimed: *"Ach, lieber Chimmy!* What an idiot, what a fool I am!" And getting up, he promptly started for the door.

"*Na, na, na!*" cried the woman. "Franz is already gone!"

So the doctor returned and sat down, shaking his head like an admonished and repentant child, and Franz came in with an armful of bottles and lined them up on the table, and for an hour the doctor and I had little chance to speak, for the woman rattled on and on about nothing of any interest until, frustrated, furious, and flushed with wine, I rose to leave.

"But you've only just arrived!" protested the woman, her face now purple and perspiring.

"I'd like to stay," I said, "but I have an officer waiting outside."

"An officer!" she cried, staggering to her feet. "Bring him in! Bring him in!"

"He doesn't speak German," I told her. "And I have to drive him into Frankfurt for lunch."

"*Na, so was!*" she said, as she and the doctor and the son followed me unsteadily out of the door and into the street. On seeing the Major in the jeep she tottered faster towards him, and before I'd a chance to introduce or defend him she had grabbed him by the hand and was trying, with a spate of alcoholic German, to drag him out of his seat and into the house.

"*Wein!*" she finally shouted. "*Wein! Velly goot!*"

"What's she talking about, Jim?" asked the Major, poor devil, clinging for dear life with one hand to the steering-wheel.

"Oh, don't take any notice of her," I said, lamely. "She's just a bit tight and wants you to have a drink."

"You telling me!" gasped the Major, still struggling in her clutches.

I quickly gripped the embarrassed, helpless doctor's hand. "I'll try and get back and see you soon again, *Herr Doktor*," I lied.

"Ach, please, please do!" said the old man, with a desperate, pleading look in his eyes.

Then I leapt into the jeep.

"I'm awfully sorry about that, Major!" I said, as we moved off. "And for having kept you waiting so long."

"That's perfectly okay, Jim," he said.

"My God!" I muttered, and let out a laugh.

"What?"

"I just thought of something," I said. "I caught sight of the lobby of the hotel there, the one I was telling you about, and I suddenly remembered, twenty-odd years ago in there, watching half-a-dozen stalwart men carry Lord Birkenhead up to bed!"

"Lord who?"

"Birkenhead," I said. "He was Chancellor of the Exchequer. A very brilliant man. And a very heavy one."

"What was wrong with the guy?" asked the Major.

"Drunk as a lord!" I said, and the Major's laughter went echoing all over the silent Spa.

Even if you were prepared for the American Military Government Headquarters, located in the sand-colored skyscrapers of the "I.G."—the *Interessen-Gemeinschaft Farbenindustrie Aktien-Gesellschaft* (in more civilized speech, a dye industry [*])—it was still a surprising sight. After you'd bumped over the roads into the center of the ruined city, entered the estate through the rolls of barbed wire, past American guards who all of a sudden clicked their polished heels, threw out their chests and chins like native robots, and you saw for the first time the acres of mown grass, the flower-beds, the trees, the undamaged mass of beige buildings, you could understand the many cracks the Germans made about this and other I.G. havens during the war: "If you want to live, go to the I.G.!" —"Join the I.G. and die a natural death!"

Inside the massive, crowded mess hall the Major seemed to breathe at last like a fish popped back into water just in time. I, on the other hand, felt not only like the New Boy at school, but one who, unfortunate enough to have arrived

[*] Baedeker (1929): "One of the largest trusts in existence."

in the company of an Assistant Master, has been ushered into the men's dining hall instead of the boys'.

At a table for four in an arena of Heaven knows how many dozen tables, I felt trapped in the Red Tape, among the Brass Hats of all Europe and America. Here, I thought, sit the world's future Prefects, sipping iced water and pecking at saucers of pallid cole slaw, while up in Potsdam the three Head Masters play an important game of political poker over brandy, vodka and champagne.

While the beribboned gentleman speaking Polish on my left carefully fished the ice from his glass, the British staff officer at the next table growled to his neighbor under the bristles: "I say, whatcher call this stuff?" and pushed away the slaw. But the rouged and powdered WAC opposite, and the Major by my side, gobbled up theirs with goggling eyes and gazed around for more.

"Have mine, Major," I said, and added: "I think, if you don't mind, I'd better be off. I don't want to keep you waiting again. Supposing I pick you up at four?"

"That's perfectly okay," the Major said, digging his fork into my saucer, "stay as long as you like. I'll go up on the roof and take a sunbath."

I drove round the mutilated streets for a while, looking for houses and hotels in which I used to live, for the "Manhattan" and the Frankfurter Hof bars, for the *Kneipen* near the Hauptbahnhof and the bank in which I'd wasted months of life—but some of the buildings were barely recognizable shells and of others I could find no trace at all.

The house in the Funk Strasse, however, was within a hundred yards of the I.G.'s barbed wire entanglement, and for this reason, perhaps, its limes and poplars were in full leaf, the street and sidewalks as good as new, its houses, so far as the eye could see, intact. I left the jeep with an MP behind the wire and rang the top bell of No. 18. I heard above me a window go up, a voice call out: *"Al-aw!"* and looking up I saw, hanging out from five or six stories high, the unmistakable head of Gisela Dunkelmann, who had married Kurt

Gessner, who had been missing since March. Taking off my cap I spoke her name, and from that height she looked down and with strangely little surprise, I thought, she spoke mine.

"I knew it was you!" she called out from the top of the house. "I dreamed last night you would come!"

This strange announcement threw before me the figure of the peculiar Dr. Dunkelmann and at once it seemed less strange, for in his world such remarks were considered no odder than his behavior at Beethoven recitals when he, the dignified Goethe-like psychiatrist, would stand up, hypnotized, in the back of the packed auditorium and with staring eyes and outstretched arms start singing until he had to be carried out in a trance. Next day, remembering nothing about the night before, he would insist on hearing every detail.

"Very interesting. Very interesting, indeed!" he would say, and start comparing the hypnotic effect the master's music had on him with that which a certain tropical plant, used as a drug, was said to have on Mexican Indians.

"Come on up!" Gisela was saying at the door. "Try not to be bothered by the number of people. We are nineteen in four rooms."

"Gisela," I said, looking at her and then at three blond children clutching at her skirt, "only your hair has changed!"

"*Ja,* gray as an old woman, *gel!*" she said, hunching her shoulders, cocking her head on one side and smiling. "Did you meet Papa?"

"Now, Gisela!" I exclaimed, "are you going to tell me you dreamed that, too?"

"No," she said, and when she let out that throaty giggle, it struck me (as it had in the old days) that she was one of the very few Germans I'd known with any appreciation of the absurd. "I just figured it out," she said, leading me upstairs with the children trailing at our heels. "Ever since I woke up, I've been wondering how you were going to find me. In my dream you weren't alone, but with Kuno and Wolfgang and Papa—"

"Kuno!" I exclaimed, remembering that this was the name

Gisela had given the friend, the Bright Young Man from London who'd stuffed the false beard into my hands in the train near Heidelberg.

"Naturally," she was saying, "I never think of you without thinking of Kuno. That was how we met. I always thought Kuno was a genius, you know."

"So did he," I laughed.

"Wolfgang didn't," she said, stopping for breath on the third or fourth floor. "Wolfgang used to say young Englishmen like Kuno never finish anything but their visky-sodas!"

"I know of worse things to finish," I muttered, and there flashed through my mind a vision of a crowd of depressingly earnest young men snapping at one another over the works of Schoenberg, Křenek and Hindemith, snapping away in a room with barely a seat to sit on and not a damned drop to drink. "Christ, my dear, what *bores!*" I heard Kuno growl as we had both made for the door.

"D'you remember," Gisela went on, "the night Kuno invited us all to caviare and champagne in the *Tanzklause?*"

"Yes, indeed," I said, "and your mother had to pay the bill!"

"And Kuno insisted on waltzing with the waiter! I don't think I've ever laughed so much in my life!" she said, and I thought that was probably and unfortunately true.

"Talking of champagne," I said, "do you remember Wolfgang's glasses?"

"Wolfgang's glasses?"

"Yes. Wolfgang was leaving for Paris in the morning, you were packing his bag, and suddenly you went into the kitchen and came back with two gold-rimmed champagne glasses and started wrapping them up."

She burst out laughing. *"Mein Gott, ja!"* she cried, shaking her head. "He never traveled without those glasses!"

"What always impressed me were the stories you used to tell about his birthdays—"

"When he invited all his wives and mistresses?"

"Yes," I said. "Did you *really* never fight, *none* of you?"

"Fight? No, never," she said, "we all had a wonderful time!"

At the top of the house she stopped and opened a door. "We have the family's few remaining possessions here," she said. "D'you remember Papa's house in the Ulmen Strasse? There's nothing left of it. Every book of his priceless medical library is gone."

"Did he lose his job in the clinic?" I asked, following her into a dark hall.

"Yes, but he's just got it back through the Americans. He's working again. He's nearly seventy-five, you know."

"Good business!" I breathed, and walked behind her into a large room full of women, children and two young men sitting together in a window. Everyone stared.

"This is Constantia," Gisela said, and I looked up into the blond open face of a girl taller than myself.

"Heavens!" I gasped. "Last time I saw you, you'd barely opened your eyes!"

She smiled shyly while I was introduced to the young men, the women, and a whole brood of children who, once I'd sat down, started climbing up my legs, over my shoulders and squabbling as to who should finally land in my lap and play with the buttons of my uniform. In the end, three of them succeeded in getting onto the chair, while I stared out over their heads at the staring women on the sofa and a bookcase jammed with books running the length of the room.

"The children have their hearts' desire at last," Gisela said, in German. "They've never stopped asking me when they'll get the chance to talk to an American soldier!"

Oh, Lord! I thought, and I happened to glance at the faces of two of the youngish women on the sofa. They were sullen faces, and when Gisela had made that remark I noticed their brows come down over their eyes and that they stared at her as though she'd dropped some particularly heavy brick. Gisela caught the look and I had the impression she flushed. Letting out a slightly embarrassed giggle, she turned quickly to me and continued, in English and in a tone which suggested she was not interested that the others should hear, her nostalgic memories of the past.

"D'you remember the Manhattan," she said, "and *Fasching,* and us all dressing up and going to the *Kostümfeste?*"

"I do, indeed," I said, with a vision of the hot, enormous halls jammed with drunken Germans in fancy-dress, and the first shock of seeing the small, dark, doorless, divaned cabins specially set aside for those couples whose intoxicated lust no longer allowed them to stand up.

"And me coming over with Kurt, before we were married, to the *Goldene Stern* where you and Kuno used to stay—Kurt's missing, you know," she added.

"So the Professor told me," I said. "Where was he during the war?"

"At the beginning he was here, trying to finish a long book. Then he was drafted and sent to Russia. Some months later he was released to continue the book—"

"What was it about?" I asked, and I noticed that her eyes were cast slightly down, and that the other women, the sullen ones on the sofa, and some more seated round in chairs, were listening silently, intently, like spectators in a court of justice, all their eyes first on Gisela, then on me.

"About the African colonies," she said.

"The old German colonies?"

"No, no, the British."

"Oh, probably the Transvaal," I said, "where Frobenius discovered the pre-historic cave-paintings?"

"Yes," she said, "but most of it, I think, was about Southern Rhodesia."

"That's interesting," I said. "The ruins at Zimbabwe?"

"That's right. How did you guess?"

"Well, they're famous," I said. "Also, I saw them, more than twenty years ago, and I've never forgotten them. Did Kurt ever go there?"

"Yes. With Frobenius."

"Is he still alive?"

"No, he died just before the war."

"I'd love to see the book," I said.

"Well," she muttered, with a just perceptible hesitation. "It was never published. . . . But he wrote another book," she added quickly.

"Really? What was that about?"

"Cannibalism," she said, with no change in her expression; but when she saw me put my hand over my mouth she burst into laughter and got up. "I'll get you a copy," she said, leaving the room.

The vision of a German calmly writing a book on man-eating men while all over Europe bombs were raining down and round the corner men were being tortured and driven by starvation even to eating the flesh of the dead inmates before they themselves died in concentration camps, did not seem to strike the ladies as grotesque enough even for a shake of the head. They just sat there in sullen silence until one of them, a plump masculine-looking figure with a head of hair like a floor-mop, asked me somewhat curtly if I would take a letter to a friend in America. When I complied, two more women produced pens and paper and started writing on their knees.

"Would there be any chance of me getting to America?" asked the plump one, looking up from her letter. "I'm actually Swiss, you see," she added.

"I really have no idea," I said.

"And I have good connections over there," she persisted. "And I wasn't in the Party. Nothing like that."

"I really couldn't tell you," I said. "I know nothing about such things."

Then Gisela returned and laid on the table beside me a tremendous tome in cardboard covers.

"My God!" I exclaimed. "All that on cannibalism! It must have taken years to write!"

"It did," she said. "He started it before the war. When it was finished, he was made editor of an anthropological magazine. Then he was called up again and sent to France. . . ." Gisela rose from her chair. "I'm afraid I've got to take the children out now," she said. "By the way, have you had anything to eat?"

"Oh, yes, thanks," I said, "in the I.G."

"Ach," she said, then muttered something I couldn't catch, and smiled a kind of secret smile and flushed and looked away.

"What was that?" I asked.

"Oh, just—d'you know what we—what the Frankfurters call it?"

"Call what? The I.G.?"

"Yes."

"No. What?"

"Das Pharisäer Ghetto!" she said, and flushed and looked away.

"The Ghetto of the Pharisees?" I repeated in English. Then, having spoken the words and grasped their import, I glanced up (no doubt my mouth agape at the outrage) and, catching sight of some of the eyes in the suddenly silent room, I held my tongue, stood mentally still, as once, years ago, while day-dreaming and unarmed on an African farm, I had stopped hypnotized in front of a familiar mopani tree. In its trunk this tree had a large round hole in which I sometimes dropped the paper wrapping from my sandwich lunch; and out of the corner of my eye that day I thought I'd seen something move in the mouth of the hole. I stopped dead, to look: and there, out of the dark hole—its evil eyes half-closed, its fangs shooting in and out—rose the head of a green mamba, one of the deadliest of all snakes.

As I had held my breath then, to see the reptile like green lightning disappear, I now held my breath in the German room, to catch what more might come. But all I caught was the sight of Gisela shooting a look at the other women, the others flashing a glance out of the corners of their eyes at her, then swiftly at me and away. And in that instant, while no one spoke or moved, I was aware of the shocking sensation of being in the presence of the Real Enemy, and that it was these people—not the illiterate DK's we'd interviewed, the *kleine Mann* or *Frau* who'd follow like sheep in the wake of any Dog which barked loud enough, believe any lie provided it was often enough repeated—but these people here, just because of their education, their superior intelligence and knowledge, who were the Responsible Ones. And with this shock came the certainty that they were still highly dangerous, as dangerous as a nest of mambas hibernating in the trunk of a tree.

LONDON TO WASHINGTON

15

"SOME of these God-damned CIC guys have swiped your plane!" I heard the sergeant say.

I sat up on the floor of the weapons-carrier, looked at my watch. I'd been asleep for an hour. Alongside me another civilian lay on his back, snoring, his legs dangling from the flap-door.

Outside in the heat, over a luggage-crammed trailer, half a dozen heads were clustered round *Kannibalismus,* which had been too heavy for my baggage. Its illustrations had also been too much for my stomach. They showed men splitting open the breasts of others still alive, cutting out their hearts, presenting the entrails to mothers for soup, which they shared later with their children. To illustrate a sixteenth century explorer's account of the Congo, a German artist of the period had drawn a Frankfurt butcher's shop where the butcher, surrounded by bleeding arms and hands, was busy chopping up a meaty human haunch. Some unfortunate gentlemen were being skinned alive and roasted, while others were bound to a stake where portions of their flesh, sliced off with shears, were being eaten raw by the goggle-eyed spectators. The victims' heads, it seemed, were always reserved for the ladies whose privilege it was to do the cooking.

The grizzly pages found such a fascinated audience among the bored civilians on the airfield that the news the sergeant brought barely registered.

"Swiped our plane!" I said.

"That's right," he replied. "Some of these high-powered guys from H.Q., they just hop into any old plane and tell the pilot to go where the hell they want him to!"

"We bin on this blasted airfield just four and a half hours!" someone said.

"Let's swipe someone else's plane!"

"Ha!" chortled the sergeant. With an eye on the snorer's legs and a couple of civilians dead-asleep in front of the weapons-carrier, he said: "I doubt any of you fellahs are likely to be taken for a VIP!"

So—our plane and the afternoon gone—the sergeant whirled us back to Nauheim again.

The following day we took precautions—or rather, whenever we saw a plane coming down we frantically waved handkerchiefs, while the sergeant shot off in a jeep with the determination of a hotel porter who has spotted a millionaire guest in need of a cab. He was as successful as the porter usually is.

Once in the air the plane, as though its pilot had a bad conscience, hummed all the way to England without stopping.

Great weather in London is so rare that a golden evening is seldom taken for granted. The women who leaned cross-armed on their window-sills, the men on chairs outside their low, soot-covered houses seemed to breathe an air of unusual content. In the gutters an odd ribbon of tinsel glittered like silver; from basement railings hung an occasional gaudy streamer; on the walls were still pasted torn Election posters: *Vote for Churchill!—Vote for Labor!* Oxford Street looked as though it were still enjoying the after-effects of a long night-out, which the people on its sidewalks did not wish to forget.

At the Terminal in Welbeck Street the atmosphere was less festive. Three Americans were arguing with the corporal behind the counter.

"Hi!" one said. "We've come to be transferred from those

lousy billets you sent us to. Six in one room with six hundred fleas!"

"I'm red all over from bedbugs!" complained another.

I had intended phoning Mrs. Craig. Instead, I withdrew from the queue and called up Julia, the wife of my young brother, who was still serving with the British army in some port on the Adriatic.

"Why, I've been expecting you for days!" she told me. "Didn't you get my letter? Come at once. Of course I've room. Perfectly good divan in the basement."

A little guiltily I slipped out of the Terminal and managed to find a cab, whose mat-covered floor seemed unnaturally high above the ground. I had just slammed the door when a face with a clipped gray mustache above an Old Etonian tie appeared at the window.

"I'm going to St. John's Wood, sir," I said. "Can I give you a lift?"

The Englishman looked me over with an air of surprise. "Oh, I say," he said, hesitating, then climbing in, "that's awfully kind of you, sir. Suits me handsomely. Promise I won't take you out of your way. Just drop me at the corner of Church Street," he told the driver.

Flags drooped from the windows along Edgware Road.

"London seems remarkably cheerful," I said, for something to say.

"Yes," he said, laying his briefcase on his knees, his bowler on the briefcase, and crossing his hands over the crook of his umbrella. "Yes, we've taken it pretty well on the whole. I'm optimistic. You'll see, these Socialist chaps 'll have a hard time, very hard indeed. They'll make the blunders. Then we'll have the swing of the old pendulum again. That's the historical process over here. . . . 'Course,' he added, half-turning to me, "I don't know what you think?"

"I think there's a good deal in what you say," I said.

"Trouble is," he continued, a faint smile on his healthy, upper class face, "trouble is, most Americans—if you will excuse me saying so—don't understand the situation. From what I've read of reports in your papers, anyone'd think we'd just had a Revolution, that the new Government is made up of a lot of these Bolshies. Not at all. Couldn't be more mistaken. Take this fellow Bevin, now. He's as English as Churchill. With diff'rent ideas, o' course. Diff'rent ideas. But do you imagine he'll let himself be dictated to by these Russians? Ha, don't you believe it, sir! Course, I don't know what you think?"

"I think Americans, sir," I said, "are inclined to judge others by themselves. It's a country of extremes."

The taxi slowed down, came to a halt.

"I say," said the Englishman, gripping his umbrella, his briefcase, and eyeing my uniform, "excuse me being personal, but—er—well, could you, sir, by any chance be British?"

"More or less," I told him, smiling. "We went to the same school!"

In his embarrassment his foot slipped on the threshold of the cab and I thought he was going to fall.

"My word!" he stammered as he recovered himself. "I really —I don't know what—I'm awfully sorry—I hope sincerely I didn't say—"

"It's I who should apologize, sir," I said, "for my disguise!"

"Not a bit of it, my dear fellow. Wise men and spies, they say, trust their ears rather than their eyes! Allow me to help with the fare—"

"Certainly not."

"Well, I'm most awfully grateful," he said, extending his hand.

"Not at all, sir," I muttered.

Out of the hole at the back I watched him walk off, smiling to himself and shaking his head.

He had left behind him a copy of the *Times*. From force of a habit broken by Geography (not Time), I turned first to the "Agony" column, then to the headlines (tucked away inside) and the leading editorial.

> *Wanted.* Has anyone a spare box of Max Factor's Pancake, No. 1 or 2? Good prices given.
>
> *Rolls Royce.* Phantom 11 or 25 h.p. Limousine required at once.
>
> COMING INVASION OF JAPAN
>
> JAPAN IN DECLINE
>
> The Allies have reached a point where they can safely warn the civil population that this or that town is on the bombing list and that its inhabitants will be ill-advised to await attack. If this and the powerlessness of the Japanese fleet to strike a blow fails to move the Japanese people, it can only be inferred that addiction to suicide is not confined to the military caste.

I'd never seen my sister-in-law's home. It turned out to be the lower half of a two-story house, off a quiet street with trees and with its own private entrance.

"What magnificence!" I exclaimed, gazing round the sitting-room, out of the window onto the patch of private, walled-in garden.

"What's so magnificent?" Julia asked, as I followed her downstairs to the basement dining-room, into the nursery, the kitchen and another patch of garden with a large elm at the back.

"The space!" I said. "In New York, you know, the rent of this place would run anywhere from five to six hundred pounds a year!"

"What?" she cried. "We pay a hundred and eighty!"

"Good God!" I said. "That's what we pay for our small three-room walk-up!"

"Walk-up?"

"You know: stairs."

"Oh, 'course, lifts."

"And you've a fireplace," I said, subsiding into the comfortable English sofa. "Does it work?"

"Work? 'Course it works—when there's something to burn. They all work."

"All?"

"Yes. We have three."

"Good God! That would raise the rent another hundred and fifty pounds! . . . Silence, space and chimneys," I said. "Just what only the rich in New York can afford. No wonder Americans are always so crazy to go out!"

"I long to go out!" Julia said. "I'm so tired of hunting for something to cook—and cooking!"

"Wonderful! Let's go out! My pocket, for the first time in years, is full!"

As I spoke, the door opened and in walked two youngish-looking British majors.

"My brothers," Julia said.

The officers made me feel very old and foreign. Calculating quickly, I realized with amazement that to neither of them was the Kaiser's War even a memory. I could not understand everything they said, for they talked, or rather mumbled in a private family jargon, breaking off their sentences and bursting into laughter over a single word. Then it began to dawn on me that the years (the war in particular) had given their generation (just as the Kaiser's War had mine) a new language, common words and idioms a new meaning. One phrase they constantly used was "had it." Oh, he or she's "had it!" they kept saying.

"What on earth does that mean?"

Then in a flash, from behind each chair and curtain, the Old Ghosts (those you thought had been laid so long ago) peeped out and grinned:

Wait and See. Watch and Pray. Silence is Golden. Patience is a Virtue. Don't speak till you're spoken to.

Where have the majors been these last years?

Don't be personal! May cause embarrassment.

(Later: "Cairo and the Middle-East. Good fun!")

Wonder what they think of the Elections?

Don't discuss politics at home! May cause unpleasantness.

(Later: "Damn good show, what! The family, of course, take a poor view!")

Wonder if either of them have been in Germany?
Don't talk shop in the drawing-room. It's rude.
Wonder what they're doing tonight?
Ask no questions, you'll hear no lies.
(Later: You never knew.)
"I say, old girl, what about running round the corner for a nip?"
"Hullo, Constable! Closed?"
"Yes, sir! Sold out."
"What's open?"
"Try the White 'Orse up the road, Madam."
"Thanks, Constable. Good night."
"Night, sir! Night, Madam."
Manners maketh Men.
"What's yours, old man?"
"No. This is mine."
"Go on. Don't be silly!"
"Gin & Lime—four Gins & Lime!"
"Cheerio! Mud in yer eye. Here's 'ow. Chin-chin."
"Same again, please, Miss."
"Coo, look at 'im! Won't 'alf feel queer in the mawnin', will 'e?"
"He's had it!"
"Well, s'long old girl, must be toddling!"
The majors vanished.

In Fitzroy Street a little old man was turning the handle of a barrel-organ—the music of London. He had no monkey.

In the small, expensive French-Italian restaurant in the cheap and tawdry street the *padrone* and his family took me for my brother.

"Well, I never! Uniforms sort of don't register any more, like. Just faces. And when we saw Madam . . . Why, just like old times, i'n't i'?"

It was. You could get almost everything you wanted. "Don't bother with the menu, sir. What would you like to eat—*canard à l'orange, pigeon petit pois?*"

Only the bill (for the wine and liqueur) was five times bigger. How odd to pay for a meal!

"Black market."

"Europe's new name."

Down Tottenham Court Road a line of WRENS marched arm in arm. In Shaftesbury Avenue G.I.s stood in the dark corners, with teen-age English girls.

"Hullo, dearie!" Strange to see prostitutes again. Groups of men stood motionless, as usual, outside the pubs.

"Someone told me today the Japs will surrender soon."

"People I've talked to say it will take another six months to a year, and that the Invasion will be terrible."

A private car drew up at the curb. "Want a lift, Bill?" the civilian driver asked. "'yde Park Corner. Only three bob!"

"They're doing that everywhere now," Julia said. "Black market gas."

"Gas?"

"Did I say that? Funny. Didn't realize it. We've probably picked up a lot in the last three years."

The Café Royal was crowded. You stood in a line for a seat. And when you got it, the man opposite at the same table reached out a huge red hand towards Julia.

"Good-looker!"

He had tiny glassy, bloodshot eyes, oiled hair and a big brown mustache the shape of handle-bars. On his khaki shoulder was stitched the word *Commando*. The girl beside him looked the other way.

"Good-looker, gimme your hand, damn you!"

"I think we'd better move."

We got up and stood in line again.

"Are most of them like that?"

"Most I've seen. Belsenites we call them."

Trained to murder without sound, and all at large. . . .

"There's another!"

He was staggering out, a huge hulk with a beret over one ear, a girl on each arm.

"Let's go."

In the dark streets round Berwick Market sheets of newspaper fluttered against the basement railings; a black cat shot across the sidewalk; girls arm in arm with men in uniform marched in line, singing. At a corner where there used to be an exclusive night-club, a garden of Ragged Robin gleamed white against a jagged wall, under the moon.

In the basement dining-room the elder major's cot was empty.

At seven in the morning, when I went out, he was snoring.

I had spent half one winter (before Hitler marched into the Rhineland) a few hundred yards from here. But you don't go far walks in London in the winter. . . . Avenue Road was empty in the early sun; the air was clear, fresh, like country air; but the trees, their leaves a dusty green, were pregnant with August. The great city was still asleep. You could hear every sleeping movement and smell the tar —the smell of London. Crossing Albert Road into the unkempt, war-weary woods of Regents Park, you could sniff the sawdust, the sweat and dung and disinfectant of caged captivity—the smell of Sunday afternoons during the last summers of the Old World.

"Cousin Charles has given you tickets for the Zoo. What do you say?"

"Thank you."

"Thank you who?"

"Thank you, Cousin Charles . . . Can we ride on the elephant? Feed the monkeys? Buy a balloon?"

From the bridge I looked down on a canal I didn't remember ever having seen. The placid water shone green, like motor oil, and along the parallel path under the trees came trudging a single heavy horse. Throwing all its weight on its forelegs, arching its great neck, it heaved, all alone, at the long flat barge on which no one could be seen.

As London slowly wakes up it begins to purr like a cat, to hum like no other city. The higher the sun rises the louder grows the hum: the cat grows into the lion, and growls the majestic growl of the king of beasts.

A line of waxen-faced, poorly-dressed women stood outside a shop whose window was bare, its door closed.

From the mail-slot in my brother's front door the *Times* stuck out.

> *Nannies* trained: prospect change & travel.
>
> *For Sale.* Lady's hack. 15½ hds. Aged. Perfect manners.

FIRST ATOMIC BOMB HITS JAPAN

EXPLOSION EQUAL TO 20,000 TONS OF T.N.T.

"RAIN OF RUIN" FROM THE AIR

"H'm. Japs copping it, what?"
"Poor swine!"
"I say, might be the end!"
"By Jove, this bread-and-dripping's good!"
" 'Forty thousand foot column of smoke!' Lummy!"

What was it that damned Red Cross nurse in Kempten said? "I know that England started the air warfare against Germany. . . ."

In Knightsbridge two gleaming Rolls Royces glided soundlessly through the roar. A sleek, hatless young man steered the open one, with his little finger, into the Park at Albert Gate.

From the top of the No. 9 bus (the one I used to take from this corner to the bank every morning twenty years ago) the sight of Grandmother's house—shuttered, sold and weeping—supplied the deepest reminder of Time, Change and Oblivion. . . . Hutton, ever-smiling in eternal tails, opening the door into the cool marble hall. The space. The flowers. The silence. On the wide, generous stairs the soft plum-colored carpet with never a sign of wear. The Canalettos and the ormolu French clock. In the enormous dining-room the sideboard under which you hid and all alone traveled the Seven Seas. The womb of Wealth and Security, the World that could never end. The morning-room. The cyclamen and the roses. The Matriarch always wise and always old. The Dresden-china tea at five; the circular egg-and-anchovy sandwiches; and Robert Browning who "used to walk over from Wimpole Street on Sundays. He was a very charming old man. . . ."

In a bombed house near Hammersmith, the head of Kuno, the Bright Young Man, was just visible beneath a mound of clothes, books, newspapers and blankets. To reach the bed you stumbled over an empty bottle and a Picasso canvas which, like everything else in the room (including the trousers and coat he was going to wear), belonged to someone else.

"Christ, my dear, it's nearly lunch time. Rudi's waiting at the Ritz. What a *bore!*"

"How did you like the RAF?"

The head rolled over and laughter poured from the pillow. "The *noise,* my dear . . . !"

"The *people!*"

"But I was jolly popular!"

"?"

"Oh, yes. Ever since the day I lost my uniform. Seems no one'd ever done that before. People are really *too* extraordinary. I just left the silly thing in a public lavvy. Like 'Köpenick.' The colonel simply wouldn't believe me. They called me Cracky after that. Cracky, indeed! Christ, where are my socks?"

"I saw Gisela."

"Gisela? Who's she? Oh, that old tart! What a *bore* the Germans are!"

"See about the atom bomb?"

"Atom? No, that's too much! 'Up Guards and at 'em!' Oh dear, oh dear!—What pretty trousers! Got a pair to spare?"

The Memorial to Albert, that ghastly shrine of the novel's Golden Age, still towered over the squat, circular Hall of Music.

> *Gentleman* (Private) requires Rolls Royce for immediate use.

> *Maltese* (miniature), three adorable little white balls of fluff, finest pedigree; prices from 17 to 25 guineas. Will exchange one for miniature Pekinese.

REPORT OF VAST DAMAGE BY NEW BOMB

PARACHUTE SAID TO HAVE BEEN USED

UNITED STATES DENOUNCED
   AS "DESTROYER OF MANKIND"

DARKNESS OVER HIROSHIMA

You felt numb, lonely, lost. Drink? Why not? What else? But in Piccadilly you couldn't get into a bar.

Star, Standard, Noos! The latest abaht the Bomb!

"All over bar the shoutin'!"

"Bloody 'oax, more likely!"

"I wouldn't wonder!"

"Strike me pink, see this?"

"What?"

" 'RUSSIA DECLARES WAR ON JAPAN!' "

"Well, I'll be buggered!"

"Yellow Peril sandwich!"

". . . pound of flesh!"

"Says Uncle Sam to Uncle Joe: Sucks ter you!"

> *Countess* wishes to sell exquisite antique rose & grey aubusson tapestry *carpet*. Price £200. Worth much more in France or America.

HIROSHIMA INFERNO

FOUR SQUARE MILES OBLITERATED

"Hya, Jim! How yer doin'?"

"Hi, Major!"

"Say, I wanna ask your advice. My girl . . ."

"Anything wrong?"

"Everything. Say, how the hell d'you get rid of 'em?"

"Run, I guess."

"I have. But she always knows where I am!"

"Mentioned marriage, Major?"

"Well . . . Ha! Guess I—"

"Oh, Major! A ring?"

"Well . . . Ha!—Say, they bin looking for you in the office for days. Couldn't find you—"

"Me?"

"You were down to fly home yesterday!"

"Hell! Excuse me, Major."

"Perfectly okay, Jim. See you on the other side!"

Star, Standard, Noos! Read abaht Russia!

RUSSIANS ADVANCE IN MANCHURIA
GOOD TANK COUNTRY
ATOM BOMB ON NAGASAKI
JAPAN'S CAPITULATION IS NEAR

In the office the captain lolled on his chair, his feet up on the desk. "Well, okay," he said, wearily, "make it the thirteenth if you like. Don't suppose anyone here gives a damn when you leave."

WASHINGTON SAYS TOKYO OFFER ACCEPTED
U.S. KEPT CALM—"JUST IN CASE"

REJOICE
> The Secretary of State . . . hopes that it may be possible for local authorities to arrange to provide bands, to light bonfires and to take other appropriate means of celebrating this historic occasion.
> It is hoped that the churches will be able to arrange for church bells to be rung throughout the country

In Piccadilly the traffic was blocked by crowds singing. There was the deafening din of the wooden rattles you used on Field Days in the OTC in the Kaiser's day. "God damn you, Stern, that's a machine-gun, not a bloody toy!"

On the scales my baggage and I were fifty pounds too heavy. Out of the duffel bag I dragged all the uniform I'd never worn, handed it to Julia. I was still overweight. Reluctantly I gave her *Kannibalismus*.

"Mail it to me, please!" I said.

"Bon voyage! Do hope you don't arrive on **VJ-Day!**"

"I'll have 'had it' anyway!"

NO CEASE FIRE YET IN PACIFIC

END MAY BE DELAYED SOME
                    DAYS, EVEN LONGER

Late News

Washington. Mr. Ross, Presidential Press Secretary . . . advised reporters to be on the alert until midnight. "We just don't know," he said, "it might come through."

In the bus, the face of the uniformed civilian beside me seemed vaguely familiar. He looked at me sideways, smiled. "How are you getting along—?" he began.

"Under the Occupation?" I laughed. *"Ach, Herr Hauptmann,* it's much better than I expected. *Wissen Sie,* we heard—"

". . . we women would be raped—"

". . . jailed, deported—"

"Aber mein Mann, my husband, he always said—"

". . . those of us who were not in the Party—"

". . . we'd be pushed off the trottoir, not allowed to breathe—oopsah!"

"Gesundheit!"

At the airport I cabled my wife to leave Vermont and meet me in New York.

In Scotland an icy wind was howling in from the Atlantic. Thirty of us sprawled on seats in a waiting-room from ten at night until two in the morning. Then we were given a lecture and shown a movie—the longest "short" I ever saw—describing in mouth-drying detail how to behave when the plane crashed in mid-ocean. Towards dawn we boarded a plane identical with that on the screen. Painted white inside, it had chromium armchairs (my first contact with "plush-seats") and a carpeted aisle down the center. A young attendant handed round peanut-butter sandwiches in boxes, coffee in cardboard cups. On my left I looked out of a square window with purple serge curtains and tasseled bands. On my right I found a gadget by which you could regulate the angle of your cushioned chair.

HIROSHIMA: THE CITY WITHOUT A SHADOW

> *Prague.* Some days ago a rumor swept through Prague that Hitler had been found alive in the small town of Hedonin, in Bohemia.
>
> But it was a false alarm. The alleged Hitler was František Holub Kysperek, a Czech tram conductor, well known as the Führer's double during the Occupation.
>
> While the Germans were there he used to make money by posing for photographs. He was especially popular with German soldiers, who posed with him and sent the snapshots home to impress their friends.
>
> Finally, the Gestapo intervened and forced Kysperek to shave off his mustache and comb his hair differently. Then they put him in prison.
>
> Kysperek has now been discovered by American film producers and has been asked to go to Hollywood to appear in films as Hitler.

Ten hours later the plane descended on the Azores airport, an area of flat rock on the edge of the ocean. We emerged into tropical heat. While sitting at a counter eating a plate of tepid canned vegetables, I heard my name called out over an amplifier. I held my breath. Patuxent. . . . "Very sorry . . ." B.O.Q. . . . New York . . . Vermont . . . B.O.Q.?

Three of us, including Turner, the civilian I'd met on the bus, stood at a desk awaiting sentence.

"Very sorry . . . There's bad weather between here and Newfoundland. The plane is overweight. Got to carry an extra load of gas. . . ."

"But I weigh only 140 pounds!"

"Very sorry. We've taken the first three names on the list. Yours happens to be the first."

"It would. When does the next plane leave for New York?"

"Ah, that we don't know."

"For Washington?" asked Turner.

"For Miami?"

"We don't know. You will be informed. Meanwhile . . ."

Meanwhile we were carried off, like jailbirds, on the floor of an open truck, across a wilderness of baking rock, to a low wooden oven, to a bare cell with cots.

"You know what they call this place?" Turner said.

"B.O.Q.?"

"No. The Island of the Lost. I once knew a couple of guys who were dumped off here on their way home. One was here six weeks. The other went off into the hinterland and was never seen again. You can't even send a cable."

Turner and the other man undressed, took a shower and shaved. I rolled over, took a sleeping draught and delivered myself up to my private God. . . .

I wasn't sure whether I'd slept an hour or a night when the door burst open and a voice shouted urgently: "Anyone here wanna go to Washington?"

Turner leapt from his cot. "I do!" he yelled.

"New York!" I said.

"Washington I said!"

"Remember what I told you," Turner warned me.

I heeded the warning.

Twenty-two of us sat on bucket-seats, lay on the floor, vomited into a pail in the rear, groaned, snored, as the plane swooped up, rocketed down, bumped, tossed and roared through the night. After six hours one of the crew came into the dark cavern and whispered to a man lying on the floor. The man sat up, rubbed his eyes, lay down, sat up again, whispered to his neighbor. The neighbor got up, lurched over the prostrate bodies as far as Turner, who had just raised his head from my shoulder. Turner looked at the man, listened to something he said, nodded his head, gave a wan smile and turned to me.

"It's over," he muttered.

I looked at him, then nodded. The sergeant next to me was not in a state to be told anything, so I repeated to myself: "It's over . . . it's over!" and wondered where my wife was and how I was to get from Washington to New York.

As we landed at Gander or Stephensville (I never knew which), I caught sight of the plush-seated plane moving off over the Newfoundland airfield—to New York.

"Jesus Christ!" exclaimed Turner, as we climbed down the ladder in the dark.

We looked up to see a house or hut or barracks on fire. A couple of G.I.s, silhouetted against the flames, were hurling bottles through a window. There was a tinkling sound of glass smashing. A third G.I. raised a bottle at arm's length, tottered, then collapsed on the ground. Some WACs began to cheer.

"Peace on earth!" I muttered.

"Good will toward men," added Turner.

In the mess we sat opposite a corporal. His right hand was round a bottle, his head on the table, an inch from a broken, bloodstained tumbler.

Between us, Turner and I ate a dozen fried eggs and bacon.

In the draughty dawn, some ten thousand feet above the coast of Maine probably, I dropped from the bucket-seat to the floor. God bless you, Turner, wherever you are, for throwing that blanket over the shivering frame! It won't forget!

In the bleak Washington airport a clock was striking nine; the mercury lay half a degree under ninety.

"You can't travel any further on those orders," the passport official told me, wiping his brow on his shirt sleeve.

"You'll have to take a commercial plane," he said. "And pay."

"I'll pay," I said.

Six girls sat in a row behind desks and telephones. They looked astonishingly clean, composed, well-dressed, as though they'd just come out of a bath and a beauty parlor.

"A seat to New York?" exclaimed the nearest girl. "Today?" She shook her curly head, picked up the receiver.

"Gee, you look kinda tired," she said, and into the phone: "Anything for New York?"

She downed the receiver and shook her head. Then she repeated the performance six times.

"It's a bad day," she muttered, smiling.

"We'll remember it."

"I'll say! Shoulda seen Washington last night!"

"And Newfoundland this morning!" I said.

She picked up the receiver again, asked the question, laid it down.

"Go take a seat," she sighed. "Only chance is a passenger not turning up. But we'll get you onto a plane somehow."

She did, two hours later. A sumptuous limousine transported me to the commercial airport, which was like a racetrack for millionaires, its grandstand a twentieth-century palace of glass and shining chromium.

Through a drugstore window I stared at a mountain of oranges and grapefruit, and tried to picture the face of a European in my place. I tried to rehearse an imaginary conversation about the continent of Europe with my wife and friends, but I didn't know how to begin. I went on staring at the oranges and grapefruit, at the empty seats in the drugstore, and I knew then that the conversation would prove futile, for I realized as never before that between those who have seen and those who haven't, there is a gulf fixed which the spoken word cannot bridge.

THE PUBLIC SLANDERERS

A Foul Thing lies hidden
In dust and dried slime
As the flame lies in light ashes.
A shower, a gust of wind
Kindles the evil life,
And out of nothingness there rise
Plague, fire and smoke.

From a dark cave emerges
A thief on the prowl;
Money-bags he craves
But better loot he gleans:
He falls upon a strife
About nothing, a confused knowledge,
A tattered banner,
A people in stupor.

Wherever he goes he finds
The void of barren times,
There he can shamelessly stalk,
And is claimed a prophet;
On a garbage heap
He plants his foxy feet,
And hisses his message
Into the startled world.

Wrapped in his baseness
As within a cloud,
Lying to the people,
He soon looms huge in power,
Surrounded by his helpers
Who, standing high and low,
Are sniffing opportunities,
And offer him their services.